Modernism, Mass Culture, and the Aesthetics of Obscenity

How did explicit sexual representation become acceptable in the twentieth century as art rather than pornography? Allison Pease answers this question by tracing the relationship between aesthetics and obscenity from the 1700s onwards, highlighting the way in which early twentieth-century writers incorporated a sexually explicit discourse into their work. Pease explores how artists such as Swinburne, Aubrey Beardsley, James Joyce, and D. H. Lawrence were responsible for shifting the boundaries between aesthetics and pornography that first became of intellectual interest in the eighteenth century and reinforced class distinctions. Her analysis of canonical works, such as Joyce's *Ulysses* and Lawrence's *Lady Chatterley's Lover*, is framed by a wide-ranging examination of the changing conceptions of aesthetics from Shaftesbury, Hutcheson, and Kant to F. R. Leavis, I. A. Richards, and T. S. Eliot. Based on extensive archival work, the book includes examples of period art and illustrations which eloquently demonstrate the shift in public taste and tolerance.

Allison Pease is Assistant Professor of English at John Jay College, City University of New York.

Modernism, Mass Culture, and the Aesthetics of Obscenity

Allison Pease

CAMBRIDGE
UNIVERSITY PRESS

PUBLISHED BY THE PRESS SYNDICATE OF THE UNIVERSITY OF CAMBRIDGE
The Pitt Building, Trumpington Street, Cambridge, United Kingdom

CAMBRIDGE UNIVERSITY PRESS
The Edinburgh Building, Cambridge CB2 2RU, UK   www.cup.cam.ac.uk
40 West 20th Street, New York, NY 10011–4211, USA   www.cup.org
10 Stamford Road, Oakleigh, Melbourne 3166, Australia
Ruiz de Alarcón 13, 28014 Madrid, Spain

First published 2000

Printed in the United Kingdom at the University Press, Cambridge

Typeface Monotype Bembo 10/13 pt   *System* QuarkXPress™   [SE]

A catalogue record for this book is available from the British Library

ISBN 0 521 78076 4 hardback

For Lee

Contents

Illustrations

List of illustrations

Preface

Explicit sexual representation became common-place in twentieth-century literature. Readers ceased to be shocked by graphic descriptions of palpitating bodies in the throes of sexual pleasure, and became unlikely to consider such images pornography. Indeed, specific and overt references to sex acts and sexualized bodies became so much a part of literature, including works of high-cultural aesthetic status, that today they seem hardly worth notice. It has not always been thus; indeed, our contemporary nonchalance in the face of sexual representations reflects a remarkable cultural and aesthetic shift. In the last decades of the nineteenth century, a middle-class reader in England would no sooner have expected to encounter detailed descriptions of sex acts or sexualized bodies in a mainstream novel than she or he would have expected its characters to pop from the pages and speak to her or him. Though pornographic novels were clandestinely distributed and sold throughout the nineteenth century, their sexual representations were carefully segregated from works with respectable public distribution. A literary work even alluding to sexuality would have raised a public outcry and been subject to legal censure, as many examples attest.

What changed? How did explicit sexual representations find their way into both literary and visual works in the twentieth century under the rubric of art? How did such representations, once the domain of pornography alone, shape the cultural imagination and our contemporary relationship to art? This book pursues these questions by looking at the history of pornographic and aesthetic discourses in the modern period, from their simultaneous emergence as publicly theorized entities in the eighteenth century to the incorporation of pornographic representations into modernist high-art novels and drawings in the late nineteenth and early twentieth centuries.

The British modernist incorporation of pornographic tropes and images into literary works of serious aesthetic aspirations is the focus of this study. This book demonstrates not simply how modernist artists were influenced by popular pornography, but also the complex and conflicted ways in which they strove to incorporate mass-cultural pornographic representations of the body, sex, and sexuality into their works even as they affirmed the aesthetic value of their appropriations of pornography, thus redefining conceptions of the aesthetic. Yet in order to understand the aesthetic and cultural implications of modernist incorporations, my exploration must begin much earlier, in the eighteenth and nineteenth centuries, when the oppositions between aesthetics and pornography, which collapsed in the twentieth century, were first put into place.

In eighteenth-century Britain, art and aesthetic experience were newly categorized and authenticated by the emergent upper-middle classes through the modern discourse of aesthetics, which explained art as that which had no practical use, but incited intellectual cognition that was both disinterested and discussible. Theorists from the Third Earl of Shaftesbury to Frances Hutcheson to Immanuel Kant conceived of a specific form of aesthetic experience that promoted the cognitive over the physical faculties. Active engagement with art was considered a rational, moral and civic-minded activity; an activity that identified one as upwardly mobile, if not already of the upper classes. If aesthetic experience as articulated in the eighteenth century allowed one to transcend the body – a particularly middle-class subject formation that relied on a disavowal of the materialism by which that class was grounded – pornography rooted one more firmly in the body. As opposed to aesthetic disinterest, pornography provoked interest, both in terms of sensual response and significant profit. In the eighteenth century, pornography gained public recognition as a genre of writing at odds with aesthetic ideals. It is my argument that pornography threatened the class hierarchies upon which aesthetic theories of the eighteenth century rested by exposing common experience in bodily sensation. Its commercial and physical associations linked it symbolically with the working and lower classes; the selfish individualism that pornography celebrated was viewed as pestilential to civility. Importantly, the discourses of aesthetics and pornography became publicly recognized at the same historical moment and were in many ways considered mutually exclusive. This opposition persisted throughout the nineteenth century, engendering the cliché of Victorian prudishness.

Though modernist works present striking examples of the appropriation of pornography under the rubric of art, precedent for the incorporation of such representations can be traced back to a handful of important Victorian figures. Forced to publish his scandalous poetry with a known publisher of pornography, Algernon Charles Swinburne represents an intriguing transitional figure whose 1866 *Poems and Ballads* began to destabilize the previously established boundaries between what could be considered aesthetic and what pornographic. Those boundaries were being simultaneously eroded by the expanding interests of the working and lower classes, whose increased education and literacy in the later nineteenth century threatened, by their demand for forms of aesthetic pleasure that fell outside of traditionally privileged forms, to marginalize the aesthetic tradition of Shaftesbury and Kant and the inherent social structures underpinning that tradition. It is those shifting boundaries, I maintain here, that allow us a fuller understanding of the social project of dominant eighteenth-century aesthetics, the tradition of Shaftesbury and Kant, specifically its efforts to exclude the body and the body politic from its economy of values. By tracing those distinctions through their historical arc into the first half of the twentieth century, the interdependent relationship between mass culture and high culture in modernism becomes more apparent than previous scholars have allowed.

When late-Victorian print artist Aubrey Beardsley, and literary modernists James Joyce and D. H. Lawrence, appropriated the tropes and images of pornography into their works, they found their sources in Victorian and Edwardian pornography. The concerns of Victorian and Edwardian pornography, curiously enough, became the concerns of modernist high art. Importantly, pornography was one of late-Victorian and Edwardian Britain's most overlooked mass-cultural products. In this book I have found it necessary to recover this dimension of Victorian and Edwardian pornography in order to correct what I see as the too-narrow assessments of its forms and distribution by previous scholars. The impact of Victorian and Edwardian pornography on sexual representation in modernist high art and, by modernism's influence, throughout twentieth-century works of literature and art is such that, to the extent that sexuality is formed through language and representations at all, twentieth-century sexuality was formed in part by Victorian and Edwardian pornography.

In recent criticism scholars have argued that British modernism was formed out of an opposition to mass culture. One of the central goals of this work is to make clear that artists such as Beardsley, Joyce, and Lawrence were not everywhere in opposition to mass culture, but in specific ways they appropriated it, incorporating the images and representational techniques of one very significant mass-cultural product: pornography. By emphasizing form over content, Beardsley and

Joyce introduced explicit pornographic tropes into their works while successfully courting high-art status. Though their texts destabilized the opposition between pornography and aesthetics, they simultaneously propagated the goals of the aesthetic tradition of Shaftesbury and Kant: to objectify the senses and make rational the body and, by extension, the body politic. As this book argues, D. H. Lawrence satirized this very practice in *Lady Chatterley's Lover*. He claimed that both aesthetic form and pornography forced an objectification of the body that, through the enabling discourse of sexology, he deemed as unhealthy.

Joyce's and Lawrence's turn toward pornographic representation reflects not only the increasingly pervasive force of the pornographic as a mode of representation, but also, in Lawrence's case, a desire to articulate subjectivity in ways previously denied by aesthetic constructions first formulated in a highly classed society. As the body began to enunciate itself within mainstream aesthetic discourse, so the body politic began to have greater access to the aesthetic through universal literacy, less exclusive university enrollment after World War I, and a newly defined relationship between the individual and the aesthetic object. Interestingly, however, the two models of sexual representation offered through Joyce's and Lawrence's work have tended to reify the very class divisions that one would have expected to be erased by the collapse of certain elements of the pornographic into the aesthetic. While Joyce's disjunctive method of sexual representation has been adopted by a smaller, more rarefied group of literary elites, Lawrence's wholistic method of sexual representation has been embraced by the entirety of twentieth-century mass culture, from romance novels to Hollywood films.

To fully appreciate how sexual representations made their way into British literature and art consumed by the middle and upper classes as high culture in the beginning of this century, this book seeks to show the role that literary critics played in adjusting the public to them. For while Joyce and Lawrence encountered enormous challenges in publishing and distributing *Ulysses* and *Lady Chatterley's Lover*, their novels were championed by literary critics such as I. A. Richards, F. R. Leavis, and T. S. Eliot. Establishment figures in literary London and at Cambridge University, these critics made broad claims for the capacity of literature to promote what they saw as the health of culture at large, and for these novels to participate in that process. Modernist critics privileged sensibility over reason, rejecting Shaftesburian and Kantian aesthetic reception based on intellectual cognition alone, and advocated sense and sensation as crucial aspects of aesthetic consumption. By training readers in methods of reading that accommodated the body, modernist criticism not only legitimated the body as part of aesthetic consumption and production, it also promoted a more completely engaged, "interested," way of approaching texts. Modernist criticism thus played a fundamental role in collapsing the distinctions set up in the eighteenth century to separate the aesthetic from the pornographic.

At stake in the argument of this book are both a revised reading of modernism's relationship to mass culture in light of its appropriations of pornographic discourse, as well as a more socially embedded view of the legacy of the Kantian aesthetic in the modern period, especially in terms of its relationship to the body and the bodies of the working classes. At the level of ideas, this book seeks to show the transition in the modern period from aesthetics in the tradition of Shaftesbury and Kant, which privileged cognitive response, to a modernist, twentieth-century aesthetic, which incorporated and demanded, even as it regulated, an embodied response. By using pornography as the frame through which to view this shift, this book also works as a cultural history, revealing the specific practices of pornography and aesthetics in the late nineteenth and twentieth centuries in order to sharpen the focus of this history of ideas. Chapters one and five provide the theoretical and historically general context through which to understand the historically specific practices explored in chapters two, three, and four.

Perhaps ironically, this argument is a continuation of the modernists' project: the legitimation of pornography by high-cultural institutions. Indeed, my argument in many ways replicates the very claim I make – that modernists successfully appropriated pornography for high art and the middle classes by idealizing its materialist urges through a formalist structure. This book serves as proof, as if such were needed, of the continued impact of modernism's complex negotiation between aesthetics and pornography. If pornography has gained a place in serious academic discourse in the last ten years, it has done so because modernism first demanded that it be taken seriously, and showed us how. Academic interest in pornography is but a continuation of the cognitive distancing inculcated through aesthetic ideals first articulated in the eighteenth century.

Pornography is a limited genre but it has much to tell us about the modern period, during which it has simultaneously been transformed from a tool of political propaganda in the seventeenth and eighteenth centuries to a private sexual practice in the nineteenth and twentieth, and from a limited circulation amongst elite circles to ever more widely distributed forms of magazines, photographs, and Internet web sites. What this book will make clear is that, whether or not an individual has ever looked at or read a pornographic text, he or she has felt its impact in untold ways.

Though altered, portions of my discussion on Swinburne in chapter two appear from my article, "Questionable Figures: Swinburne's *Poems and Ballads*," *Victorian Poetry*, 35:1 (spring 1997): 43–56. This book has had many incarnations and I am grateful to those who have offered their time, thought, and collegiality in order to help the book find its current shape. Foremost, I thank John Maynard for his tireless generosity over the life of this project. I would also like to thank Carolyn Dever and Jeffrey Spear for their support and suggestions at various points along the way. Thanks to Perry Meisel for his interest, and Marvin Taylor at the Fales Library for an enthusiasm about his collection that led to an entirely different form of research for me. I am grateful also to a 1996 Gordon Ray Fellowship which allowed me to do research in the British Library, and to my chair, Bob Crozier, and to Provost Basil Wilson at John Jay College for providing financial support for the book's illustrations.

I owe a debt of time and patience to Mary Poovey, David Simpson, and the late Walter Kendrick for reading chapters and offering useful criticism. Regenia Gagnier helped complicate my ideas on aesthetics by sharing her 1996 MLA paper with me when I asked. Christopher Snodgrass and Linda Gerstner Zatlin were incredibly helpful to me in tracking down Beardsley illustrations and I thank them. Members of my wonderful reading group supported this project in ways immeasurable (and not just with the scotch). Thanks go to Tim Carens, Peter Chapin, Anjali Gallup-Diaz, Minu Tharoor, Bill Tipper, and Anne Wilson. Members of New York University's Victorian Studies Group, especially Gita Panjabi and Sarah Blake, were helpful with work on the second chapter. I want to express my gratitude and adoration to friends, Tita Chico, Betsy Duquette, and Karen Kligerman, who willingly helped me move this project along in its earliest stages through discussion, reading chapters, and boisterous cheerleading.

My love and thanks to my family, Pat, Hugh, Kate, Laura, Lowell, Brooke, Owen, Myra, Jerry, Neal, Ellen, Joe, C. J. and Carly for their support and good humor about this project. Finally, I owe my largest debt of gratitude to Lee, who gave me love, shelter, encouragement and M. D. There is a sentence in this book that remains purely his.

1 Civil society: aesthetics and pornography in the eighteenth century

As aesthetic philosophy emerged and created the modern notion of the art object in the eighteenth century, so pornography as we understand it today came into prominence in the Age of Reason. They emerged in Britain not as mutually exclusive entities, but as mutually generative ones that relied conceptually on interest and disinterest for their completion. Theorized versions of pornography and aesthetics also participated in a larger cultural debate about the formation of a new ideological, political, and economic order after the Glorious Revolution of 1688. In doing so, their development contributed to and commented on reformulating tensions between public and private, sense and idea, individual and community, Whig and Tory. By looking at their mutually constitutive emergence in this chapter, I seek to avoid representing what was categorized as pornographic or aesthetic as either liberating or repressive. Instead, I demonstrate how they emerged as conceptually interdependent, and how they challenged, while they constituted, each other's ability to make meaning.

Since the eighteenth century, what is aesthetic and what is pornographic have repeatedly been defined as mutually exclusive, pornography often marking a boundary or frame within which "true" aesthetic texts operate. One important distinction between the two has characteristically been the level of physical response elicited from them. Pornographic texts work to create embodied readers, readers whose awareness of their own body is heightened as they consume pornographic texts. Aesthetic texts are characterized in the modern period by their ability to create an experience of disembodiment, a movement away from sense toward rational or intellectual pleasure. In a post-Kantian paradigm that helps to articulate the interdependence of dominant aesthetics and pornography in the modern period, T. W. Adorno suggests that the aesthetic encounter is always a wresting away from, if not simply an objectification of, the physical interests of the body:

> Perhaps the most important taboo in art is the one that prohibits an animal-like attitude toward the object, say, a desire to devour it or otherwise subjugate it to one's body. Now, the strength of such a taboo is matched by the strength of the repressed urge. Hence, all art contains in itself a negative moment from which it tries to get away. If Kant's disinterestedness is to be more than a synonym for indifference, it has to have a trace of untamed interest somewhere. Indeed, there is much to be said for the thesis that the dignity of works of art depends on the magnitude of the interest from which they were wrested.[1]

Adorno's text, aided by psychoanalysis's notion of repression, suggests that what is aesthetic exists in dialectical unity with an almost devouring sensuousness, the grounding impulse of pornography. Though Adorno is intrigued by the "animal-like" sensuousness that threatens to unravel the moment of aesthetic apprehension, he makes it clear that it is the cognitive work of transferring the sensuous to the intellectual that guarantees what one apprehends is art.

The project of the dominant Western tradition of modern aesthetics, beginning in the eighteenth century with Shaftesbury and carried further in the nineteenth century after Kant, was to derealize the body even as democratization and pornography were working simultaneously to *realize* the body and the body politic.[2] Aesthetic philosophy developed out of moral philosophy in the late seventeenth and early eighteenth centuries. Working to maintain social order in the changing landscape of a post-Revolutionary England, moral philosophy espoused self-control as the condition of granting civil liberty in an increasingly egalitarian society. Aesthetic philosophy in the Kantian tradition maintained that level of internal subjection even as it made abstract the social order upon which moral philosophy grounded itself, creating in its stead an idealized set of aesthetic referents. In what I will call in this work the aesthetic tradition of Shaftesbury and Kant – the aesthetic tradition that has dominated Western art for the last two hundred years – art functioned as a substitute body, but was only legitimated when it entered into the realm of judgment, knowledge, or reason, the harmonious, purposive purposelessness of the aesthetic. In the aesthetic tradition forged by Shaftesbury and Kant, the play of the aesthetic permits the illusion of a freedom from materiality while in fact relying quite specifically on materiality.

Pornography developed simultaneously as both an extension of, and a counter to, modern aesthetics. On the one hand it was an absolute objectification of and substitute for the body and in this mirrored, or perhaps even exaggerated to the point of parody, the aesthetic; on the other hand it remained quite distinct from the aesthetic in that it elided the reflective or contemplative distance invoked by it. Instead, the pornographic functioned, as Adorno suggests above, by provoking an "animal-like" attitude in the subject, whose primary aim became the subjugation of the representation to the body's interests. To be sure, if the aesthetic operated as a sublimation of the senses, pornography's effort was to de-sublimate the senses.[3] In opposition to the aesthetic, pornography was and still is characterized by interest, both in the sense of sensual desire and commercial profit, its use and exchange values.

Before the eighteenth century, sexually explicit works were regulated in England primarily through the licensing acts. They were found problematic not because of their content, but because pornographic publishers reaped large profits from works without paying appropriate licensing fees.[4] In 1580, for example, William Lambard proposed "An acte to restrain licentious printing" in which he condemned books that "set up an arte of making lascivious ungodly love." His motives were commercial as well as moral. He objected that sexually explicit literature sold well "to the manifest injurie of the godly learned, whose prayse woorthie endevours and wrytings are thearfore lesse read."[5] Pornography, it appeared, was more popular than divinity. Though Lambard viewed this as creating private catastrophes for ignored authors, by the eighteenth century many educated or propertied individuals would come to see pornography as threatening a broader group of interests. The emergence of pornographic texts in the seventeenth and eighteenth century signified the burgeoning abundance of private interests, both commercial and personal, that threatened the propertied and educated elite who composed the public sphere. Simultaneously, the propertied and educated elite were creating new forms of representing themselves to themselves through an economy of values circulated within a newly defined category of experience, the aesthetic. In the modern period, the use and exchange values of the pornographic form a necessary complement to the apparent disinterest and inutility of the aesthetic, whose only capital is cultural. More than a mere coincidence of chronology, the aesthetic and the pornographic emerged as distinct genres in the eighteenth century through a mutually generative dialectic whose terms relied upon one another for completion.

Civil society

4.

Pornography in the time of the aesthetic

The technology of modern pornography's appeal to the senses was fostered in part by the European philosophical shift in the seventeenth century towards an empirical, subject-based epistemology that privileged individual sense experience as the source and basis of all knowledge.[6] Though language problematizes its ability to do so, pornography offered itself as pure sensation. It tendered description after description of physical sensations which were then refracted through other sensations, seen or felt. As pornography gradually evolved into its modern form throughout the eighteenth century, its features distinguished themselves from those of a simultaneously emerging view of the aesthetic.

Though forms of pornography have existed and been distributed narrowly for centuries, they were until the eighteenth century primarily imported into England from the Continent, and were often ancillary to other causes, political or religious. As Lynn Hunt has argued, pornography in early modern Europe, between 1500 and 1800, was most often a vehicle for using the shock of sex to criticize religious and political authorities.[7] The oft-quoted 1668 diary entries by Samuel Pepys regarding his purchase and, some interpret, masturbatory use of *L'Ecole des filles* prove that pornography from the Continent was available in London bookstores in the seventeenth century, and those who could read in French or Latin had access to it.[8] David Foxon, in *Libertine Literature in England, 1660–1745*, has suggested there were three Continental works that received a fairly wide distribution in England in the second half of the seventeenth century: *La Puttana Errante* (1650), *L'Ecole des filles* (1655), and *Satyra Sotadica* (1660).[9] Term Catalogues advertised a number of licensed titles that indicate sexually incriminating works of a political or religious bent were also being printed in English. The catalogues include: *The Nuns Complaint Against the Friars* (Easter, 1676); *The London Jilt; or The Politick Whore* (Easter, 1683); *The Ten Pleasures of Marriage* (Trinity, 1683); *Eve Revived; or The Fair One Stark Naked* (Michaelmas, 1683); *The Confessions of the New-Married Couple* (Michaelmas, 1683); *The Amorous Abess, or Love in a Nunnery* (Easter, 1684).[10]

The content of pornographic texts in this period resembled modern pornography in several fundamental aspects: through the naming of parts and sensations the texts overtly set out to sexually stimulate their readers; they posited a physical, sexual reality of individual selfishness in order to expose "hypocritical" social conventions, especially those of the church; and they created a self-contained, hedonistic world of sensual gratification that cut off individuals from any higher moral authority.[11] Enabled by the new discourses of science, pornography participated in the view that valorized nature and the senses as sources of author-ity. Indeed, pornography's aim to provoke a physical response in the reader formed part of its attack on the public's denial, or sublimation, of individual, sensual interest, for a reader's arousal forced an acknowledgment of what other-wise proved socially problematic because of its potential to disrupt community: the senses form a powerful part of one's subjective response.

The belief in an embodied, private subjectivity played into the political strat-egies of the libertine ideas spreading across Europe in the wake of the Reformation and Counter-Reformation. Pornographic works of the late seven-teenth and early eighteenth centuries positioned the material "truth" of sex against the "hypocritical" conventions of church and society. As David Foxon notes, these pornographic stories took "place within a tightly knit family circle, with the shocking suggestion that all the conventional relationships are merely a facade for personal gratification, into which even the local priest enters."[12] Early modern pornography was never simply solitary or homosocial male pleasure inspired by writing on or across the sexualized body. Rather, that body was always also configured as the body politic, the body of the people.[13] The sexually explicit literature of this period insisted that selfish interest and material gain were at the heart of any individual act. These works collapsed every public figure or act into a private one, thereby threatening emergent conceptions of social order.[14]

The bawdy plots of English Restoration drama as well as the notoriously explicit works of the Earl of Rochester may be said to be continuous with, or to have participated in, this general movement toward a more libertine outlook. However, as a public backlash ensued and drama became more chaste by the turn of the eighteenth century, pornography written in English disproportionately absorbed sexual discourse and began to resemble what we would now recognize as modern pornography: texts written with the specific purpose of sexually stim-ulating their readers. Pornography began to achieve a wider, though publicly segregated, distribution as print technology increased and authors began to write not for patrons, but for a relatively new, autonomous market supported by the emerging wealth of the middle classes. While these texts did not acquire the name pornography until well into the middle of the nineteenth century, works of an explicit sexual nature were printed, sold, and occasionally prosecuted throughout the eighteenth century.[15]

In the second half of the eighteenth century and even more so in the nine-teenth century, the ability of sexually explicit texts to produce interest – that is, to provoke both personal interest in the form of sexual excitation and commer-cial interest in the sense of profit – began to take precedence over their political content. Though still used for political attack in the early nineteenth century, pornography was increasingly identified as a commodity with a specific use in the form of the solitary sexual experience it engaged. One nineteenth-century text, *The Adventures of Lady Harpur* (1894), shows modern pornography's awareness of this aspiration by having its title character relate that the impetus for her story is solely to stimulate her readers:

> The intention of all Literatture [sic] of this kind is to excite and gratifying [sic] our amorous inclinations, therefore those descriptions which do most surely and speedily produce the desired effect will be the most satisfactory and successful; and as the employment of such names and expressions are in common use, even those which are generally considered coarse and vulgar, is universally found most provocative of amorous emotion, they are the best suites [sic] to the purpose.[16]

As Lady Harpur indicates, modern pornography concerns itself with the intensification of bodily sensation through naming. Pornography works to write the body in as many minute variations as possible, to evoke its materiality and palpability for the sexual imagination of its readers. While Steven Marcus contends that pornography constantly tries to escape language, such an assertion seems counter to the entire project of written pornography which, by writing the body and sexual acts, extends, proliferates and continues the body and the sexual acts in a never-ending stream of words.[17] Pornography in the eighteenth and nineteenth centuries was primarily constructed in language and its technology was utterly rooted in a faith in the materiality of language.

For this reason, influenced as English pornography was by works from the Continent, it participated in what Foucault has characterized as a broader cultural move toward self-examination: "the nearly infinite task of telling – telling oneself and another, as often as possible, everything that might concern the interplay of innumerable pleasures, sensations, and thoughts which, through the body and the soul, had some affinity with sex."[18] The reader of pornography deploys a practice of reading which opens a relation to the self and the body by querying the insinuations of the flesh. The reader is encouraged to mimic the pornographic narrative's voyeur figure – more thoroughly explored below in this chapter and in chapter three – by engaging in an act of sensual self-scrutiny, gauging the body's complicity with the mental recitation of sensations or voluptuous imaginings, and in doing so achieving sexual stimulation and gratification. Pornography, by this account, is not so much a representation of sexuality as a specific practice of it.

The narrator of *The Whore's Rhetorick* (1683) shows that looking at sexually explicit pictures is an act continuous with sexual performance:

Besides the Male Picture prescribed for your use, you must be stockt with others of a different nature to operate on your visitants more effectually than the similitude of your Ganymede could affect your self . . . These obscene images do produce marvellous effects toward the propagation of Love, they insinuate at every Pore of the Eye an extravagant desire to gratifie the sensitive appetite, they spur Men on by an irresistible impulse toward the venereal Bed; from whence he ought at no time be suffered to come off a winner.[19]

As this text makes clear, pornography values embodied response above all else. Tellingly, this passage glosses the relationship between the empirical and the theoretical so that any cognitive excitement is understood only as empirical. Images penetrate the body, as it were, physically. They "insinuate at every Pore of the Eye." Once "inside the body," these images purportedly create a desire to mimetically recreate the sensations they portray. No art validates the mimetic so profoundly as pornography, and this is its most powerful and threatening aspect.

The voyeur figure, one of pornography's most classic and consistent tropes, offers a model for the reader to engage with, and reproduce for his or her private use, the pleasures of the seen and heard. Such a technology can be seen at work in the eighteenth-century pornographic classic *Fanny Hill*, when Fanny accidentally finds herself in a closet next to a bedroom occupied by a prostitute and her client. This scene depicts Fanny's physical awakening as she witnesses the sexual act for the first time and then responds to her body's demand for sexual satisfaction:

I instantly crept softly, and posted myself so that, seeing everything minutely, I could not myself be seen . . . As he stood on one side, unbuttoning his waistcoat and breeches, her fat brawny thighs hung down, and the whole greasy landscape lay fairly open to my view; a wide open-mouthed gap, overshaded with a grizzly bush, seemed held out like a beggar's wallet for its provision.

But I soon had my eyes called off by a more striking object, that entirely engrossed them.

Her sturdy stallion had now unbuttoned, and produced naked, stiff, and erect that wonderful machine, which I had never seen before, and which, for the interest my own seat of pleasure began to take furiously in it, I stared with all the eyes I had: however my senses were too much flurried, too much concentrated in that now burning spot of mine, to observe anything more than in general the make and turn of that instrument, from which the instinct of nature, yet more than all I had heard of it, now strongly informed me I was to expect that supreme pleasure which she had placed in the meeting of those parts so admirably fitted for each other . . . and now the bed shook, the curtains rattled so, that I could scarce hear the sighs and murmurs, the heaves and pantings that accompanied the action, from the beginning to the end; the sound

Civil society

and sight of which thrilled to the very soul of me, and made every vein of my body circulate liquid fires: the motion grew so violent that it almost intercepted my respiration . . .

Whilst they were in the heat of the action, guided by nature only, I stole my hand up my petticoats, and with fingers all on fire, seized, and yet more inflamed that centre of all my senses: my heart palpitated, as if it would force its way through my bosom: I breathed with pain; I twisted my thighs, squeezed, and compressed the lips of that virgin slit, and following mechanically the example of Phoebe's manual operations on it, as far as I could find admission, brought on at last the critical ecstasy, the melting flow, into which nature, spent with excess of pleasure, dissolves and dies away.[20]

This scene is notable for the excess of sensation that Fanny both produces and consumes, an economy highlighted by the "circulation" of liquid fires throughout her body. Sensation as knowledge is excessively detailed in this passage, Fanny citing carefully all that she sees and hears. She gives preeminence to the "centre" of her senses, notably not her mind, but her genitalia. Fanny takes a privileged position as voyeur, seeing "with all the eyes" she has, while not herself being seen. The knowledge precipitated by what she sees induces her to explore her own body, creating a form of physical self-knowledge that can only be produced when sensation is perceived as a primary agent in the epistemological process. The body is constructed here as the site of affect, which in turn can manufacture a form of knowledge-as-sensation, the only form of any importance in pornographic writings.

As this archetypal passage conveys, pornography invites readers to indulge their own sensations through a mimetic imaginative practice extended and complemented by the physical act of masturbation. Pornographic texts repeatedly celebrate their own technology, their own ability to self-reflexively create the sensations they describe. For instance, in *A New Atlantis for the Year One Thousand Seven Hundred and Fifty Eight* (1758) the narrator describes how reading pornography assists a young woman toward sexual self-knowledge:

Having soon reached her teens, and by the means of her chambermaid got a translation of Ovid's *Art of Love*, Rochester's Works, and the *Memoirs of a Woman of Pleasure*, all her doubts about her inward feelings vanished; she was convinced what use she was designed for, and made acquainted with the canal thro' which it was to be admitted; which, with her new-disciplined fingers, she used frequently to explore.[21]

Ever aware of its ability to induce sexual arousal, if not masturbation, pornography reinforces this power through repeated textual example. Significantly, terminology for solitary sexual practices was established in English in the eighteenth century. The first record of the word onanism noted by the *Oxford*

English Dictionary was in 1727, and self-abuse appeared in 1728. The first use of the word masturbation was recorded in 1766. The emergence of these terms in the eighteenth century indicates that the concept of solitary sexual stimulation entered British parlance at the same time that those pornographic literary practices that encouraged a solipsistic engagement with the senses began to find a reading public.[22]

Distinguishing itself as a distinct genre in the late eighteenth century, the sexual self-interrogation that is pornography can be seen as an aspect of the wider shift to the reflexive self-interrogation that encompassed the Romantic movement.[23] Just as Romantic artists were concerned with the imaginative interplay between the self and the seen, so pornographic readers imaginatively "read themselves into" the works they read. Indeed, just as Romantic writers focused on the power of vision to imaginatively link a speaker to what he or she saw, so pornographic narrative relied on visually imagined descriptions to verbally emplace its readers. Most written pornography depends on vision to accomplish a sensational replication, as the passages above from *The Whore's Rhetorick* and *Fanny Hill* suggest. In *Venus in the Cloister* (1724), two nuns discuss the masturbatory transports of another nun in language that shows the importance of visual emplacement:

> Angelica: "*Thou woulds't have seen* that innocent, half naked, her mouth smiling with those amorous, gentle contractions of which she knew not the cause. *Thou woulds't have seen* her in an ecstasy, her eyes half dying, and without any strength or vigour fall beneath the laws of undisguised nature, and lose in defiance to all that care that treasure, the keeping of which had cost her so much pain and trouble."
>
> Agnes: "Very well, and it is in this that I should have placed my pleasure, *to have considered her thus naked and curiously to have observed* all the transports that love would have caused in the moment she was vanquished."[24]   (my emphasis)

The text continually prods the reader to approach the material with a visual imagination. It does not describe sexual ecstasy as an emotionally or physically experienced phenomenon, but rather verbally cues the reader that it must be experienced visually. This passage also makes clear pornography's insistence on the replication of sensation as a form of knowledge. To be sure, the readership of an early eighteenth century piece like *Venus in the Cloister* (published first in the late seventeenth century) would have been as interested in the anti-authoritarian, anti-clerical sentiments as the sexual ones. But increasingly, sexually explicit works were produced for sensual stimulation only. To those in the eighteenth century concerned with maintaining civic order as well as the exclusive privileges of literacy and polite culture, the emergence of the pornographic as an English prose genre prompted serious questions about the category of art, its purposes and appeals.

In eighteenth-century England, pornography became both a crime and a business. In 1727 the King's Bench declared that selling sexually explicit literature was a common-law misdemeanor, fining Grub Street hack and bookseller Edmund Curll £43 for selling *Venus in the Cloister* and placing him in the pillory at Charing Cross for an hour. In 1749 Ralph Griffiths published *Fanny Hill, or Memoirs of a Lady of Pleasure* by John Cleland with only minor legal incident and with legendary commercial success. Griffiths's profits from the book, reputedly as high as £10,000, enabled him to indulge in a flagrant display of social climbing in which he purchased a large country estate and maintained two coaches.[25] Cleland was arraigned before a Privy Council for writing *Fanny Hill,* where he pled poverty as his excuse. The Earl of Granville, President of the Council and a relation of Cleland's, determined the case by settling upon him a £100 annuity with the request that he not write anything like *Fanny Hill* again. Though Griffiths's profits on *Fanny Hill* are surely exaggerated myth, the myth reveals an important shift in the public perception of pornography as a commercial enterprise: in the eighteenth century pornography began to be seen as a lucrative business.

At the same time that popular reading materials like the novel and the periodical entered the newly autonomous market in the eighteenth century, pornographic texts began to surface within the market with their own specific aim of moving readers sexually. By doing so pornographic texts created physical interest – stimulation – in the bodies of their readers while creating financial interest, profitable returns on their investments – for their publishers.[26] Directives, such as one given by the Marquis de Sade, reinforced the notion that there is an end, a use, to such narratives:

> Your narrations must be decorated with the most numerous and searching details; the precise way and extent to which we may judge how the passion you describe relates to human manners and man's character is determined by your willingness to disguise no circumstance; and what is more, the least circumstance is apt to have an immense influence upon the procuring of that kind of sensory irritation we expect from your stories.[27]

The end product of pornography is a form of "sensory irritation." The increasing commodification of cultural products, whether novels, periodicals, or pornographic works, provided an impetus to move customers to purchase such products. Pornography proved the most facile of consumer products in that it reproduced itself for the buyer, whose consumption of a pornographic work could produce an empirically realized physical stimulation and, potentially, satisfaction. Its commercial and individual utility were central to its gradual distinction from the aesthetic.

Civil society and the arts in the time of the pornographic

British theories of taste in the eighteenth century were an outgrowth of secular, moral philosophy which, in the wake of Hobbesian proclamations of a ubiquitous self-interest, sought to relate those private interests to the public good and to find in the disposition of the senses, so often seen as a product of providence, a harmony akin to an idealized social order. British theories of taste were therefore imbricated with the ideas that sought to justify civil society. Many refuted the claims of Hobbes and Mandeville that individual desires prevent society from having naturally common or harmonious ends. Proponents of civil society, like many British theorists of taste, argued that reasonable choices were governed by a logic which ensured the common good.[28] Theorists such as Shaftesbury, Hutcheson, Kames, Hume, and Burke, thinkers who shaped what Linda Dowling has called the "Whig aesthetic," but what I will broadly call taste in the Shaftesbury tradition, defined aesthetic experience as a model for disinterested, socially generous behavior against the philosophical and pornographic claims of an individually interested and sensually selfish social order.[29] Though each of these thinkers represented aesthetic experience diversely in its particulars, they shared a general consensus about the broad nature of taste and the subject's experience of it. What I will call taste in the Shaftesbury tradition are theories of taste that: attempt to posit a universal agreement or, as Hume termed it, "standard" of taste; assert a subject's disinterested pleasure in apprehending an object of beauty; locate aesthetic pleasure in rational and reflective rather than sensual faculties; emphasize the importance of form in producing beauty; find objects of beauty autonomous and irreducible to utility.

In the eighteenth century, taste became a self-identifying behavior through which gentlemen could demonstrate their participation in what John Barrell has called "The Republic of Taste," a group of like-minded citizens able to abstract the true interest of humanity, the public interest, from the labyrinth of private interests which were imagined to be represented by disordered detail.[30] The perceived need to conceptualize and stand apart from the particularities of material experience followed from the empirical philosophy of Locke which, in asserting that all knowledge derives from the senses, played a role in the shifting cultural order. Locke's philosophy was emblematic of the new ways of understanding the construction of knowledge, belief, and opinion in the late seventeenth and early eighteenth centuries. Knowledge was no longer perceived as emanating from a center, but was seen as forming collectively in a new social space, the sphere of public opinion.[31] Aesthetic appreciation played a central role in concretizing this symbolic realm of the public sphere by exposing and thereby tacitly ratifying the mutual understanding of rational individuals. Like pornography, British theories of taste in the eighteenth century took as a given that the senses formed the fundamental basis of the epistemological process. However, while pornography both began and ended with the senses, theories of taste in the Shaftesbury tradition acknowledged sense only to seek to show its eventual irrelevance in any "true" aesthetic interaction. Where sense led inward into private experience, aesthetic experience was theorized as that which moved individuals away from sense into an objectified, rational public sphere.

With the goal of affirming a *sensus communis*, a shared public sense, many theories of taste in the eighteenth century that were later integral to Kant's appraisal of the aesthetic sought to prove that art's appeal to the senses was limited. Beginning with Shaftesbury's widely read ideas on taste in *Characteristics of Men, Manners, Opinions, Times* (1711), the measure of a work's value shifted from its pleasurable effects on an audience, or affect, to such purely intrinsic considerations as the "perfection" and "harmony" of the work itself. Shaftesbury's work, notably influential in Germany, explicitly stated that "provoked sense" was antithetical to the contemplation and judgment necessary to appreciate what is truly beautiful. Beauty, Shaftesbury claimed, could not be the object of sense. In language that suggests a political analogy between sensual subjects and the mob, Shaftesbury claimed that only "the riotous mind" was "captive to sense," and could "never enter in competition, or contend for beauty with the virtuous mind of reason's culture."[32] Shaftesbury's language reveals a central issue underlying the concept of taste after the settlement of 1688: political accountability. As Linda Dowling has argued, beneath the debate between sense and reason in matters of taste was the "question of how legitimacy is to be achieved in the liberal polity, how a state that derives its authority from the consent of its people may pretend to be founded upon anything more secure than – as its enemies kept warning – the restless, irrational appetites of an ignorant population."[33] To counter such irrational forces, Shaftesbury conceived of taste as a force that educated one to choose virtue and reason over pleasure, thereby fostering an ideal political order.

Building on Shaftesbury's theories, Kant's philosophy of aesthetic judgment placed artistic consumption in explicit opposition to the kind of sensual consumption by which the pornographic reader made use of his "art," claiming that "A pure judgement of taste has, then, for its determining ground neither charm nor emotion, in a word, no sensation as matter of the aesthetic judgement."[34] Disinterested aesthetic contemplation was figured as antithetical to the kinds of physical reaction prompted by the pornographic. Throughout the eighteenth century, the aesthetic was viewed in its most dominantly understood forms as an invisible social contract. The aesthetic was no hedonistic cult of individual sensibility, as it came to be figured later in the nineteenth century, but rather a binding structure between what Kant saw as "on the one hand, the universal feeling of sympathy, and, on the other, the faculty of being able to communicate universally one's inmost self – properties constituting in conjunction the befitting social spirit of mankind, in contradistinction to the narrow life of the lower animals" (CJ 226). Art was that which allowed the growing community of educated and propertied individuals to represent itself to itself.

As the market for cultural products gained relative autonomy in the first half of the eighteenth century, theories of taste sought to discriminate between modes of consumption, and in doing so to define the boundaries of polite society. Taste was figured in the writings of Shaftesbury, Hutcheson, Jonathan Richardson, and Addison, among others, as that which gave purchase to the polite society of gentlemen. In an article in the *Weekly Register*, Shaftesbury declared that "So much depends on true Taste, with regard to eloquence, and even morality, that no one can be properly stil'd a gentleman, who does not take the opportunity to enrich his own capacity, and settle the elements of taste, which he may improve at leisure."[35] Taste became a sign of conspicuous leisure through which one displayed one's distance from certain types of work through polite conversation about the arts. Taste, however, did not simply display one's leisure, but leisure rigorously and morally applied toward the secular arts.[36]

In a more clear example of taste as upward mobility and a mark of cultural distinction, Jonathan Richardson advised in his 1715 treatise *A Discourse on the Dignity, Certainty, Pleasure and Advantage of the Science of the Connoisseur* that taste in the arts promotes morality:

> If gentlemen were lovers of painting, and connoisseurs, this would help to reform themselves, as their example and influence would have the like effect on the common people. All animated beings naturally covet pleasure, and eagerly pursue it as their chief good; the great affair is to choose those that are worthy of rational beings, such as are not only innocent, but noble and excellent. Men of easy and plentiful fortunes have commonly a great part of their time at their disposal, and the want of knowing how

to pass those hours away, in virtuous amusements, contributes perhaps as much to the mischievous effects of vice, as covetousness, pride, lust, love of wine, or any other passion whatsoever. If gentlemen therefore found pleasure in pictures, drawings, prints, statues, intaglias, and the like curious works of art; in discovering their beauties and defects; in making proper observations thereupon, and in all the other parts of a connoisseur, how many hours of leisure would be profitably employed, instead of what is criminal, mischievous, and scandalous![37]

From this excerpt it is possible to see why Ronald Paulson has remarked that in the eighteenth century "Aesthetics is religion empirically challenged, belief turned into appreciation of beauty, [and] good manners."[38] Taste in the arts was figured by Richardson as a secular alternative to scriptural morality. However Richardson did not emphasize the moral lessons of individual works of art so much as the forms of pleasure available through the process of engaging with them, pleasures "worthy of rational beings." In doing so, he signaled an important shift in eighteenth-century aesthetic philosophy. Where classical aesthetics was primarily oriented toward the work of art, modern aesthetics was, and still is, concerned with the subject enjoying the art; modern aesthetics endeavors to gain a knowledge of the subject's inner state and to describe it with the instruments of empiricism.[39] Richardson was no philosopher, but he implicitly addressed a central concern of most theories of taste in the eighteenth century: how to direct empirical stimuli toward positive, rational, ends. If pornography showed how aesthetic consumption could gratifyingly indulge sensation, theories of taste in Britain, and later in Germany of the aesthetic, offered an alternative view that relied on subjugating the body's interests to those of the mind.

The senses were thus figured as both a problem and a solution in aesthetic theories of the eighteenth century. Given the etymological meaning of the term aesthetic – things material and perceptible to the senses – the project of aesthetics in the tradition of Shaftesbury and Kant, their efforts to limit or transcend the sensual, appear counter-intuitive. However, to understand the importance of limiting the powers of sense in aesthetic theories, one should understand the relationship between the project of taste and the creation of a public sphere of (predominantly Whig) gentlemen.[40] Political authority in this period was granted to those who could abstract ideas out of the raw data of experience and think in general terms. To think generally was to be able to consider the good of the whole over one's personal good. John Barrell has explained that men of independent means in the early eighteenth century were thought to be above private interest, and therefore more worthy to act on the public's behalf. In contrast, a man with an occupation might discover a desire to promote the interests of his occupation, and this would prevent him from discovering what is good for man in general. The experience of such a man would be considered too narrow to serve as a basis of ideas general enough to be represented as true for all mankind. Because mechanical arts (and pornography was considered a mechanical art) are concerned with things, material objects, it was thought they could not offer an opportunity for the exercise of a generalizing and abstract reason. Barrell claims that men of the public sphere believed: "The man of independent means . . . who does not labour to increase them [his means], will be released from private interest, from the occlusions of a narrowed and partial experience of the world, and from an experience of the world as *material*."[41]

If a gentleman considered himself free from materiality, he saw the common man as wallowing in it. James Harris in *Philological Inquiries* (1780–1781) commented that "The vulgar . . . [are] merged in sense from their earliest infancy, never once dreaming anything to be worthy of pursuit, but what either pampers appetite, or fills their purse."[42] Materiality was seen as anathema to politics and gentleman-like behavior. It was vulgar. By extension, it was unsuitable to displays of taste and aesthetic consumption, the activities of the gentleman.

Materialism and selfishness were perceived as forces that worked against polite society and the new breed of gentlemen-rulers who composed the public sphere. As Shaftesbury wrote in *Characteristics*, "A Man of thorow *Good-breeding*, whatever else he be, is incapable of doing a rude or brutal Action. He never *deliberates* in this case, or considers of the matter by prudential Rules of Self-Interest or Advantage. He acts from his Nature."[43] One's "Nature" Shaftesbury argued in his works, is not derived, as Hobbes would have it, from self-interest, but born of a moral "sense" and "natural affection" for society, an ethical sociability that disapproves of individual pleasure.[44] Lawrence Klein has suggested that Shaftesbury and his contemporaries frequently connected Hobbes with the sort of sexual libertinism represented by the Earl of Rochester. The two were associated after an account of Rochester's deathbed conversion circulated the idea that Rochester confessed reading Hobbes had turned him into a voluptuary.[45] Associating Hobbesian individualism with sensual indulgence, Shaftesbury asked,

> Who is there who can well or long enjoy anything, when *alone*, and abstracted perfectly, even in his very Mind and Thought, from every thing belonging to Society? Who wou'd not, on such Terms as these, be presently cloy'd by any sensual Indulgence? Who would not soon grow uneasy with his Pleasure, however exquisite, till he had found means to impart it, and make it *truly pleasant* to him, by communicating, and sharing it at least with some *one* single Person?[46]

Implicit in this and countless other shapings of the experience of taste is an attack against the sensually solipsistic pleasures of pornography. Acquiring, having, and displaying taste is always a communicable, communal activity.

One of the objectives of the philosophies of taste in the Shaftesbury tradition was to discriminate between the proper and improper use of sensations, showing how to abstract the senses into reason or understanding so that they could be articulated as/for communal experience. Philosophers of taste in the Shaftesbury tradition each began from sensuous perception, but worked outward from individual perception toward a conformity with higher laws, often those of divinity, in order to reconcile individual with community, sense with idea. Taste in the Shaftesbury tradition was disembodied as it was abstracted into a sense provided by God. Caygill has suggested that equivocation over whether taste was sensible or ideal issues from the providential foundation of British theorists who claimed that individual judgment was an intuition that was given the status of an idea through providence. Shaftesbury, Hutcheson, Kames, and Burke all claimed that providence could be experienced immediately, like a sense. "In this way," Caygill claims, "the freedom and autonomy of the individual at the level of sense is reconciled with the lawlike characteristics of universality and necessity at the level of idea." However, the result of this conclusion was "the disembodiment of taste; it became an intangible medium of exchange between the rational will of providence and the irrational individual sentiment."[47]

The search for conformity between sentiment and reason, individual sense and universal law that Caygill observes in the thinkers of the Shaftesbury tradition is often expressed as a *je ne sais quois*, or gift of providence. Ironically, the *je ne sais quois*, through its divine provision, grounds the sense of taste as a rational principle, legitimating subjective sentiment by showing its accordance with (divine) law. Shaftesbury articulates the *je ne sais quois* as that which defies analysis and can be described only in terms of the effect it produces:

> However difficult or desperate it may appear in any Artist to endeavour to bring Perfection into his Work; if he has not at least an *Idea of* PERFECTION to give him Aim, he will be found very defective and mean in his Performance. Tho his Intention be to please the World, he must nevertheless be, in a manner, *above it*; and fix his Eye upon that consummate *Grace*, that Beauty of *Nature*, and that *Perfection* of Numbers, which the rest of Mankind, feeling only by the Effect, whilst ignorant of the Cause, term the *Je-ne-scay-quoy* [sic], the unintelligible, or the I know not what; and suppose to be a kind of *Charm*, or *Inchantment*, or which the Artist himself can give no account.[48]

The *je ne sais quois* is supposed to demonstrate the union of sense and reason that reflects the laws of a universe over which God, who gives reason to mankind, presides. But the inability to posit a logical explanation for the relationship between reason and sense leaves the aesthetic *je ne sais quois* vulnerable to the attack of at least one pornographic text, *Venus in the Cloister* (1724). *Venus* mocks the *je ne sais quois* by intimating that it reflects a natural order over which one's own sensations, not God or reason, have sovereignty. The narrator relates:

> After this moment do they kiss who truly love each other, by amorously darting their tongue between the lips of the beloved object. For my part, I find nothing in the world more sweet and delicious when one does it as one should do, and I never put it in practice but I am ravished with ecstasy and so feel all over my body an extraordinary titillation and a certain *je ne sais quoy*, which I am not able otherwise to express than only by telling thee that it is a pleasure which pours itself out with a sweet impetuosity over all my secret parts, which penetrates the most profound recess of my soul, and which I have a right to call the sovereign pleasure.[49]

Sovereign in this passage is not God or reason, but sensual pleasure. This passage shows clearly how pornographic texts viewed themselves in dialogic opposition to the theories of taste and morality of their time. Perpetually asserting the dominion of sense over reason, they frequently attempted to expose the class biases of such theories.

Notably, William Hogarth departed from the Shaftesbury tradition in politically decisive ways that revealed his more solidly middle-class origins. In the *Analysis of Beauty* (1753), he invited *all* readers into his analysis, "Ladies, as well as gentlemen," and stated that "no one may be deterr'd, by want of such previous knowledge, from entering into this enquiry."[50] In doing so, he attacked the very thing which educated gentlemen, as educated males, relied on to assert their ability to judge – abstraction. By opening up the faculties of taste to anyone, Hogarth's treatise ran counter to Hutcheson's notion in *An Inquiry into the Original of our Ideas of Beauty and Virtue* (1735) that though "the noblest Pleasures of the internal Senses, in the Contemplation of the Works of Nature, are expos'd to every one without Expence . . . there are Objects of these internal senses, which require Wealth or Power to procure the use of them as frequently as we desire; as appears in Architecture, Music, Gardening, Painting, Dress, Equipage, Furniture; of which we cannot have the full Enjoyment without Property."[51] Hogarth's *Analysis* worked against much of the early eighteenth-century aesthetic tradition. He suggested that physical stimulation is at the heart of all aesthetic encounters, and that the objects themselves are more important than rules and theories.

Ronald Paulson has done much to recuperate and recontextualize Hogarth's interesting ideas in *The Beautiful, Novel, and Strange: Aesthetics and Heterodoxy*

(1996) and his introduction to the reprinted version of *Analysis of Beauty* (1996). Paulson argues that Hogarth's theories were an antidote to the ideological elitism of the Shaftesbury/Hutcheson school of thought:

> Hogarth, the astute mirror of his society, recognized, [that] Shaftesbury's aesthetic dis-interestedness had a political underside: the alliance of monarch and church is corrected by a government of disinterested (because property-owning, well-off) civic humanist gentlemen; royal patronage of art is corrected by similarly disinterested connoisseurs (the same persons). The only people who can *afford* to appreciate virtue and beauty are the Whig oligarchs – the "many" which the Shaftesburys wanted to balance the "one" of the monarch.[52]

However, as Paulson notes in his introduction to the treatise, "The *Analysis* was not, like Hogarth's prints, a best-seller. There was only one edition in his life-time."[53] By contrast, eleven editions of Shaftesbury's *Characteristics* were printed between 1711 and 1790. Though in hindsight, as subsequent chapters of this book will implicitly show, Hogarth looks like a visionary of twentieth-century aesthetics, his materialist and democratic aesthetics were out of step with his time, and Monroe Beardsley claims they were generally considered "single-minded and simple" by his contemporaries.[54] The critical censure of Hogarth's ideas provides more evidence of the prevailing ideology that aesthetic reception should demonstrate a rational effort to balance or subjugate the effects of sensory stimuli, and in doing so lay claim to one's subject position as a disinterested gen-tleman of the public sphere.

One motivation for the push against pure sensation was England's increasing wealth in the eighteenth century. As John Guillory has argued, the cultivation of taste in the cultural domain became a means of checking the greed and social irresponsibility associated with luxury and uncontrolled consumption.[55] To counter the individual interest in material properties or bodies, appreciation of art had to be realized as that which led away from the particular toward the general. In the tradition of Shaftesbury, Lord Kames argued this idea in *Elements of Criticism* (1785):

> To promote the Fine Arts in Britain, has become of greater importance than is gener-ally imagined. A flourishing commerce begets opulence; and opulence, inflaming our appetite for pleasure, is commonly vented on luxury, and on every sensual gratification: selfishness rears its head; becomes fashionable; and infecting all ranks, extinguishes the *amor patriae*, and every spark of public spirit. To prevent or retard such fatal corrup-tion, the genius of Alfred cannot devise any means more efficacious, than the venting opulence upon the Fine Arts; riches employ'd, instead of encouraging vice, will excite virtue.[56]

Kames's statement exemplifies the way philosophies of taste and morality vilified the senses for their invitation to selfish, anti-social behavior, a behavior troped in the language of sexuality, "inflaming," "exciting," and "begetting." Kames's text also clearly links the project of the aesthetic to the creation of a public sphere. If religion could no longer be relied on to incite virtuous acts of public-spirited beneficence, art had to take its place through an internal disciplining of the aesthetic subject.

An earlier version of this view appeared in Addison's essay *The Pleasures of the Imagination* (1712). The essay's description of the aesthetic as a form of occupational leisure provided an alternative to the drinking and gambling notable in both the aristocratic and lower classes. Because there were "but very few who know how to be idle and innocent," Addison said, virtue had to be cultivated through proper use of the imagination:

> Of this Nature are [the pleasures] of the Imagination, which do not require such a Bent of Thought as is necessary to our more serious Employments, nor, at the same time, suffer the Mind to sink into that Negligence and Remissness, which are apt to accompany our more sensual Delights, but, like a gentle Exercise to the Faculties, awaken them from Sloth and Idleness, without putting them upon any Labour or Difficulty.[57]

If the arts were to become an alternative form of leisure to those that inculcated sloth and sensual indulgence, their mode of consumption had to be regulated in such a way that turned the feelings and sensations produced by art not inward upon the subject, as in pornography, but outward toward the idea of universality. Through this perceived universality a public bond could be created that was based on one's seemingly innermost subjectivity. Though the object of a private and intimate feeling, beauty, as it was represented in theories of taste, purportedly awakened the *idea* of reason present in everyone. In this way it transcended private subjectivity and represented the experience of a *common* sense.

Ironically, British empirical philosophy started out by its own opposition to reason and its belief in sense, but as one classic text of aesthetics notes, "little by little and in various ways [it] allowed the animal frame to absorb reason again, to do its work, and to wear its colors."[58] Thus the work of British empirical philosophies of taste led quite naturally into the conclusions of Kant, who insisted that the fundamental feeling of beauty be perceived "not as a private feeling, but as a public sense" (*CJ* 84) and that beauty's production of the idea of understanding, or reason, necessarily transcends the personal. Kant denied the title of philosophy to British theories of taste because they didn't properly account for the universality and necessity of judgments, but he was nevertheless deeply read in them, and his work shows traces of their thinking, notably, Shaftesbury's.[59]

Kant and modern aesthetics: excising sense

As I have shown, taste in eighteenth-century Britain was really a code of behavior signaling membership within a distinct group of individuals who were in the process of redefining the social order. Though these individuals also likely formed part of pornography's readership, it was central to their public ideal of a civic society that they display taste in a manner distinct from the consumptive patterns of pornography. As the century progressed, the aesthetics of manners became less prominent than theoretical contributions to aesthetics. Frances Ferguson has argued that "The aesthetic, in the process of coming to be defined as something potentially distinct from taste as a particularly demanding version of consumption, becomes less important as social and sociological phenomenon and more important for representing a distinct kind of experience."[60] Kant distinguished himself from British theorists of taste by rigorously attempting to define the aesthetic as a philosophical category. Eighteenth-century Germany differed socio-politically from Britain. Germany had no large urban center, no central authority, nor an educated middle class. While in Britain proponents of taste reflected a mainstream, increasingly dominant view of the social order, in Germany aestheticians reflected an increasing alienation on the part of artists and intellectuals.[61] The mercantile and social differences of the two countries account for some of the distinctions between theories of taste and what in Germany was called the aesthetic.

Throughout this book I will use Kant's *Critique of Judgement* as the focal text for examining the concept of art and aesthetic experience in the modern period. Though since the early eighteenth century there have been a number of different aesthetics whose values are both diachronically and synchronically contingent, as of course are Kant's, no text has dominated modern Western aesthetic thought as Kant's has. The purpose of modern aesthetics was to categorize and distinguish the fine arts as a separate sphere of human activity, distinct not simply from the sciences, but notably from commerce and base sense.[62] Kant's third *Critique* concretized many of the ideas British theories of taste in the tradition of Shaftesbury had sought to establish, and generated the modern conception of art and aesthetic experience that dominated the nineteenth and twentieth centuries. Because of the dominance of aesthetics in the tradition of Shaftesbury and Kant in the nineteenth and early twentieth century, the emergence of explicit sexual representations in the twentieth century and the modernist critical embrace of sense in aesthetic apprehension must be seen as an important break with that tradition. To foreground that break, I want to trace the critical ideas of Kant's aesthetics in his own work and in some of the nineteenth century's most influential thinkers.

In the *Critique of Judgement* Kant balances the tensions between sense and idea in aesthetic reception by creating both a subjective rationale for individual aesthetic judgments, and a universal agreement in those judgments. Aesthetic judgment, while based on private sensations of pain and pleasure, also lays the foundation for the formation of community by extending to everyone individual judgments of taste. Starting from the concept that a judgment of taste is individual, Kant moves toward the idea that "The beautiful is that which, apart from concepts, is represented as the object of a UNIVERSAL delight" (*CJ* 50). While he acknowledges that that universality cannot spring from concepts because there can be no transition from concepts to feelings of pleasure or displeasure, he claims that a judgment about beauty demands the same delight from others:

> By the judgement of taste (upon the beautiful) the delight in an object is imputed to *everyone*, yet without being founded on a concept (for then it would be the good), and that this claim to universality is such an essential factor of a judgement by which we describe anything as *beautiful*, that were it not for its being present to the mind it would never enter into anyone's head to use this expression, but everything that pleased without a concept would be ranked as agreeable. (*CJ* 53)

The key phrase proposed here by Kant is "present to the mind." The beautiful according to Kant is that which engages the mind in a mode of free play that elevates it beyond individual interest toward the *idea* of universality. The concept of "free play" is imagined as a form of disciplined freedom in which a private individual response can be explored in reference to a larger metaphysical (not transcendental) framework. Instead of regarding art as a means of bringing morality to civil society, Kant believes art represents the same natural law which directs individual moral judgment. Individual judgment is ordered not by the institutional representation of natural law, but by an intuition or inner sense of it.[63] Paul de Man argues that in Kant the beautiful shares a moral component manifested in "the autonomy of aesthetic pleasure with regard to sensuous pleasure, a form of freedom and thus, in Kant's system, where morality is always linked to liberty, at least potentially a form of moral judgment."[64] Aesthetic free play as manifest by the beautiful always implies a formal/ethical disciplining of the subject.

Kant presents the beautiful in distinct contrast to the agreeable, which rests solely on private sensation and individual taste and so elides the communal. Kant defines agreeable art as that in which "pleasure should accompany the representations considered as mere *sensations*" (*CJ* 165). The agreeable never transcends the sensible. The agreeable, in fact, poses a threat to judgment (a middle term in the Kantian lexicon between understanding and reason) and "where agreeableness is of the liveliest type a judgement on the character of the Object is so entirely out of place, that those who are always intent only on enjoyment (for that is the word used to denote intensity of gratification) would fain dispense with all judgement" (*CJ* 45). Kant defines the agreeable as the irrational pleasures built solely upon personal sensation and "what GRATIFIES a man" (*CJ* 49). In doing so, he clearly marks a boundary between the pornographic and the aesthetic.

What raises an object from the merely agreeable to the beautiful is a finality of form that allows the mind in its free play with that form to achieve a disinterested, or non-personal, delight that is universally communicable. Communication, in fact, grounds Kant's assessment of aesthetic pleasure. The concept of the universal communicability of a pleasure implies that the pleasure does not arise out of mere sensation but out of reflection; in doing so, pleasure enables community (*CJ* 166). Central to the communicability of aesthetic experience is the form that enables it. In apprehending the beautiful, the subject's mind is characterized by restful contemplation and disinterest. His or her mind is set into a mode of free play by the finality of form offered in the beautiful object. Form does not gratify by sensation, but merely pleases, the fundamental prerequisite for taste.[65] By focusing on form as a necessary validation of the aesthetic exchange, Kant finally excises the senses from the aesthetic. Through aesthetic pleasure form allows for an understanding that can be universally communicated, and by which one can judge taste subjectively, but also as universally appreciable. Shaftesbury makes a similar claim for the importance of form in his argument that the value of beauty lies in what it reveals in the realm of form. The animal, which is irrevocably subject to the power of its emotional response, is excluded from the world of pure forms. Form, Shaftesbury maintains, can never be understood and assimilated unless it is distinguished from mere effect and made an independent object of aesthetic contemplation.[66]

The agreeable, with its gravitational pull toward irrational, sensual pleasure, threatens to undermine "pure" judgments of taste. What distinguishes the agreeable and the beautiful in the apprehending subject is interest or disinterest. The subject of the agreeable has an interest in that agreeable object. The subject of the beautiful is, in Kant, as in the Shaftesbury tradition, described as disinterested.[67] The economically charged vocabulary of aesthetic consumption reveals the efforts of this line of aesthetic philosophy to remove the aesthetic from the sphere of commercial value into its own, seemingly transcendent, autonomous sphere of aesthetic value, what in the nineteenth century comes to be associated with the Art for Art's Sake movement. A striking example of the attempt to make this distinction can be found in Shaftesbury's *Characteristics,* where a Socratic character relates one of his dialogues, informing his pupil that formal treatment of an object, rather than the value of an object, is responsible for aesthetic value:

> I know, good Philocles, you are no such admirer of wealth in any kind as to allow much beauty to it, especially in a rude heap or mass. But in medals, coins, embossed work, statues, and well-fabricated pieces, of whatever sort, you can discover beauty and admire the kind. True, said I, but not for the metal's sake.
> 'Tis not then the metal or matter which is beautiful with you? No. But the art? Certainly. The art then is the beauty? Right. And the art is that which beautifies? The same. So that the beautifying, not the beautified, is the really beautiful? It seems so.[68]

As this excerpt makes clear, Shaftesbury specifically distinguishes economic from aesthetic value, practical interest from aesthetic contemplation, the object, even as artistic object, from the shaping artistic intention.

Disinterest relies on one's ability to remain outside of any personal interest, whether that interest signifies a bodily desire or, as the word often implied in the eighteenth century, an obligation through one's position. One's ability to remain disinterested, then, often implied one's position of social advantage. In a circular logic, this advantage was further supported through one's ability to exemplify taste. In its earliest incarnation as an aesthetic principle, disinterest signified the connection between Shaftesbury's political and aesthetic concerns. For it was the property owner, the civic humanist, who was thought to be above considerations of ambition, possession, consumption, and desire, and therefore capable of a "rational and refined contemplation" of both morality and beauty – capable, as Ronald Paulson has shown, of both governing men and judging art.[69]

Theories of taste that advocated aesthetic disinterest arose in conjunction with the increased production of cultural goods. As Guillory has pointed out

> The division of labor, the employment of wage-labor, vastly increased the accumulation of commodities, but it did not necessarily increase their fineness; it rather exposed the apparent aesthetic inferiority of commodities to works of art. Hence the qualitative distinction between the work of art and the commodity could be coordinated with class distinction as the distinction between taste and the lack of it.[70]

Kant's aesthetic denied personal interest, involvement, or an enjoyment of the senses, and in doing so set up a hierarchy of consumptive modes. Pierre Bourdieu has suggested that this hierarchy duplicates itself in the social sphere and that

Civil society

> The pure aesthetic is rooted in an ethic, or rather, an ethos of elective distance from the necessities of the natural and social world . . . The detachment of the pure gaze cannot be dissociated from a general disposition towards the world which is the paradoxical product of conditioning by negative economic necessities – a life of ease – that tends to induce an active distance from necessity.[71]

Taste classifies the classifier, and Kantian judgments of taste were based on a class that could distance itself from material necessity, the bourgeois elite. In *The Structural Transformation of the Public Sphere*, Jürgen Habermas has represented this elite as the emergent bourgeois public characterized by the "rational-critical debate of private people in the *salons*, clubs and reading societies" whose activities were "not directly subject to the cycle of production and consumption, that is, to the dictates of life's necessities."[72] Important to understanding the social divide between aesthetic and pornographic reception, the bourgeoisie were increasingly associated with the economic and aesthetic distancing characterized by the reflective judgment demanded in Kant's third *Critique*.

A salient example of this distancing can be found in Addison's and Steele's periodical, *The Spectator*. The title already suggesting a remove from necessity, Addison's first editorial piece declares, "I live in the world rather as a spectator of mankind than as one of the species."[73] Addison's distancing gaze constitutes itself as at once respectable and superior by substituting observation for participation.[74] What's more, Addison's aesthetic model claims that a form of cultural capital is earned through the specific mode of aesthetic consumption based on elective distance. "A man of polite imagination," Addison says, "is let into a great many pleasures that the vulgar are not capable of receiving . . . It gives him, indeed, a kind of *property* in everything he sees, and makes the most rude uncultivated parts of nature administer to his pleasures" (my emphasis).[75] Notably, Addison's gaze resembles the pornographic in its voyeuristic interest, its subjugation of experience to the visual sense. However, Addison's reaching after "a kind of property" should also be seen as an attempt to claim an economy of symbolic or cultural capital based on an appropriative aesthetic gaze.

Eighteenth-century philosophies of taste that relied on disinterest constituted a social hierarchy between those who had taste and manifested it through an elective distance, and those who lacked taste and manifested it through a sensually and economically interested mode of consumption. This differentiation reified the burgeoning split between high and low culture, or, as it was often labeled, between culture and nature. "The antithesis between culture and bodily pleasure (or nature)," Bourdieu offers, "is rooted in the opposition between the cultivated bourgeoisie and the people, barbarously wallowing in pure enjoyment."[76] Distinctions between high and low culture have continuously been made on this dialectic well into the twentieth century, the high typically manifesting itself in some form of passivity and distance, the low in active immediacy.

While Kant inherited a philosophical tradition beginning with Plato that registered a deep mistrust of the senses, it is interesting that he accorded a place, albeit low on the scale of aesthetic experience, to sensual encounters. By doing so he effectively reinscribed social delineations of the bodily and sensual as low (and lower class) and the mental and intelligible as high (and upper class). Slippage between the agreeable and the beautiful, in their individual associations with pleasures, vulgar and refined, was problematic to Kant. While such slippage carries the obvious implication of the mixing of the classes, it also implies the more critical aspect of art's subject-rendering function. That is, in art's mirror-like ability to confirm in the gaze of its viewer or reader the taste and values sought there, an agreeable charm captures its subject in and through interest and violates both the subjective and the cultural order proposed by Kant's aesthetic. The Kantian cultural order relies on the disciplining freedom of the aesthetic for its maintenance. Art creates a demand for subjectivity, and reformulates the question of the utility of art as a question of the motivelessness of subjectivity itself.[77] The sensuous charms of the agreeable pose a threat to that subjectivity-as-motivelessness, as Kant here implies:

> Charms may be added to beauty to lend to the mind, beyond a bare delight, an adventitious interest in the representation of the object, and thus to advocate taste and its cultivation. This applies especially where taste is as yet crude and untrained. But they are positively subversive of the judgement of taste, if allowed to obtrude themselves as grounds of estimating beauty. For so far are they from contributing to beauty, that it is only where taste is still weak and untrained, that, like aliens [fremdlinge], they are admitted as a favour, and only on the terms that they do not violate that beautiful form. (CJ 67)

Kant grants alien status to the sensual charms of the agreeable as long as they facilitate the revelation of form and remain accidental to the "true" judgment of beauty. Kant's ideas share with early nineteenth-century German philosophers Hegel, Schiller, and Schopenhauer, among others, a drive to stave off the forces of interest, desire, and irrationality from a pure sphere of understanding. The senses are constantly disavowed in favor of a disinterested mode of reason. Yet as Jean-Luc Nancy has pointed out, a deep self-enjoyment arises out of what he calls "the supreme and secret interest" of reason: "The disinterestedness of the judgement of beauty, caught in the logic of *ratio artifex*, is a profound interestedness:

one has an interest in the being anticipated of unity, in the (pre)formation of the figure, in the avoidance of chaos."[78] The unity Nancy speaks of is a fiction of unity that allows one's subjectivity to be reified in the apprehension of the object, thus creating (at least the anticipation of) a unified, symbolic self.

Judgments of taste perform a perpetual reconstitution of such subjectivity, demanding not simply an object with qualities that can be said to exist *a priori*, but rather a specific attitude or set of practices in conjunction with that object, in this case, a distancing that allows for a free play of the cognitive faculties (which, Bourdieu makes clear above, are the conditions of a certain economic ease). When Kant said that "the agreeable in no way conduces to our culture," (*CJ* 117) he delineated a mode of cultivation that allowed one to distinguish oneself through a form of disinterested pleasure experienced in the cultural consumption of aesthetic objects that, at the least, sublimated their affect. "Pure pleasure," Bourdieu claims, "ascetic, empty pleasure which implies the renunciation of pleasure, pleasure purified of pleasure – is predisposed to become a symbol of moral excellence, and the work of art a test of ethical superiority, an indispensable measure of the capacity for sublimation which defines the truly human man" as created through aesthetic philosophy.[79]

It hardly needs to be said that pornographic representations of sexual acts, in their direct appeals to the senses and their propensity to elicit extreme reactions of physical interest in their subjects, would fall outside of Kant's notion of the beautiful. Pornography was among the spectrum of other arts, or cultural commodities, of affect that the Kantian aesthetic demarcated as outside the realm of aesthetic value. True or fine art demonstrates, in Kant's famous dictum, "purposiveness without purpose." The fine arts are characterized by inutility, creating merely "play" within the faculty of judgment. In contrast, pornography produces affect, a form of bodily work in its consumers. It remains firmly within the commercial.[80]

What both British empiricists and German idealist philosophers of the eighteenth and nineteenth century acknowledged, and what seemed to create a problem for them, is the material presence of the human body in all aesthetic interactions (phrased differently, materiality is the primary consideration from which they create their philosophies of purity and of mind).[81] While Kant begrudgingly created a category for sensuous experience under the idea of the agreeable, he did not allow the category to enter into the cultivated experience of fine art. It remains lowly, outside, "alien." Kant's determination is philosophically overdetermined and can be found in much of the philosophy of the eighteenth and early nineteenth centuries.[82] For instance, Hegel leaves the body outside of the privileged sphere of the beautiful. In his lectures on art, which appeared in 1835, he said, "Mind, and mind alone, is pervious to truth, comprehending all in itself, so that all which is beautiful can only be veritably beautiful as partaking in this higher sphere and begotten of the same."[83]

The Hegelian dialectic, however, is better able to confront the body through its double mode of incorporation and transcendence. Hegel created in the category of fine art the primary bond of mediation between that which is exclusively external, sensuous, and transitory, and the medium of pure thought (*PFA* 388). He sought a unity between material, sensuous phenomena and reason, the mind. But his was an unequal union where the only experiences that could be said to be true were those in which the idea transcends the medium, where thoughts are delivered from their sensuous media.

In *Philosophy of Fine Art* Hegel framed "purely sensuous sensation" as inimical to the intelligence that is the prerequisite of individual freedom, the liberal autonomy for which the aesthetic stands as a model. Desire, the product of the mind turned sensuously inward upon itself, isolates the individual and disrupts the social order. Of this Hegel said:

> In this negative relation desire requires for itself not merely the superficial show of external objects, but the actual things themselves in their material concrete existence . . . its [desire's] craving is just this to force it to annihilate this self-subsistency and freedom of external facts, and to demonstrate that these things are only there to be destroyed and devoured. But at the same time the particular person is neither himself free, begirt as he is by the particular and limited interests of his desires.   (*PFA* 406)

Freedom according to Hegel is to escape the "particular and limited interests" of one's desire, to master the body by way of the mind. Freedom from materiality is necessary to autonomy.

This passage helps to elucidate the overlapping concerns of both Hegel and Kant and the participation of these themes in the hegemonic Western aesthetic ideas of the eighteenth and early nineteenth centuries. The order set up by both philosophers is based on a lack of bodily need, a disavowal of desire, control over objects through cognitive distance, and a belief in the possibility of universal consensus in the experience of the beautiful. Art's "true function," Hegel said, "is exclusively to satisfy spiritual interests, and to shut the door on all approach to mere desire" (*PFA* 407). Why this vilification of desire? Perhaps more significantly, how did desire come to be so naturalized? The interpretation of desire as a fundamental ordering principle was concomitant with the rise of the volitional, empirical subject and the capitalist order in the seventeenth and eighteenth centuries. This shift toward empirically realized desire was the enabling moment of the pornographic, and that from which the aesthetic recoiled.

Kant and Hegel trope sensuous desire as "alien," uncannily using the same word to demarcate the boundaries of disinterested aesthetic experience. In one of the passages from *Critique of Judgement* quoted above, Kant distinguished the sensuous charms of the agreeable from the more austere experience of the beautiful, arguing that "So far are they from contributing to beauty, that it is only where taste is still weak and untrained, that, *like aliens [fremdlinge]*, they are admitted as a favour" (my italics, *CJ* 67). That passage closely resembles one in *Philosophy of Fine Art* where Hegel made the claim that art's value lies in its ability to remove the viewer from the conditions of his own passions and to provide an admirable objectivity:

> [art] places before the vision of the mind pictures of passion . . . a power of amelioration is contained therein . . . The man in this way contemplates his impulses and inclinations, and whereas apart from this they whirl him away without giving him time to reflect, he now sees them outside himself and already, for the reason that they come before him rather as objects than a part of himself, he begins to be free from them as *aliens [fremdlinge]*. (my italics, *PFA* 419)

It is striking that both men used the word alien [*fremdlinge*] to describe subject-centering forms of aesthetic experience. For certainly there were sectors of the populace that were alien to the disembodied disinterest that formed this culturally dominant matrix. Indeed, as the body was so frequently figured in dominant discourse as the working or lower classes (and in pornography as the body politic), the disavowal of the senses, and by extension the body, in the aesthetic interaction suggests a cultural mode of distinction that operated under the principle of limited access to cultural goods, an access dependent on a superiority to economic necessity. While Kant figured these aliens as absolutely outside the realm of the beautiful, Hegel interestingly designed a model in which the alien, that which induces or is desire, exists *within* the subject. His model made way for increasingly modern interpretations of desire and the desiring body by Schopenhauer and Freud that likewise locate the alien within.

Though Schopenhauer's *The World as Will and Idea* was written in 1819, before Hegel's aesthetic work was known, it was not popularized until the revised version appeared in 1844. Terry Eagleton has heralded Schopenhauer as perhaps the first major modern thinker to place the abstract category of desire itself at the center of his work.[84] It was Schopenhauer who declared with great Romantic gloom that, "So long as our consciousness is filled by our will, so long as we are given up to the throng of desires with their constant hopes and fears, so long as we are the subject of willing, we can never have lasting happiness nor peace."[85] Art's purpose, according to Schopenhauer, is to lift its viewer out of the "endless stream of willing" beyond subjectivity to a mode whereby the subject can know the object purely. The will taints knowing and idea, but man is necessarily of twin urges, "at once impetuous and blind striving of will (whose pole or focus lies in the genital organs), and eternal, free, serene subject of pure knowing (whose pole is the brain)."[86] As in the aesthetic philosophy of Kant and Hegel, Schopenhauer conceived art as a middle term between absolute sensuousness and absolute reason. He imagined art as a realm of disciplined freedom wherein the subject tamed his or her sensuousness through its own objectification. This led Schopenhauer to say that "*we ourselves are* the will whose adequate objectification at its highest grade is here to be judged and discovered."[87] This objectification is central to modern aesthetics and its relationship to the senses. As will be shown later in this book, when modernist artists began to represent explicit sexuality in their texts, part of their success in doing so under the rubric of art lay in their ability to create an objectified distance from such representations.

While German thinkers were building on Kant's ideas and developing a tradition of Idealism, British philosophers and artists of the nineteenth century were absorbing and assimilating Kantian aesthetics to their own empirical tradition. English adaptations of Kantian philosophy in the first half of the nineteenth century, with the exception perhaps of Coleridge, frequently translated it into the framework of British orthodoxy, as René Wellek has pointed out.[88] Though not universally accepted, Kant's influence on British thought became widespread after Carlyle's popularization of German ideas, including Kant's, in *The Life of Friedrich Schiller* (1825) and in the English translations of Kant's works that appeared in the 1830s. W. David Shaw notes in *The Lucid Veil* Kant's direct and indirect influence on such central Victorian figures as Arthur Hallam, Alfred, Lord Tennyson, J. S. Mill, H. L. Mansel, David Masson, H. G. Lewes, Robert Browning, and Arthur Hugh Clough.[89] Kant's thought was well absorbed into British aesthetic thought by the end of the nineteenth century, as I will explore in chapters two and three. On the Continent, the dialectic between sense and reason continued to be probed in significant ways, as I explain below.

The nineteenth century: the aesthetic and the pornographic in dialectic

Reflecting an important shift in dominant thought, several thinkers in the nineteenth century began to accommodate, indeed to validate, the body as the basis for a positive social order. As the body was "realized" in philosophical discourse (some aesthetic, some not), the attempts of the aesthetic to derealize the body through reflective judgment were undermined. Marx, Nietzsche, and Freud all participated in a philosophy that begins with the body and finds bodily episte-mological and aesthetic experiences valid. In doing so, they reflected significant changes in the social order, as will be explored in subsequent chapters.

Marx's thinking provides an apt example of the mutually generative dialectic between sense and reason in the nineteenth century. While his political philos-ophy is deeply rooted in sense perception and the body as the valid foundation of being and knowing, his aesthetic philosophy tends to reify the conclusions of the idealist philosophers (against whose work he rebelled) in concluding that the arts ought to bring objectivity to the senses. In the *Economic and Philosophical Manuscripts of 1844* he wrote,

> Only through the objectively unfolded richness of man's essential being is the richness of subjective *human* sensibility (a musical ear, an eye for beauty of form – in short, *senses* capable of human gratifications, senses confirming themselves as essential powers of *man*) either cultivated or brought into being . . . The *forming* of the five senses is a labor of the entire history of the world down to the present.[90]

The language of the quote is unstable and can be read as either that which confirms the conclusions of a necessary objectivity in Kant, Hegel, and Schopenhauer, or as that which undermines objectivity by suggesting an ulti-mate power in the subjective senses. Though Marx allowed for a gratification of the senses, that gratification had to arise through an objectification. In this way he appears to have stressed the opposition of art and the senses as did Kant and Hegel.

Similarly, Marx described beauty as that which surpasses animal need. Making the distinction he said:

> The animal is immediately identical with its life-activity. It does not distinguish itself from it. It is *its life-activity*. Man makes his life-activity itself the object of his will and of his consciousness. He has conscious life-activity . . . An animal produces only itself, while man reproduces the whole of nature. An animal's product belongs immediately to its physical body, while man freely confronts his product.[91]

Marx conceived of art, or any product of work, as the objectification of the senses, or, as he said, the making "conscious" of one's life activity; porno-graphy is little different in the sense that it induces a sexual practice that is the making conscious of one's responsive sensual impulses. Yet the pornographic is so frequently figured as a reflexive rather than a reflective activity that, in the terms Marx proposed above, he participated in asserting the aesthetic as oppositional to the animal production of the physical body, and hence the pornographic.

To assert the other side of the dialectic, Marx wrote in his *Economic and Philosophical Manuscripts* that "*sense perception* must be the basis of all science. Only when science starts out from sense perception in the dual form of *sensuous* consciousness and *sensuous* need – i.e. only when science starts out from nature – is it *real* science."[92] Indeed, in Marx's vilification of commodifying abstraction, he assumed an aesthetic position ideally responsive to particularity, specifically sensuous particularity, the opposite of the Kantian aesthetic. The separation of use from pleasure is a privileged realm of disconnection from material determinacy (a realm disavowed by the pornographic), a form of consumption that only the idle rich can afford to enjoy – the consumption of their own acts of pleasurable consumption. While Marx saw the human senses as an end in themselves, he saw the human body under capitalism tragically divided between the utter biologistic and material need in which sensuous existence is stripped bare (the have-nots), and the complete lack of need in which sensuous existence is bloated by whim and becomes "perversely self-productive, a matter of 'refined, unnatural, and *imaginary* appetites'"[93] (the haves). In either case, sensuous existence is the fundamental medium through which one's economic circumstances are experienced. Those circumstances shape human experience and there is no form of transcendence, save capital itself.

Nietzsche, too, insisted on the body as the fundamental, unavoidable fact around which idealist philosophy had drawn its abstractions. He was quick to point out the failure of idealism to maintain barriers between mind and body, art and sense. In the aptly titled chapter from *Beyond Good and Evil*, "On the Prejudices of Philosophers," Nietzsche remarked that philosophers "rank the credibility of their own bodies about as low as the credibility of the visual evidence that 'the earth stands still,' and thus, apparently in good humor, let their securist possessions go (for in what does one at present believe more firmly in than one's body?)."[94] He decentered the Kantian aesthetic by saying, "Behind all logic and its seeming sovereignty of movement, too, there stand valuations or, more clearly, physiological demands for a certain type of life."[95] Those physiological demands arise from the material conditions that produce the subject of an aesthetic judgment. In consecrating the sensible world, Nietzsche denied the intelligible world that Kant had maintained as an idea necessary to reason. As they were for Marx, bodies to Nietzsche were always already politicized and sensuous bodies, and they meant the impossibility of disinterested speculation.

Marx and Nietzsche articulated what became increasingly common in the social and intellectual sphere as the nineteenth century progressed, a loss of faith in the centered, rational subject. As Nietzsche argued in *The Gay Science*, "because the subject is fractured, our evaluations, our points of view, our interpretations of the world can never be grounded on any kind of reference to absolute knowledge in its strict meaning (that is, unrelated to life's historicity)."[96] Though Nietzsche came to his conclusions from a different political perspective than Marx (Nietzsche being an advocate of the aristocratic body, Marx the working class), their work served to reduce the importance of judgment, reason, and knowledge, while making the body the site of political accountability.

Freud clearly put sense experience into dialectic with aesthetic experience. Whereas sensuous experience was seen in Kant as the irrational, that which has no pretense to reason, Freud created a rational narrative for the irrational in his theory of the unconscious. As Leo Bersani has suggested, "Psychoanalysis is an unprecedented attempt to give a theoretical account of precisely those forces which obstruct, undermine, and play havoc with theoretical accounts themselves."[97] The unconscious formulates an antagonism internal to thought itself. It portrays rationality as perpetually threatened from unknowable sources within. Freud said, "We have found . . . that very powerful mental processes or ideas exist (and here a quantitative or *economic* factor comes into question for the first time) which can produce all the effects in mental life that ordinary ideas do (including effects that can in their turn become conscious as ideas), though they themselves do not become conscious."[98] The body in Freud becomes the stage upon which the irrational acts out its strange drama of instability, thereby reinscribing the body as completing the logic of the irrational (as manifest, for instance, in symptoms). In this sense the body becomes associated with a more profound truth than the mind, whose reason is "exposed" by Freud as a tool of the irrational, always already destabilized by the irrational faculty of desire.

In the realm of the aesthetic, Freud dealt another death blow to the Kantian notion of the serenely balanced subject of disinterested inquisition. Recalling the derivation of the word aesthetic from the Greek *aisthesis*, or sense perception, Freud implicated all of human experience in the realm of aesthetics, aesthetics being about intense bodily sensations and the figurative imaginings that seek out and try to reproduce those sensations (or the ego they perpetually create). "The ego is ultimately derived from bodily sensations," Freud claimed in *The Ego and the Id*, "it may thus be regarded as a mental projection of the surface of the body."[99] In his creation of id, ego and superego, Freud deftly reinscribed the tradition of moral and aesthetic philosophy onto the individual subject. The long-standing problem of moral and aesthetic philosophy, the relation between the sensible and the intelligible, was essentially transferred in Freud's conception to an internalized battle that demonstrates the success of aesthetic philosophy in shifting the problems of social responsibility from the state to the self-regulating subject. Like the modern notion of the aesthetic artifact, the modern bourgeois subject is autonomous, the law having been inscribed within. The ego reduplicates the aesthetic even as it undermines the premises upon which it was created; so far as it is a "mental projection of the surface of the body," the ego is essentially a reenactment of the mental objectification of the body that is a necessary constituent of the aesthetic in the tradition of Shaftesbury and Kant. Like the subject of the aesthetic who represses its sensuous call, the ego is perpetually figured as "wresting away" from the sensual forces of the id. But as Freud said, the ego is a "bodily ego." In saying so, Freud privileged the body as the site of accountability.

Desire in Freud, embraced as the law under which all humans operate, creates a subversion of idealist aesthetics not simply because of its insistence on interest in every artistic exchange, but also because of its place in decentering the subject through its complicated paths to fulfillment. The subject is no longer an all-controlling ego, but a system of forces continually displacing one another in competition for the gratification of different "drives." As opposed to the Kantian or Schopenhauerian notion of the subject who has desires that are simply transcended in the face of the beautiful, which further stabilizes the subject, the always already desiring Freudian subject is always decentered, already alienated from a centered self by the perpetual movements of desire within. Whereas in the classical aesthetic model desire is generally conceived as generating from individual needs or wishes, desire in Freud operates as an anonymous system of laws, the rules of which are unpredictably based upon individual experience. Aesthetic experience can never reify the subject because there is no stable subject to confirm.

In *Civilization and its Discontents* Freud described the aesthetic in a way that reflects the aesthetic tradition of German idealism, yet clearly violates its general principles:

> The enjoyment of beauty has a peculiar, mildly intoxicating quality of feeling. Beauty has no obvious use; nor is there any clear cultural necessity in it. Yet civilization could not do without it. The science of aesthetics investigates the conditions under which things are felt as beautiful, but it has been unable to give any explanation of the nature and origin of beauty, and, as usually happens, lack of success is concealed beneath a flood of resounding and empty words. Psychoanalysis, unfortunately, has scarcely anything to say about beauty either. *All that is certain is its derivation from the field of sexual feeling.*[100] (my italics)

Civil society

Published in German in 1930, this passage counters much that Kantian aesthetics sought to establish. While maintaining its inutility, the aesthetic is no longer
self-producing, but produced by sexual feeling. Sexual feeling elides the aesthetic
as a social project. It implies a personal, bodily interest, the very sensual interest
that the culturally dominant philosophies of taste and the aesthetic from
Shaftesbury to Kant set out to limit. Yet what Freud propagates in common with
Kant is the notion of a universality in the form of a libidinal impulse common
to all (it differs significantly from Kant in that it is not necessarily articulable).
By doing so he assures the homogeneity of bodily desire, making all bodies equal
under the laws of physiology. As is asserted in much pornography, sex is a social
leveler. The cultural distinctions that eighteenth-century aesthetic philosophy
set out to create for art are here quickly folded back into their foundation. Freud
collapses the apparent opposition between the pornographic and the aesthetic
back into dialectical relation in order to show their common basis in sense and
desire.

The aesthetic of the obscene

Having very broadly sketched the dialectic of the pornographic and the aesthetic
from the eighteenth century to the turn of the twentieth century, I have showed
their common roots in the seventeenth-century shift toward empirical epistemology, their opposition in the eighteenth- and early nineteenth-century
philosophies of, among others, Shaftesbury, Hutcheson, Kant, Hegel, and
Schopenhauer, and then their collapse back into dialectic in the works of important nineteenth-century thinkers such as Marx, Nietzsche, and Freud. The
remainder of this book will look at that dialectic through the prism of an artistic development within the British literary tradition in the second half of the
nineteenth century that flourished in the twentieth: the aesthetic of the
obscene.[101]

What I will call the aesthetic of the obscene is a mode of sexual representation that, while potentially affecting the sensual interests of its readers, does not,
as opposed to pornography, seek sexual arousal as its main purpose. I will primarily address the literary form of this aesthetic, though because Aubrey
Beardsley's drawings participate so completely in this aesthetic, I include his
work as an important example. Pornography, a genre of sexual writing that in
itself constitutes a sexual practice, enjoyed at the turn of the twentieth century
a select upper-middle and upper-class readership of collectors in its most rarefied
form, as well as a mass audience in its leaflet and visual forms. Pornography was

not and never has been part of the dominant cultural order. Since 1727 it has been labeled obscene, offensive to publicly accepted taste and morality. I use the word obscene to acknowledge the social dimensions of an objectified public taste in the late nineteenth and early twentieth centuries. For it was in this period that charges against obscenity in literature (mostly, though not solely, pertaining to sexualized representations) became publicly visible.

In contrast to the pornographic, the aesthetic of the obscene seeks to be accepted into the cultural mainstream, and it does so by mediating its own materialist interests with idealist artistic techniques that promote the kind of consumptive practices associated with the aesthetic. Though an offshoot of the culturally outcast genre pornography, the aesthetic of the obscene developed within the context of dominant cultural traditions, what we categorize as canonical literature. The introduction of explicitly sexualized (often genitally focused), desiring bodies onto the page in publicly esteemed literature marked a redistribution and appropriation of pornographic and aesthetic forms. That which in its pure, repetitive form would be called pornography is excised and displaced into a larger social and ethical context – a poem, novel, or drawing. As such, the would-be pornographic forms part of the body of the work of art. In its new, contextualized space, the pornographic is no longer solely obscene, or offensive to taste, but aestheticized through a contextualization that works to objectify and distance its appeal to the senses. I call it an aesthetic of the obscene in an attempt to capture the seemingly paradoxical nature of representing the "unrepresentable." The cohabitation of the aesthetic and the obscene as manifest in pornography is the culmination of their mutually generative dialectic.

The aesthetic of the obscene works in many ways antithetical to the aesthetic of the beautiful, that which we have come to identify as "the aesthetic," in that it provokes a particular and individual, often bodily, response from a specific, not necessarily idealized, object of sexual interest. While not by necessity aiming to address an individual viewer or reader in his or her sensual particularity, its effect is such that it registers decidedly individual sensual impact that cannot necessarily be universally communicated. In this way it promotes a turning inward upon the subject. Yet this focusing inward upon the sensual self, when brought into alignment with the ethical and other social concerns of the literary work as a whole, can also be seen as a movement outward, yet another way of bringing the sensations and emotions into the realm of reason. The aesthetic of the obscene continues to objectify and distance the senses, and in doing so it perpetuates the project of the aesthetic traditions I have outlined. Such a distancing, however, is only effective when brought into conjunction with specific reading practices. Such reading practices will have to be placed historically, as this book sets out to do, in order to understand how the aesthetic of the obscene gains high-art status.

The aesthetic of the obscene, as it develops at the turn of the century, is a culmination of the mutually generative dialectic of the pornographic and the aesthetic, one that brings the two together while maintaining their individual identities within their union. It is at once material – displaying and therefore provoking bodily desire – and ideal – rendering the senses vulnerable to the rational faculties through formal, idealized techniques. The representation of the sexual is legitimated through the assertion of form which holds off the collapse into the pornographic.[102] Such representations are made titillating by the careful balancing acts they perform between legitimate and illegitimate culture, perpetually laying bare the risk of going beyond permitted boundaries. Indeed, as many texts show, there is no guarantee of the suppression of interest on the part of the reader, and the pornographic often works to destabilize the aesthetic by which it is circumscribed. Lynda Nead has commented that erotic art, as opposed to pornography, succeeds in addressing the viewer as a unified and rational subject, much like the beautiful in the Kantian scheme.[103] However, in order for a subject to have a notion of a unified and rational self, that subject must be interpenetrated by a larger cultural order that creates the idea of such a subject, a symbolic self, as it were. The aesthetic of the obscene participates in the dominant cultural order by simultaneously creating subjects while it is created by them. Crucial to its success in the twentieth century has been the establishment of a legitimating body of ideas by which it is to be read, which in turn created its reading subjects. The fact that today one rarely picks up a book that doesn't contain what is now commonly called "the obligatory sex scene" would suggest that that ideology has successfully penetrated our cultural consciousness.

2 Victorian obscenities: the new reading public, pornography, and Swinburne's sexual aesthetic

Edmund Gosse characterized the British poetry scene in the 1860s as a time of almost deadening quiescence. Tennyson had settled into the tasteful repose of his laureateship, Browning was squirreled away producing *The Ring and the Book*, and minor writers were remaining resolutely so.[1] Looking for the next great poetic genius, literary London began to place its hopes on one particularly promising young poet, a Pre-Raphaelite with a preternatural ear for melody and an uncommon breadth of reading. In May of 1866, Monckton Milnes, Lord Houghton, celebrated this promising talent at the Anniversary Dinner for the Royal Literary Fund, gathering together the likes of Anthony Trollope, Charles Kingsley, and Leslie Stephens. Seeking to answer the question of who might best represent England's poetic future, a Royal Literary Fund spokesman declared that, "The representative of that future generation [of poets] is, I say without fear or hesitation, Mr. Swinburne. He alone, of his age, has shown power to succeed in the highest walks of poetry."[2] Algernon Charles Swinburne replied to the numerous accolades bestowed upon him that night with his usual blend of brilliance and conceited brio, delivering a brief, memorized lecture on his preferences for the "sunburned" pleasures of the French troubadors over Dante's sterner lessons. At that point it seemed clear that Swinburne was destined for poetic greatness.

Three months later Swinburne's life and reputation would be changed forever. With the publication of *Poems and Ballads* in August, Swinburne went from being hailed as the next great poet of England to being vilified as "the libidinous laureate of a pack of satyrs."[3] *Poems and Ballads, First Series* was vehemently attacked in the press as recklessly sexual and anti-Christian. Reviewers were unwilling to swallow what Richard Burton characterized as "so much undiluted paganism."[4] When his publisher, J. Bertram Payne of Moxon, learned that *The Times* was preparing an attack on the book that would demand criminal prosecution, he curtly informed Swinburne that he was withdrawing *Poems and Ballads* from sale.

Before publication Swinburne had been urged to expurgate his poems by his friends. George Meredith had implored him; "I, who love your verse, would play savagely with a knife among the proofs for the sake of your fame; and because I want to see you take the first place, as you may if you will."[5] Dante Gabriel Rossetti had worried that the language of *Poems and Ballads* would "make a few not even particular hairs stand on end, to say nothing of other erections equally obvious."[6] But Swinburne refused to bowdlerize his work. When Moxon withdrew the volume, Swinburne was forced to choose between a quiet retreat into obscurity or dubious notoriety by publishing with a questionable imprint. He chose to publish his poems with John Camden Hotten, a publisher known in London for such titles as *An Exhibition of Female Flagellants* and *Lady Bumtickler's Revels.*[7] Swinburne's association with a known publisher of pornography begged the question his poems had already provoked: were they art or pornography?

Nineteenth-century Britain inherited the oppositions between pornography and aesthetics that were created in the eighteenth century. Until Swinburne, few artists violated the ideological boundaries separating disinterested aesthetic apprehension from a provocation of the senses. But Swinburne was writing in a rapidly changing world. Nineteenth-century Britain was characterized by an awareness of two very divided cultures: a mass culture associated with the working and lower classes, and a high culture associated with the middle and upper classes. Mass-cultural representations were viewed as gratifying the emotional, physical, and financial interests of their producers and consumers at the expense of a socially oriented reason. Advocates of high culture in the nineteenth century had to contend with an increasingly consumer-oriented culture. They feared that the gratifying pleasures of mass-cultural media would circumvent the less immediate routes to disinterest upon which the liberal aesthetic and by-then traditional, social order depended.

While there was an increased emphasis on consumption and sensation in aesthetics of the late Victorian period, there was, importantly, a disciplining of that consumption in accord with the earlier project of Shaftesburian and Kantian aesthetics to bring the body more overtly into the realm of culture by objectifying the senses and making them rationally intelligible. What may have appeared to be a move toward a hedonistic or solipsistic aesthetic, "Aestheticism," which as a critical outlook distinguished itself by a lack of conviction in social utility or productive value, in fact opened the way for an ethical, productive aesthetic. This aesthetic operated by distancing readers and viewers from the sexualized representations they apprehended through a critical reception that privileged representational form rather than content. In order to produce an acceptable aesthetic of pleasured bodies, Swinburne and his supportive critics invoked a Kantian formalism by which the sexual content of his works was subordinated to an ascesis of form, a disciplining of both the subject and object of the artistic representation. As such, the sexualized representations within Swinburne's poems could be seen to serve other than physically titillating purposes.

Before addressing the aesthetic debate around Swinburne's *Poems and Ballads*, this chapter will show how a new, diversified reading public played a central role in provoking high-cultural anxieties about aesthetic reception and the social order. The discussion of nineteenth-century pornography that follows argues that Victorian pornography needs to be understood as a mass-cultural form that, like those who fear the demise of high culture, is preoccupied by the working-class body. The potential of the working-class body to disrupt the social order lies underneath much of the aesthetic debate in the latter half of the nineteenth century, and no genre makes that more clear than pornography. The blurred lines between interested and disinterested bodies in Swinburne's work thus foreground the increasingly charged dialectic between aesthetics and pornography that are the concerns of this book.

Literacy and the cultural divide

Until the eighteenth century high culture distinguished itself by also being literate culture. However, increasing literacy in the nineteenth century challenged literate high culture to further differentiate itself. One response, as I elaborated in chapter one, was to cultivate the aesthetic as a separate, symbolic economy dealing in cultural capital. In the nineteenth century near-universal literacy was achieved in Britain, allowing considerable access to literary high culture for many. Simultaneously, a new literary culture for the masses was created which threatened to marginalize high culture itself. Education underwent vast reforms in the nineteenth century and many of those who previously had no claim to an education, the working classes and women, gained access to one.[8]

Though the expansion of education made great strides, discrepancies between female and male literacy did not begin to level until well after the Endowed

Schools Act of 1869 and the Elementary Education Act of 1870.[9] Accurate literacy statistics are hard to come by, but one way to measure the changes in literacy is to assess the numbers of people unable to sign their own name into marriage registers. An article published in *The Nineteenth Century* (March 1894) tracked such changes. Its numbers reveal a decided lag in female literacy until the 1890s:[10]

Year	Males	Females
1843	32.7%	49.0%
1853	30.4%	43.9%
1863	23.8%	33.1%
1877	15.3%	20.9%
1891	8.4%	7.3%

In addition to the remarkable leveling of gender imbalances, these figures show that literacy enjoyed a steady and dramatic rise throughout the century.

While the working classes had the most to gain from the expansion in elementary education, the middle classes also benefited. The increase in industrial wealth within the gentry and professional classes created a growth in the public schooling system, founding thirty-one classical boarding schools between 1837 and 1869.[11] This created greater educational opportunities for middle-class boys, and essentially assured their integration into a system of elite values. Girls of the middle class were predominantly overlooked until around mid-century. When at this time it was discovered that the female population was outnumbering the male population by numbers upwards of fifty for every one-thousand males, the need for female education to ensure self-sufficiency was satisfied by the creation of colleges for women where they could prepare for careers as governesses. With the growing legitimation of such schools, public boarding schools for girls were opened in the 1860s and 1870s, and in the 1870s university education for women was accepted as an experiment that never ended.[12]

The upper classes preserved their own educational segregation by schooling their girls either at home or in small academies (as shown so well in the Brontë novels), and sending their boys to the Seven Great Public Schools (Winchester, Eton, Henry VIII, Charterhouse, Harrow, Shrewsbury, and Rugby). These schools maintained their social exclusivity through high fees and a classical curriculum. Evidence of the erosion of this exclusivity, however, can be seen as early as 1833 when E. G. Bulwer Lytton observed that:

The long established custom of purchasing titles, either by hard money or the more circuitous influence of boroughs, has tended to mix aristocratic feelings with the views of the trader; and the apparent openness of honours to all men, makes even the humblest shopkeeper, grown rich, think of sending his son to College, not that he may become a wiser man or a better man, but that he may *perhaps* become my lord bishop or my lord chancellor . . . While the rank gained by intellect, or by interest, is open but to few, the rank that may be obtained by fashion seems delusively to be open to all.[13]

Here Lytton details the role that education played in allowing the working middle class to rise socially. Whether at the Great Seven or one of the less established public schools, middle-class boys were rapidly attaining a classical, public education and earning the privileged title of gentleman along with it. At the same time the sons of the newly moneyed industrial class were internalizing the superseded values of an agrarian, aristocratic, and Christian society; adopting – in the opinion of Peter Miles and Malcolm Smith – the anti-materialist position that disguised the role they played in legitimating the burgeoning economic domination of the social class from which they emerged, the sons of the working class were receiving a much simpler education from the state that essentially prepared them for their stations in life.[14]

The consequence of this bifurcated educational system (to eliminate women for the moment) was to prevent the rise of a unified national culture even as economic differences between the classes were slowly eroding. As a result, a process of political socialization that could have included the working classes was prevented. The working classes were becoming literate, but they were still denied access to the values and training of gentlemen. The vast majority of women were, likewise, excluded from integration into the dominant educational values of elite males. To argue that the classes and genders were socialized discretely through formal education suggests that individuals from various classes went about their lives in hermetically sealed "class bubbles." This is obviously not true. In fact, the increased mixing of the classes in urban centers and workplaces, and the differences between sex and class which education increasingly blurred as the century progressed, created anxiety in those who perceived that their culturally dominant position, and/or the set of beliefs that accompanied that position, were under threat.[15] The very fractured nature of the socialization process promoted cross-class and cross-gender mistrust. For those socialized within the anti-materialist tradition of the public schools, all behavior save their own was suspect. Women and the working classes were believed to be tainted by the material, either in the form of material interests which threatened the economic dominance of the middle and upper classes, or in the form of a dangerous material sensuality which represented moral and racial degeneration.[16]

Victorian thinkers like Matthew Arnold, William Morris, John Ruskin, and Algernon Charles Swinburne, aware of the split between an idealized cultural unity and the reality of cultural segregation, reproduced in their writing schizophrenic desires for an egalitarian society based on the moral-aesthetic ideals fostered in elite, classical education. In her book, *The Vulgarization of Art: The Victorians and Aesthetic Democracy*, Linda Dowling has argued that advocates of what she calls "aesthetic democracy," Ruskin, Morris and Arnold, were at once motivated and repulsed by the possibility of an aesthetic sense common to all. Within the desire for a pleasure in aesthetics that could be shared by all, as expressed by Ruskin, Morris, and even Wilde, lay "an ideal aristocratic sensibility unrecognized as such."[17] For what threatened this ideal was the "loss or emptying out of meaning that occurs in any context where 'noble' or 'aristocratic' is no longer permitted to function in relation to a set of terms – the ignoble, the vulgar, the base – in opposition to which it had originally assumed its meaning."[18] In other words, proponents of aesthetics had relied on its oppositional status to popular, commercial and lower-class arts for its identity as such. What was aesthetic was necessarily elevated. The desire to see England culturally and aesthetically unified was, as Dowling sees it, the product of aristocratic sensibilities projected as a democratic endowment.[19] As a result, high-cultural advocates remained ambivalent about envisioning aesthetic capacities in everyone. Judith Stoddart finds this paradox in the works of Swinburne and Ruskin, noting, for instance, that Ruskin's "Letters to Workmen and Labourers," in *Fors Clavigera* (1871–1884), reveals a decided "ambivalence in its declared intention of social involvement on the one hand, and its Latin title and preoccupation with fine art and artists on the other."[20] Intellectual socialists like Ruskin were in many ways the victims of their own elite educations.

Matthew Arnold's critical work similarly reveals a conflict between an egalitarian spirit and a cultural predisposition that prevented him from truly embracing the working-class people whom he called "The Populace." While on the one hand he hoped for a national cultural renewal for all members of society based on "the best that has been known or thought in the world," on the other hand he saw a mockery made of the ideal of perfection by the very signs of a materially based lower class. In "The Function of Criticism at the Present Time," Arnold noted that mixed in with "the best in the whole world" and England's "unrivalled happiness" lay "a touch of grossness in our race . . . the workhouse, the dismal Mapperly Hills . . . the gloom, the smoke, the cold," and unwanted illegitimate children born to the young girls of the workhouses.[21] His example of Wragg, a young girl who strangled her illegitimate child after leaving a workhouse was intended to show how England's debased nature prevented it from attaining a moral-aesthetic ideal. The elements lurking in Wragg's story, sexual relations out of wedlock and a manual-labor job at a workhouse factory, aligned her with the material, bodily existence that asserts itself as at odds with his attempt to suggest a higher mode of being in "non-practical" life. His story, like Bulwer's quote above, calls attention to the juxtaposed existence of wealth and poverty, aristocrat and trader in nineteenth-century British society. Both writers were aware that the ideological boundaries of privilege were being threatened by the very bodies that had been needed to define privilege itself.

As economic and educational circumstances began to alter dramatically the social landscape of the nineteenth century, the idea of a shared culture provoked anxiety in those who believed themselves its guardians. The modern understanding of culture as the training, development, and refinement of mind, taste, and manners is a product of the eighteenth century, but its first use is recorded in the *Oxford English Dictionary* as 1805.[22] Arnold's use and promotion of the concept in *Culture and Anarchy* as well as other essays represents an attempt to name and demarcate culture in order to enforce its boundaries. In keeping with the project of eighteenth-century moral and aesthetic philosophy to bring individual bodies into an objectified, rational public sphere, Arnold's culture seeks to make "reason and the will of God prevail" and "places human perfection in an *internal* condition, in the growth and predominance of our humanity proper, as distinguished from our animality."[23] As such, Arnold's project in *Culture and Anarchy* and his critical essays is to resituate the terms of eighteenth-century aesthetic theory back into the social sphere from which they had been disconnected after Kant. Arnold's cultural aesthetic continues the project of modern aesthetics to bring individual bodies into the realm of reason through a universal subjectivity based on the idea of culture. Arnold's aesthetic, in the tradition of Shaftesbury and Kant, works under the principle that objectified bodies abstracted from their own senses create the illusion of a universally shared public sphere.

The individualized objectives of aesthetic moralists like Arnold, Ruskin, and Morris to create a refined popular culture are but the more widely recognized examples of such efforts. The feeling that the new cultures being created by the increased wealth and literacy of the working classes had to be integrated into a worthy, unified national culture was widespread among the educated classes.

Evidence of this attitude can be found in speeches, reviews, and books throughout the 1880s and 1890s. What commentators saw rising in place of their conception of culture was a mass culture that threatened to engulf the values of old.
James McNeill Whistler derides the rise of a mass, popular culture in his speech
"Ten O'clock," where he says:

> The world was flooded with the beautiful, until there arose a new class, who discov-
> ered the cheap, and foresaw fortune in the facture of the sham.
>
> Then sprang into existence the tawdry, the common, the geegaw.
>
> The taste of the tradesman supplanted the science of the artist, and what was born
> of the million went back to them, and charmed them, for it was after their own heart;
> and the great and the small, the statesman and the slave, took to themselves the abom-
> ination that was tendered, and preferred it – and have lived with it ever since!
>
> And the artist's occupation was gone, and the manufacturer and the huckster took
> his place.[24]

Here Whistler places the beautiful and the commercial in opposition, just as
thinkers in the tradition of Shaftesbury and Kant had done a century and a half
earlier. Whistler figures mass culture as that which gratifies or charms its recip-
ients, and in doing so corresponds to their bodies in either sensually pleasing or
charming them in an occult and non-rational manner. In this way he aligns mass-
cultural forms of consumption with those traditionally associated with the pornographic, those that address the senses rather than the intellect.

For the high-cultural reading public, the problem of increased literacy manifested itself in a new, self-spawning mass culture which began to proliferate in
the form of newspapers, magazines, and penny fiction. Articles decrying the rise
in frivolous reading materials created primarily by and for the literate working
classes were published repeatedly throughout the later years of the century.[25] An
article published in 1894 entitled "Elementary Education and the Decay of
Literature" argued that while "It was with reason expected that multitudes who
hitherto had occupied their leisure with degrading excitements would find in
reading a more agreeable and more elevating amusement," the true result of
increased literacy in the working classes had been the growth in decadent fiction
and "weekly papers of a scrappy character" which encouraged sensationalism.[26]
Listing the most prominent new journals created between 1878 and 1892, the
author marveled over their mass circulation: "Most of these publications have
been published to circulations counted by hundreds of thousands, and concur-
rent with their growth has been the establishment of newspapers combining
with the ordinary news the same scrappy and sensational elements."[27] Mass
culture was seen not as an acculturating panacea, but as a marginalizing threat.

The tremendous volume of printed materials circulated among the working classes was a point of almost hysterical concern for many commentators, as an 1890 review of penny fiction in the *Quarterly Review* makes clear:

> The number of penny weekly papers, leaving newspapers, trade journals, and professedly religious organs wholly out of account, is literally enormous, and their circulation almost fabulous. There is probably no family of the classes rather absurdly described as "working" and "lower middle" in which one at least of these prints is not bought as regularly as Saturday night comes around. In many such families three, four and even more are taken by various members and lent out to one another. Including such as may be seen at the counters of public-houses and the tables of coffee taverns and cheap restaurants, we are probably well within the mark in saying that every copy sold is read by six persons. Now as one of these prints boasts a circulation of 334,000 a week (?), another modestly announces its sale as "a little under half a million" (?), a third claims a quarter of a million, and several are known to sell over 100,000 weekly – it is obvious that the family penny papers combined must be one of the greatest social forces in the kingdom.[28]

As revealed here, the new literary industry's apparent influence over popular culture and the majority population was the source of both fear and envy for the educated elite. One article written in the *North American Review* and then reprinted by W. T. Stead in his *Review of Reviews* noted that newspapers rapidly were becoming the literature of the masses. "It is not too much to say," Mr. E. L. Godkin asserted, "that they are, and have been for the last half-century, exerting more influence on the popular mind and the popular morals than either the pulpit or the book press has exerted in five hundred years . . . The new generation which the public [state-run] schools are pouring out in tens of millions is getting its tastes, opinions, and standards from them, and what sort of world this will produce a hundred years hence nobody knows."[29] To the literary mind turned in upon the changes wrought by an autonomous lower-class market, the rising dominance of mass culture in the form of mass-produced, ephemeral reading materials meant the necessary erosion of the cultural memory that had been so carefully preserved through the tradition of elite education into moral-aesthetic values. In its increased marginalization, literary high culture had to seek ways to colonize the new market created by Britain's modern reading public. The difficulty arose in balancing the urge to preserve old cultural territory while seeking new.

Arnold's plea in "The Function of Criticism at the Present Time" for a disinterested English criticism that allows for the free play of the mind was the plea of an English gentleman raised on classical ideals, for disinterestedness is one of the hallmarks of the English gentleman (a gentleman defined as one who had attended public school and therefore knew Greek and Latin).[30] To counter the ill-effects of Britain's increasingly fragmented culture, Arnold proposed disinterest as a way to unite the public sphere and to deny fractious interests. In doing so he drew on the Shaftesburian and Kantian aesthetic tradition. Finding in disinterestedness a moral imperative, Arnold reconnected Kantian terminology with its generating principles in eighteenth-century British moral-aesthetic philosophy. As this suggests, disinterest did not propose to renew all segments of society, but continued to propagate the interests of Arnold's so-called "Philistines," the middle class. By following Arnold's prescription for "keeping aloof from practice," one removed oneself from the interests of the reformist, capitalist present, or "interest," and freed one's mind for "play." "Without this free disinterested treatment of things," Arnold claimed, "truth and the highest culture are out of the question."[31]

Arnold's prescription was indicative of the severance between cultural and practical life in the nineteenth century as fragmented segments of the middle class became responsible for both the capital and cultural realms. While high culture maintained continuity – disinterestedness as the privilege of those without economic necessity – economic necessity increasingly became the order upon which society was run. Disdain for industrialism and commercialism, one of the hallmarks of the Aesthetic movement in the late nineteenth century, was the relic of the anti-materialist, aristocratic ideals of the eighteenth century which were perpetuated by an elite educational system that tried to cut itself off from the means of production. Interestingly, disdain for the industrialism and commercialism that produced a mass culture also created an identity for the defenders of high culture.[32] William Morris clearly understood these conditions in 1880 when he commented that, "The lapse of time, which through plenteous confusion and failure, has on the whole been steadily destroying privilege and exclusiveness in other matters, has delivered up art to be the exclusive privilege of the few."[33]

In contrast to the gentlemanly code of disinterestedness, working-class behavior was frequently identified by the middle classes as materially interested. In *Culture and Anarchy*, Arnold characterized what he calls "The Populace" as "that vast portion, lastly, of the working class which, raw and half-developed, has long lain half-hidden amidst its poverty and squalor, and is now issuing from its hiding-place to assert an Englishman's heaven-born privilege of doing as he likes, and is beginning to perplex us by marching where it likes, meeting where it likes, breaking what it likes."[34] As opposed to the images of stasis and self-restraint so often favored by the middle classes, the working classes are frequently described in images that imply movement and a lack of restraint. The young Sigmund Freud, in a letter written in 1883 to his fiancée, Martha Bernays, justified lower-class material interest as compensation for the barrenness of their lives:

> It is neither pleasant nor edifying to watch the masses amusing themselves; we at least don't have much taste for it . . . I remember something that occurred to me while watching a performance of *Carmen*: the mob gives vent to its appetites, and we deprive ourselves. We deprive ourselves in order to maintain our integrity, we economize our health, our capacity for enjoyment, our emotions; we save ourselves for something, not knowing what . . . Our whole conduct of life presupposes that we are protected from the direst poverty and that the possibility exists of being able to free ourselves increasingly from social ills . . . Why should they scorn the pleasures of the moment when no other awaits them? The poor are too helpless, too exposed, to behave like us. When I see the people indulging themselves, disregarding all sense of moderation, I invariably think that this is their compensation for being a helpless target for all the taxes, epidemics, sicknesses, and evils of social institutions.[35]

While the compassion of Freud and other nineteenth-century liberals was able to justify the behavior of the masses, such observations and the numerous tracts written throughout the second half of the century on poverty and the working class, such as Engels's *Condition of the Working Class in England* (1845), Henry Mayhew's *London Labour and the London Poor* (1862), Andrew Mearn's *The Bitter Cry of Outcast London* (1883), Charles Booth's *Life and Labour of the People of London* (1891–1903), and B. S. Rowntree's *Poverty: A Study of Town Life* (1901), continued to reinforce notions of the working-class poor as a degraded, unrestrained, pestilent group of over-breeders. Edwin Chadwick's report on the sanitary conditions of the laboring population in 1842 found that not only did "the ravages of epidemics and other diseases . . . tend to increase the pressure of population," but that the adverse circumstances of poverty tended "to produce an adult population short-lived, improvident, reckless, and intemperate, and with habitual avidity for sensual gratifications." Such "habits lead to the abandonment of all the conveniences and decencies of life," contributing to "the most abject degradation and . . . demoralization of large numbers of human beings."[36] Associated with disease, the lower classes were seen as an aggressive, all-consuming force, threatening to eat away at the cultural body. Their perceived disease-ridden and sensually ensnared lifestyles identified them with their bodies, bodies specifically out of control and therefore signifying a potential threat to the personal, spatial, and ideological boundaries so carefully maintained by the middle class and its favored aesthetic modes.

As class identity became more pronounced, the activities of the working classes became a subject of interest to the middle and upper classes. In an article in the *Contemporary Review* (1886), Walter Besant worried over the leisure-time activities of the working-class youth, who typically left school at age ten or eleven:

> The street is always open to them; here they find the companions of the workroom; here they feel the swift strong current of life; here something is always happening; here there are always new pleasures; here they can talk and play unrestrained, left entirely to themselves . . . As for their favourite amusements and pleasures, they grow yearly coarser; as for their conversation, it grows continually viler; until Zola himself would be ashamed to reproduce the talk of these young people.[37]

Focusing on their pleasures, Besant frets that for working-class youth such experiences are entirely unrestrained. The author of *The Quarterly Review* article on penny fiction likewise showed anxiety over the impressionability of partially educated youth, complaining of penny papers that "this foul and filthy trash circulates by thousands and tens of thousands week by week amongst lads who are at the most impressionable period of their lives, and whom the modern system of secular education has left without ballast or guidance."[38] Both articles highlight the roles circulation, interest, and pleasure play in the lives of the working classes.

In chapter one I suggested that circulation, interest, and pleasure were also central to the technology of pornography in *Fanny Hill* and other texts. The middle-class writers who focused on the circulation of pleasure and interest among the working classes saw such qualities as at odds with the preservation of their own cultural-aesthetic legacy. The circulation of interest and pleasure formed a separate economy that, in its alignment with the rise of democratic-capitalist society and the working classes as viable members of the economic and political community, signified a marked shift in British society from a culture of producers to a culture of consumers.[39] Regenia Gagnier has characterized this shift towards a consumer culture in the latter half of the nineteenth century as one that privileges an individual's insatiability rather than his rationality.[40] The diminishment of reason, to those educated into the moral-aesthetic tradition of Shaftesbury and Kant, represented a dangerous shift. Troped as disease, a material manifestation, the masses were seen by middle-class cultural defenders as a poisonous force vitiating the privileges and institutions of the entrenched elite.

In their alignment with disease, the masses shared a denomination with pornography, that most material of literary forms that worked in ways antithetical to high-cultural literary ideals. When pornography was spoken of in public discourse in the nineteenth and early twentieth centuries, it was often figured as poison or, like the lower classes, disease. As Walter Kendrick suggests, if middle-class cultural defenders believed that good art soothes and elevates, acts as a medicine upon the cultural body for its own good health, then bad art, including pornography, was considered a poison.[41] Max Nordau, in a classic example of late nineteenth-century thought on the evils of pornography, echoed this sentiment in *Degeneration* (1892):

> The systematic incitation to lasciviousness causes the gravest injury to the bodily and mental health of individuals, and a society composed of individuals sexually over-stimulated, knowing no longer any self-control, any discipline, any shame, marches to its certain ruin, because it is too worn out and flaccid to perform great tasks. The pornographist poisons the springs whence flows the life of future generations. No task of civilization has been so painfully laborious as the subjugation of lasciviousness. The pornographist would take from us the fruit of this, the hardest struggle of humanity.[42]

In his reference to a society composed of individuals that become "flaccid," Nordau makes clear the cultural association between individual bodies, the body politic, and pornography. The individual bodies of the working classes, perpetually figured as "sexually over-stimulated, knowing no longer any self-control, any discipline, any shame," threatened the hopes for a public sphere composed of disinterested bodies. So did pornography. The lower classes and pornography were viewed as uncontrollable, diseased, or poisonous forces that threatened to penetrate the healthy social body.

When in 1857 Lord Campbell learned to his horror that "a sale of a poison more deadly than prussic acid, strychnine or arsenic was being openly carried out in Holywell Street," he exemplified the entrenchment of a sensibility that Ian Hunter *et al.* describe as the intersection of two agencies: "First, a metaphorics of contagion and a mapping of 'dangerous places,'" that "traced the population in terms of a set of overlapping threats to its health, decency, good order and well-being," and "Second, the specialist knowledges of moral psychology and sexual medicine," that, "through a moral physiology . . . transformed medical pathology into a source of admonitory images used for an ethical discipline of the self while simultaneously bringing the latter within the confessional sphere of the doctor-patient relationship."[43] Evidence of the self-disciplining engendered by these cultural metaphors is abundant in discussions of pornography. In the introduction to his pornographic bibliography, Henry Spencer Ashbee distanced himself from its poisonous content, asserting that,

> Improper books, however useful to the student, or dear to the collector, are not "virginibus puerisque"; they should, I consider, be used with caution even by the mature;

they should be looked upon as poisons, and treated as such; should be (so to say) distinctly labelled, and only confided to those who understand their potency, and are capable of rightly using them.[44]

To exemplify participation in the disembodied, high-cultural public sphere, Victorian readers of pornography figured themselves in the roles of critical scientist or medic.

By using a "scientific" approach, even pornography's grossly material bodies could be brought into the sphere of reason, or at least that is the gesture indicated by their high-cultural readers. For instance, Iwan Bloch observes in *The Sexual Life of Our Time* (1908) that, "These obscene writings may be compared with natural poisons, which must also be carefully studied, but which can be entrusted only to those who are fully acquainted with their dangerous effects, who know how to control and counteract those effects, and who regard them as a natural means of research by means of which they will be enabled to obtain an understanding of other phenomena."[45] Bloch's concern for "poisons," control, and observational research, suggests that by the turn of the century, the medico-moral concern for pornography (and the creation of a "disinterested" space for study of the genre – the need to scientifically classify such study revealing the anxiety inherent in pornography's gravitational pull) was still firmly in place.

Replacing a governmental concern for acts of sedition endangering the social balance in the eighteenth and early nineteenth centuries, the concern for monitoring the availability of pornography became later in the nineteenth century, in part, one of bourgeois self-policing for moral and medical harm. The medico-moral concern for policing boundaries, literary, social, and personal, was imbricated within a middle-class ideology that feared contamination of the treasured cultural body. Keeping in mind the aesthetic and social alignments of pornography and the masses, I now want to explore how pornography of the period was in fact produced, and in what ways it constructed its relationship with the lower-class body. By detailing pornography's complicated relationship with the working classes and the working-class body in the nineteenth century, I will lay the groundwork for understanding the social significance of modernism's incorporation of explicit sexuality discussed later in this book.

Victorian pornography

It has become a truism of Victorian pornographic studies that pornography – works written with the intention of sexually stimulating their readers – was written by and for an elite, aristocratic and upper-middle-class clientele of gentleman-bibliophiles.[46] There is plenty of evidence to support this fact, residing primarily in the famous series of erotic bibliographies compiled by Henry Spencer Ashbee under the pseudonym Pisanus Fraxi: *Index Librorum Prohibitorum* (1877), *Centuria Librorum Absconditorum* (1879), and *Catena Librorum Tacendorum* (1885). This privately printed set of bibliographies lists a multitude of highly priced, limited editions of pornographic works, those in Ashbee's ken. Likewise, the list of leading English collectors of erotica since the middle of the nineteenth century is said to include Campbell Reddie, William S. Potter, Frederick Hankey, Richard Monckton Milnes (Lord Houghton), Coventry Patmore, Henry Spencer Ashbee, the fifth Earl of Rosebery, the second Marquess of Milford Haven, Edward Heron-Allen, and Michael Sadleir. This is a remarkable list which, according to pornographic historian H. Montgomery Hyde, includes "a generous literary patron who was President of the London Library; the Victorian poet who wrote 'The Angel in the House'. . . a liberal Prime Minister, a great grandson of Queen Victoria; a fellow of the Royal Society; and a distinguished contemporary novelist."[47] These facts together, along with a lack of concrete evidence regarding sales of pornography to the working classes, reinforce the idea that pornography in Victorian England was solely the domain of a small elite.

Evidence that contradicts this, however, are the vast numbers of pornographic materials recovered by the police and the Society for the Suppression of Vice throughout the century. Between 1834 and 1880, the Vice Society absconded more than 385,000 obscene prints and photos, 80,000 books and pamphlets, five tons of other printed matter, 28,000 sheets of obscene songs and circulars, stereoscopes, copper plates, and the like.[48] According to the Vice Society, in 1834 there were fifty-seven pornography shops open in Holywell Street (now Aldwych, near to Waterloo Bridge), the main thoroughfare for the pornographic trade, particularly in the first half of the century before the Obscene Publications Act succeeded in shutting many of them down.[49] In 1845, a raid on the premises of one purveyor in Holywell Street yielded 383 books, 351 copperplates, 12,346 prints, 188 lithographic stones, and 3,752 pounds of type font.[50] In 1874 a raid was made at the home of Henry Hayler, a pornographic photographer, and 130,248 obscene photographs and 5,000 slides were seized and destroyed.[51] The vast amount of material absconded can realistically be said to represent only a small portion of that which was actually produced and sold throughout the century. Given these numbers, the likelihood that such material was relegated solely to elite, upper-class males seems slim. According to the 1851 census, roughly 81 per cent of adult males belonged to the working classes and about one-half of the 16.9 million inhabitants of England and Wales lived in urban environments.[52] While that would seem to indicate a still sizeable potential market of elite buyers for pornography in London (from which most of the above pornography figures originated), figures estimating the number of "really comfortable families" from which a guinea library subscription might be expected in 1872, were estimated by *The Spectator* to be no more than 60,000.[53] What all of this suggests is that pornography had to be penetrating more markets than the traditionally assumed one. Certainly it is obvious that pornographic photographs and prints were reaching a wide segment of the population, and it is not unreasonable to assume that pamphlets and books were broadcast as well. By the mid-to-late nineteenth century, pornography was a mass-cultural product, cutting across class lines.

That works were available for all segments of the population is further supported by Ashbee's introduction where he notes, "I do not hesitate to notice the catchpennies hawked in the public streets, as well as the sumptuous volumes got up for the select few, and whose price is counted in guineas."[54] Peter Gay, who argues that pornography was the domain of the elite, also acknowledges that "It is not possible to reconstruct a dependable map across space and time of nineteenth-century pornography: too much has been lost, especially of the cheaper titles, and the expensive collections of rich amateurs which are now behind locked doors in great libraries of the world are not necessarily representative."[55] Lynn Hunt has provided research suggesting that pornography was democratized in France at the time of the French Revolution, as pornographic pamphlets of sixteen pages or less then began to gain mass audiences.[56] The influence of pornography's democratization must have spread to England. Francis Place's diary confirms that in England in the 1780s, quite respectable shops sold pornography and pornographic prints "to any boy or any maidservant."[57]

Ashbee's bibliographies, though containing a majority of works that would have interested a collector – finely bound, lavish presentations of rare erotica[58] – do indeed house a number of "catchpennies," or less expensive works that would have been within the reach of more than just gentleman-collectors. *The Mysteries of Flagellation* (1863) was priced at just twopence, and *The Wedding Night* (1841) cost three shillings.[59] Less than the two-guinea price that was a standard for volumes published by renowned pornographic publisher William Dugdale, *Kate Handcock*, privately printed in 1882, and *The Confessions of a Young Lady*, printed by Dugdale around 1860 "For the Society of Vice," were each sold for a little more than £1.[60] Catalogues advertising pornographic works at the turn of the twentieth century show a range of prices, from ten shillings for "pocket editions" of *Kate Handcock* and *The Voluptuous Night* to £40 for a rare copy of *My Secret Life*. While these are the prices printed in the catalogue, it must be noted that the majority of catalogues preserved in the British Library advertise, in handwriting, discounts of 25 to 50 per cent off the listed price, and so were probably less expensive than we have previously understood them to be.[61] Walter Kendrick has suggested that the average biweekly wage of a lower-middle-class family around 1880 was £110.[62] Spending £1 out of £220 on a book in one month does not seem out of the question, much less twopence or a shilling on a French postcard or a cheaply bound volume.[63] Wages rose in the latter half of the nineteenth century, and what had been likely out of reach for a large percentage of the population before 1850 or so, became increasingly within reach.

   Mass production continued to make many of these items cheaper. Through evidence in Ashbee's bibliographies, there appears to have been a sharp rise in the production of two- to ten-shilling "catchpenny" pamphlets around 1870, some with pornographic content, some merely promising it. Ashbee's bibliographic commentary regarding *Intrigues and Confessions of a Ballet Girl* (c.1870) in *Catena Librorum Tacendorum* suggests that this pamphlet was one of many:

> This is one of the worthless catch-pennies advertised in the low class newspapers, at a high price, to attract ignorant young people in search of something "racy." There is absolutely nothing in the book; it is not obscene, nor does it fulfill in any way the promises put forth in its highly-spiced title. I notice it as a specimen of a class of publication largely produced some ten years ago, its only object being to obtain the transfer of money from the pockets of the simple to those of the sharping publishers.[64]

Intrigues and Confessions of a Ballet Girl does not depict any explicit sex, being more a tale of low life and loose morality than a pornographic representation. It does suggest, however, one of the ironies of the middle-class construction of the lower classes as more susceptible to embodied subjectivity: in nineteenth-century pornography, the cheaper the pornography, the less body and acts were portrayed. Until later in the century, the lower classes had less access to the more genitally focused, grossly material forms of written pornography. Tracy C. Davis, in her article on the actress in Victorian pornography, has noted that erotica rich in theatrical imagery was an integral part of the penny illustrated weeklies, and that a postcard set depicting a nude gymnast on the swing and trapeze could be purchased in the 1890s at a cost of one shilling for thirty-six poses.[65] Pornographic stereographs (cards with three-dimensional images) are listed in a sales catalogue circa 1860 for prices ranging from 1s 6d to 3s each. Stereoscopes, popular three-dimensional viewing apparatuses which could and often did contain pornographic images, ranged from 2s 6d for simple tin models to 50s for deluxe ebony models.[66] Explicitly sexualized representations were clearly finding a market among the middle and lower classes.

The likelihood of a working-class audience for pornography is even more probable given the history of pornography's growth early in the nineteenth century. In his book *Radical Underworld: Prophets, Revolutionaries and Pornographers in London, 1795–1840*, Iaian McCalman makes the case that as the radical press lost its audience after the French Revolution, many of the journalists who had been radical pressmen began to sell obscene publications in the 1820s and 1830s.[67] Though some pornography was being produced for private consumption, obscene literature produced in this period often contained a political dimension, displaying a bawdy or obscene populism, that, "whatever its commercial objectives, intended to amuse, shock or disgust readers by exposing the crimes, vices and hypocrisies of the ruling classes. In style, tone and price it also borrowed heavily from traditional street literature."[68] By street literature McCalman means the bawdy song-sheets, chap-books, squibs and prints that were commonly hawked on the streets by and for the proletariat.[69] In 1848, a journalist for *The Times* commented that by looking at Dugdale's shop windows, the literature of the working classes would seem to consist of "a melange of sedition, blasphemy and obscenity."[70]

Cannon and Dugdale, whose often lavish pornographic works figure prominently in Ashbee's bibliographies, are two widely known publishers to have come out of the tradition of the radical press, and whose ideas were influenced by the spread of libertine ideas from the Continent. McCalman has suggested that libertinism's central tenets, its hostility to political and religious authority and its advocacy of a hedonistic morality based on sexual instinct, were reinforced by the ideas current in post-Revolutionary romanticism.[71] With its participation in libertine radicalism, nineteenth-century pornography flourished alongside other democratic-artistic movements of the first half of the century. Lynn Hunt has made a broader claim for pornography by suggesting that it can be associated with the entire democratizing movement of modern European culture. Hunt claims, "Pornography developed democratic implications because of its association with print culture, with the new materialist philosophies of science and nature and with political attacks on the powers of the established regimes. If all bodies were interchangeable – a dominant trope in pornographic writing – then social and gender (and perhaps even racial) differences would effectively lose their meaning."[72]

The radical presses generated a populist style of pornographic narrative that became a staple of Victorian popular culture and was eventually incorporated into newspapers and penny fiction: *chroniques scandaleuses*. Such works were usually cheap, paraphrased versions of the confessions, real or spurious, of famous courtesans, that were used as vehicles for exposing upper-class vice and corruption. Scandal in high places was a regular feature in Victorian "crim.con." periodicals and, once developed, the taste for sexual scandal was further fed with the introduction of divorce announcements after the 1857 Divorce Act in popular newspapers as well as the specialized *The Divorce News and Police Reporter*.[73]

Such periodicals, while not purely pornographic, introduced sexual narrative to a large portion of the population. As Thomas Boyle makes clear, "The police reports of mid-nineteenth-century newspapers consistently offer graphically detailed accounts of sexual misbehavior of all classes," and include stories of "seduction, rape, adultery, transvestitism, illegal abortion, bigamy, sadism, and indecent exposure."[74] While the taste for sexual scandal may have developed out of radical press practices, it spread democratically to such an extent that, while certain segments of the population may not have approved of such narratives, they were available to all who could purchase a paper or penny pamphlet and read its contents.

The limited radical audience for bawdy populism, melodrama, and libertine literature of the early nineteenth century became, through the broadening influence of the press, a mass audience in the latter half of the nineteenth century. Judith Walkowitz's work, *City of Dreadful Delight*, shows the numerous strategies Grub Street publishers used to build a mass reading public through exposing the "exotic culture of the metropolitan underworld."[75] Because of a morally critical attitude toward his subject which fostered a gentleman-like detachment from the sexual material he presented, W. T. Stead, in his publishing blitz "The Maiden Tribute of Modern Babylon," and the journalists who quickly imitated him, were able to present material that until then had been the illicit domain of pornography's sexual narratives. The success of this venture, however, is more clear in our time than it was in Stead's. As Walkowitz explains, class became a focus of Stead's narrative and a public debate ensued as to whether his articles on child prostitution in London embodied the language of a penny dreadful or an expensive libertine volume: "Whereas Stead's opponents bracketed the *Pall Mall Gazette* with 'gutter publications,' written in the terms of the 'ignorant and uneducated,' Charles Braudlaugh's *National Reformer*, equally dubious of Stead's motives, criticized his 'callous adhesion to the verbiage of the

56.

upper classes.'" Bradlaugh, who had suffered prosecution for distributing Knowlton's "dry physiological tract" on birth control, was particularly resentful of the apparent tolerance of Stead's "'highly colored adaptations' of expensive 'works printed abroad,'" a clear reference to pornography.[76]

As these assignations make clear, sexual narrative was associated with the lower classes or the libertine aristocracy, but rarely with the middle class. The body was always other. The aristocracy had a libertine tradition accompanying the rise of middle-class cultural domination in the late seventeenth and early eighteenth centuries. Through the *chroniques scandaleuses,* the lower classes had adapted and inverted that tradition to their political needs at the turn of and in the early decades of the nineteenth century. The middle-class Victorian imagination continued throughout the century to associate the lower and aristocratic classes with the unrestrained sexual body and its literature, pornography. It becomes especially interesting then that it is the middle class who eventually appropriated and transformed the explicit sexual narrative for the category of art early in the twentieth century.

Sexual narrative and the working-class body

The *chronique scandaleuse* originated out of more sexually explicit pornographic works related to political causes in France and England in the first half of the nineteenth century, but changed forms throughout the century in ways that confirm a shift toward a medically and morally self-policing Victorian culture. In its typical form early in the century, according to McCalman,

> The courtesan "authors" – invariably from humble but respectable backgrounds – began by describing how they had been tricked by aristocratic or royal libertines into parting from their true loves. They had then been seduced and forced into prostitution. Thereafter they had become mistresses to a succession of corrupt, perverted and cruel aristocrats, against whom their only recourse was . . . to play one off against the other . . . to turn private sexual knowledge to blackmailing/publishing advantage.[77]

A signal example of *chronique scandaleuse* narrative was published in the inaugural issue of the pornographic magazine *The Exquisite* in 1842. Priced at four-pence, *The Exquisite* is representative of a populist, mass-media form of pornography.[78] In a regular feature, the magazine celebrated the individual stories of London prostitutes: "Star of the Salons, Rosa Lygns, Hadlow St., New Road" is described as typical in her path to prostitution. Her story is intended both to titillate and to evoke populist glee at Rosa's revenge against power. After coming to London at age eighteen with her maiden aunt, Rosa is sought after by a barrister of the Old Bailey:

> As the account of Rosa's seduction is nothing more than the everyday occurrence of those sorts of affairs, we shall content ourselves with saying, that after repeated visits, accompanied by presents of much value, made under the pretence of honest intentions, he one evening took advantage of Rosa's friends to advise her to close the shop and accompany him to Drury Lane Theatre, and upon leaving she accompanied him to a neighboring supper room, in order to partake of slight refreshment. She drunk freely, and beyond this she remembers nothing, a sickening stupor overcame her, and she fell insensible on the ground. Upon her recovery, she discovered when too late that the wine had been drugged, and the gentleman of the long robe had her conveyed a few doors higher up, viz. to Mrs. A's, Charles Street, Covent Garden, where he effected his purpose . . . [she is kept by her seducer until] The barrister, growing tired of her, left her.[79]

The story ends with lower-class, feminist revenge: Rosa discovers that her seducer is a barrister, she blackmails him into a stipend, and she sets herself up in high-end prostitution.

This narrative is replayed with slight but telling differences throughout the century in newspaper reports of criminal proceedings, pornographic works, and moral tales written for respectable journals. In the end, the *chronique scandaleuse* is always about the working class (and importantly also the aristocratic) body and its sacrifice to, or struggle for, discursive control, the domain of the middle and upper classes. This type of narrative reveals how the working-class body was used as a focal point for nineteenth-century sexuality. It operates by staging cross-class desire, thus engaging the *frisson* of transgression so important to stratified British society, while simultaneously exposing the equally dangerous potential of a leveling of the classes. Later, modernist writers who incorporated explicit sexuality into their works maintained a trace of this narrative. To further understand this narrative, I will show the discursive construction of the working-class body throughout the nineteenth century in examples from a newspaper story, the pornographic work *My Secret Life*, and the respected journal *New Review.*

The newspaper case comes from a collection of "Various Trials Cut From Newspapers" by a Scottish lord, W. Bell MacDonald, in the mid-nineteenth century.[80] The name of the paper is not available. The news article details a case at Kingston in 1855 in which a fifteen-year-old "young gentleman" named Elton was accused of "feloniously assaulting" Mary Elizabeth Crawley, a seventeen-year-old servant at the rectory home of his clergyman uncle, with the assistance of two other servants, Elphick the groom, and Miss Fenn, the cook. The account is as follows:

> While witness and Miss Fenn were undressing, Elton came in and passed to his own room, and witness locked the door. She and Fenn then went to bed and directly afterwards Elphick came into the room, and unlocked Elton's door, and said to him, "George, you come in and lie on Fenn's side." Witness said that if they did so, she would tell Mr. Sudgeon [her master, husband of Elton's sister], and Elphick replied, "Oh no, you won't." Elton then came to her bedside. He was undressed and he got into bed. Witness screamed as loud as she could, and the prisoner Fenn put her hand over her mouth, and Elphick held her while Elton committed the assault with which he was charged . . . Fenn [then] told her it was no use complaining, it was done now, and could not be undone. Elphick then told her that unless she consented to similar treatment a second time she would be sure to be in a family way and Fenn confirmed what he said; [and then] Elphick assaulted her in the same manner Elton had done. This all took place without her consent.

After the defense claimed that Mary Elizabeth Crawley was sexually experienced at the time of her rape, the jury found the gentleman "not guilty."

To readers of pornography, the above account, though not genitally or sensuously explicit, would have been quite familiar. In nineteenth-century pornography, servants are frequently treated as easy sexual prey and, while they sometimes appear more willing, the power imbalance between master and servant is always the impetus from which the story originates and recapitulates its transgressive *frisson*. The territory that is conquered and discursively exposed (in an iteration of the colonial narrative) is the working-class body. While some versions of *chroniques scandaleuses* celebrate an eventual narrative triumph over the upper-class aggressor, the price paid is a mutual exposure into narrative itself, through which control is surrendered to the discursive techniques by which the body is rendered/tendered and to the consumptive practices through which it is consumed. At the level of plot, Crawley's working-class body is "consumed" and discarded by Elton *and* the jury because it is "used." The penny newspaper that reports the court case is used in similar fashion, consumed and discarded when used. The working-class body is a disposable good, but in being so it is fashioned for consumer, i.e. middle-class, use. What is striking about this particular case is that it appeared in a public newspaper, available to all for around a penny. Sexual narratives were increasingly popularized throughout the nineteenth century provided they were relayed within a distancing context.

In the pornographic novel *My Secret Life* (*c.*1880), the narrator, Walter, repeatedly takes advantage of the servants in his employ, seducing or forcing himself upon them in ways that look only marginally more kind than the above account.[81] One of the distinguishing features of Walter's story, as compared with the "scandalous confession," or the quasi-neutrality of the newspaper account above, is that it is given not by the sexual victim, but by the sexual perpetrator. The sympathetic voice is that of a gentleman of privilege, and it can be assumed that it was aimed at a similar reader.[82] Walter's attitudes and assumptions, his position within what Steven Marcus calls the "nexus of sex, class, and money," are made clear throughout his eleven-volume narrative.[83]

In one particular episode, Walter is left to look after a neighbor's servant girl while they are away at the seaside. In common pornographic fashion, he wears down her resistance to his sexual overtures through lewd conversation and a copy of *Fanny Hill* (an instance of the self-reflexive nature of pornography; the subject is always a voyeur, even to his own voyeurism). Walter arrives one afternoon during a thunderstorm and insists that Jenny, the servant, soothe her nerves with several glasses of sherry. Just as in the stereotypical narrative relayed by McCalman above, Jenny has a sweetheart with whom she hopes to marry and open a grocer's shop. Insisting that the young man needs to know nothing of their sex play, Walter solicits a kiss from her on the promise that he won't be rude again. Walter's conscience, unlike most pornographic narratives, is touched by the girl's innocence, though not above his own desires. "She was one of the simplest and most open girls I have ever met with," he says, "and once a half-feeling of remorse came over me about my intentions, whilst she was talking about her future; but my randy prick soon stopped that."[84]

After he chases her about the house, forcing a sovereign, which she refuses, into her pockets, and then ten sovereigns, Walter is clear in his conscience that he is entitled to do what he likes with her. The narrative becomes more decidedly sexual as he homes in on his prize, and begins, as is typical of pornography, a series of verbal repetitions. Walter relates of Jenny that "She forgot all propriety in her fuddled excitement, and whilst screeching from my tickling, repeated incoherently baudy words as I uttered them" (*MSL* 161). He elicits an incitatory echo from Jenny, but then must overcome her with the gushing stream of his own "entire baudy vocabulary, 'prick,' 'cunt,' 'fuck,' 'spunk,' 'pleasure,' 'belly to belly,' 'my balls over your arse,' 'let my stiff prick stretch your cunt,' – everything that could excite a woman" (*MSL* 161–162).[85] Such a scene suggests the power of discursive sex as it grows in importance in the nineteenth century; the transformation, as Foucault has implied, of all desire into discourse.[86] The repetition of, and continual search for, sexual words in order to proliferate, detail, and stimulate the interplay of pleasure, sensation, and thought becomes the task of both

Walter for Jenny and the sexual narrative for its readers. In this way the sensuous technology of pornography performs a separate function from other forms
of sexual narrative, such as trial accounts in newspapers, as it lingers on repetitive details of anatomy in order to stimulate the sexual imagination of its readers
and elicit a bodily response.

While Jenny seems to resist his forwardness, "She took to yelling and even
hitting me" (*MSL* 162), Walter is not to be deterred. After much repetitive dialogue, he forces himself upon her and completes sexual intercourse. At this
moment the narrative returns to the themes of the *chroniques scandaleuses*. After
taking Jenny's virginity he questions, "Then I came to my senses, where was I?
had she let me, or had I forced her violently?"(*MSL* 164). His conscience,
however, is dwarfed by his desire to sexually dominate Jenny, as is revealed when
he repeats a common pornographic trope of this period, that of the woman as
a horse to be mastered:

> She was a most extraordinary girl. After the first fuck she was like a well-broken horse;
> she obeyed me in everything, blushed, was modest, humbled, indifferent, conquered,
> submissive; but I could get no conversation out of her . . . She cried every ten minutes
> and looked at me.   (*MSL* 166)

This passage confirms Coral Lansbury's claim that a shift occurred in nineteenth-
century pornography, from a narrative voice of a woman in the earlier years of
the century, to a late-century narrator that "can best be described as a riding
master," who exercises a "lust to dominate, to assert his authority, to control and
subdue.[87] Lansbury observes that the "riding master" narrative is dependent
upon the maintenance of a categorical social difference between oppressor and
victim. Whereas novels and stories of the early nineteenth century frequently
celebrate a female of the lower class getting the better of her upper-class
employer, just as Rosa Lygns successfully blackmailed her seducer in the vignette
from *The Exquisite* above, works in the late nineteenth century feature servants
as the playthings of their master.[88]

There is indeed a marked shift in pornographic narrative from an association
with the working classes (as typically associated with a woman) to an association
with the upper classes (as typically associated with a man) as the century pro-
gresses.[89] While class boundaries were gradually eroding in society, they were
being more carefully observed in pornographic narrative to the extent that the
working-class body could not be the subject of pleasure, only its object. This
shift, however, did not occur until the last two decades of the nineteenth and
the early decades of the twentieth century, and one can infer that the effects of

mass education and feminism were taking their toll on the male defenders of cultural hegemony.

A text that confirms this shift is a short piece entitled "From the Maid's Point of View" published in 1891 in *New Review*, a journal that at this time was also publishing short works by Henry James, Thomas Hardy, and Joseph Conrad, and believed itself to be upholding high literary standards in its time. The narrative is remarkable for what, in contrast to the works above, does not happen and is not said. What is said is frequently cliché. Adopting the language of *chroniques scandaleuses*, religious conversion, and melodrama, the heroine-narrator, Maggie, begins the piece with a statement about her archetypal background, "I was born of poor but honest parents, in a small village near Carlisle."[90] She titillates the reader by suggesting that "as I have some rather promiscuous things to tell – things 'terrible but true' – I do not think it would beseem my pen to give the names of my masters and mistresses" ("MP" 170). Her parents' teaching is strengthened by that of her first employer and from this she declares "I was thus able to withstand the various temptations and 'ills that flesh is heir to' as I progressed in life, and to hold fast by the Cross which has been my staff and the prop of my failing steps" ("MP" 171). The abundance of interpolated quotes and the cliché language make clear that the narrative can find no language of its own, and must rely on a pastiche of various narrative modes in order to construct itself. Maggie's story is in fact a parody of the *chronique scandaleuse*, a parody of the lower-class mindset that consumes and regurgitates such narratives unreflectively. This suggests that not only has the narrative mode of the *chroniques scandaleuses* become quite tired by this point in the century, but that, in its pastiche, the narrator's working-class mind is perceived to be nothing more than an amalgamation of culturally constructed narratives. She is the unthinking victim of her reading, an opinion that most members of the elite-educated classes held with regard to the working classes and "their" mass-cultural media.

After her first mistress instructs Maggie "to be a good girl and never let a gentleman look at me as he shouldn't," she takes up a new position where she encounters the first threat to her innocence. "The reader will pardon me if I hasten over this part of 'my life and experiences,'" she says, but "'the wound still bleeds' [an ironic construction of Maggie's experience given that the relationship is never consummated] and I must crave indulgence for my tears. For I shall never forget him" ("MP" 172). The narrative continues as follows:

> The "fierce light" of experience beats on my memory and strives to show my dear Mr. Algernon in colours "black as Erebus", but my heart is faithful as "the needle to the

pole," and refuses to convict my earthly idol of sin. I loved him. Can I say more? Ought I to say less? He said he loved me and I believed him. He was a fine rash young man reading at Oxford; I was a tall slip of a girl as fair as a lily . . . He wanted to run off with me and marry me, but I remembered what Lady Eveline had said when she bid me good-bye, and I said, "No. If I was good enough to marry at all, I was good enough to marry in the face of day." It did not quite suit my mind to run off like a thief. I loved Mr. Algernon as I never thought I could love any man, for I do not hold much with men and least with gentlemen; but that was no reason why I should do anything under-hand, and forget father and mother and Lady Eveline and all and perhaps bring a curse instead of a blessing on my head. So I said Mr. Algernon No; and reasoned him out of hand, as it were; and kept free of guilt and shame; and always could say my prayers; and look at myself in the glass, not being ashamed of what I saw.   ("MP" 172)

Once Maggie has taken this type of narrative as far as it can go, she drops the autobiographical style and launches into her impressions about the way servants are treated by their masters and mistresses. Maggie's attack on the wealthy alters from the archetypal methods of the *chronique scandaleuse*; rather than exposing their sexual greed, she deplores how masters and mistresses continue to ignore the humanity of their servants and lead hypocritical lives. This more subtle attack suggests a shift toward the internalized policing of morality that becomes access-ible to all classes by the end of the century.

"From the Maid's Point of View" is significant in several ways. To begin, the sexual narrative so typically associated with *chronique scandaleuse* is averted through a new strength of character attributed to the working-class girl. The piece is a morally prescriptive work that suggests not only a new subjective iden-tity among the working classes, but also what was considered acceptable reading for the middle and upper-middle classes at this time. While it operates on one level as a middle-class parody of working-class moral pride, it operates on another level to endorse this pride. The story shows how the middle class had by this point in the century taken over the *chronique scandaleuse* in a gesture of moral self-policing. Interestingly, however, the cliché phrases and sayings suggest a gap between ideal narrative and actual experience. They expose the represent-edness of all experience, allowing the middle-class reader to believe and disbe-lieve the narrative. While the morally self-policing segment of the middle class might have supported Maggie's actions and therefore preferred to interpret the narrative at face value, a less earnest group of readers might have read the stan-dardized language as ironic, preferring to see in a narrative such as *My Secret Life* a more realistic mode of representation.

The story gives voice to the maid and, by airing her opinions on her employers, grants her a certain power over them. However, her power in this instance is not simply derived from knowledge of their sexual misdeeds, as in the early *chroniques scandaleuses*, but rather from a moral superiority that allows her to say, "My word! if some mistresses were only half as respectable as their maids the world would go better than it does now!"("MP" 178). The narrative of "From the Maid's Point of View" is indicative of the changing mores of the working class towards the end of the century. Jeffrey Weeks has claimed that, "In the last decades of the nineteenth century we can observe a greater decorum amongst the working class as a whole, and articulation of clear respectable standards amongst important strata of it."[91] The story raises the possibility of working-class control over their bodies and their representations even as it pokes fun at the complete lack of control so evidently displayed in the use of cliché language.

"From the Maid's Point of View" was published in a culturally prominent journal just three years after *My Secret Life* was published and distributed clandestinely. The publicly accepted story offers a striking contrast to the pornographic work in terms of class, gender, and literary identities. It is difficult to theorize which work might have represented the greater cultural fantasy. No doubt *My Secret Life* would have been banned or destroyed had it ever reached a circulating library. "From the Maid's Point of View," however, represents a more complicated position on the part of its middle-class audience, who would have enjoyed having it both ways, viewing Maggie as laughable virgin or laughable whore. Regardless of the sophistication of the reading applied, at issue is the working-class body and its ability – or not – to restrain itself.

In each of the versions of *chroniques scandaleuses* above, it is quite clear that the working classes had little discursive control of their bodies. Their bodies, real or imagined, were offered up to the sacrifice of middle-class cultural control. In the nineteenth century, the working-class body offered up the secret of its sexuality in order to be exposed, decoded and recoded for middle-class consumption. The *chronique scandaleuse* is the paradoxical genesis of this middle-class recoding.

Ironically, at the same time that pornographic literature of the sexual body was being vilified by defenders of high culture, writers and artists identified with high culture were beginning to experiment with the sexual body in their works with the intent that they should be called art and included in the realm of legitimate culture (as opposed to pornography which has always been considered illegitimate). Such inclusion, however, could be said to enact a form of control. By taking the pornographic discourse and formally controlling it within the confines of one's aesthetically, and hence ideologically, stylized art, an artist could be said to be making sex and the sexualized body safe for the middle class and the realm of high art. It is with that in mind that I now turn to a discussion of Swinburne as a transitional figure in introducing sexual representation to a high-cultural, and eventually mainstream, middle-class audience for literature.

Introducing the sexual aesthetic as art

Given my description in chapter one of pornography as a repetitive proliferation of words about the body and sexual acts, it would seem that some Victorian poets and writers would have to be classified as pornographers. Specifically, Swinburne, with poems that repetitively catalogue lips, limbs, and shuttering kisses, could be, and was, accused of creating a version of pornography. Swinburne's work directly challenged Arnold's dichotomy between interest and disinterest as representing low and high culture respectively. By introducing the sexually explicit, panting bodies typically associated with pornography (that which incites interest in its readers), while still maintaining the form and cultural capital typically associated with the aesthetic, or high culture (that which purportedly incites disinterest in its readers), the boundaries between high and low, disinterest and interest, were made less clear. In doing so, Swinburne ushered in a new era of sexual representation in British art while ironically drawing from what he claimed were older classical and aristocratic traditions of bodily representation. His poetry simultaneously represents what Raymond Williams calls residual and emergent culture, either of which stands outside of the dominant culture and must in some way be incorporated lest they continue to pose a threat.[92]

The threat of Swinburne's verse was in its assimilation to pornography. Lines from "Faustine," for example, resemble a line from *The Lustful Turk* in which a sexually domineering dey says of a sexual partner, "There alone she existed, all lost in those delicious transports, those ecstasies of the senses . . . In short she was a machine (like any other piece of machinery) obeying the impulses of the key that so potently set her in motion."[93] Compare *The Lustful Turk* to the lines of "Faustine" which declare, "You seem a thing that hinges hold / A love-machine / With clockwork joints of supple gold" (lines 141–143). Each uses a typical pornographic trope of the woman as machine, a body emptied of any potential resistance to the incessant gratification of male desires. "Laus Veneris" suggests the necrophiliac in the speaker's pronouncements, "But though my lips shut sucking on the place, / There is no vein at work upon her face" (lines 5–6). Perhaps the most reputedly racy of Swinburne's poems is "Anactoria," where a passionate, sadistic Sappho lustily exclaims:

Ah that my lips were tuneless lips, but pressed
To the bruised blossom of thy scourged white breast!
Ah that my mouth for Muses' milk were fed
On the sweet blood thy sweet small wounds had bled!
That with my tongue I felt them, and could taste
The faint flakes from thy bosom to the waist!
That I could drink thy veins as wine, and eat
Thy breasts like honey! that from face to feet
Thy body were abolished and consumed,
And in my flesh thy very flesh entombed! (lines 105–114)

The poem vacillates between "abolishing and consuming" the sexualized body. It lists body parts and actions that can easily be found in pornographic description – lips, breasts, tongues, flesh; kissing, tasting, pressing – only to dangle them between descriptive words that work to erase their physical impact. Lips are "tuneless" and thus emptied of their sensuous impact. Nipples are not material presences, but metaphorical "bruised blossoms." The poem participates in and suggests, but does not complete, the pornographic. It uses metaphor to evade pornography's insistent metonymy.

The list of sexually suggestive quotes in *Poems and Ballads* (1866) continues, from the masochistic poem "Dolores," which resembles Swinburne's clandestinely published poems of flagellation, to the sexually enumerated body of "Fragoletta." There is no doubt that the verse of *Poems and Ballads* proliferates the discourse of the body, and specifically sexual bodies in a repetitive manner that suggests some of the very techniques of pornography. By looking at the arguments surrounding Swinburne's poetry, I hope to clarify the aesthetic and social demarcations between pornography and art in the second half of the nineteenth century, and to show how those boundaries were changing.

Swinburne's poetry was released just as women and the working classes were forming a new reading public in the second half of the nineteenth century. How the "unrestrained" bodies of this new reading public would react to Swinburne's sexualized verse was at the heart of the public debate over his poems. The middle-class pressmen who reviewed *Poems and Ballads* made clear in their reviews their belief that literature had a responsibility to raise and uplift its new mass readership. The upper-middle-class and aristocratic members of the educated elite took their cues from the older tradition of libertine aristocracy (based on the right of the aristocracy to do with bodies – its own and others' – what it pleased) and argued that literature's sole responsibility was to a liberal, masculine spirit of privilege and tradition. Both sides of the debate took a pejorative view of the new reading class, but viewed its obligations to that class differently.

Writing for the *Saturday Review*, the moderate liberal John Morley took umbrage that Swinburne was "so firmly and avowedly fixed in an attitude of revolt against the current notions of decency and dignity and social duty that to beg him to become a little more decent, to fly a little less persistently and gleefully to the animal side of human nature, is simply to beg him to be something different from Mr. Swinburne."[94] In saying so, Morley revealed his belief in literature as a model for the new reading classes whose path away from Darwinian animality needed to be illuminated by civilizing culture. He asked, "Whether there is really nothing in women worth singing about except 'quivering flanks' and 'splendid supple thighs,' 'hot sweet throats' and 'hotter hands than fire,' and their blood as 'hot wan wine of love'? Is purity to be expunged from the catalogue of desirable qualities?"[95] Morley's list reveals the seemingly pornographic quality of Swinburne's writing. He made that association more overt when he asserted that the volume is "crammed with pieces which many a professional vendor of filthy prints [such as the Holywell Street vendors so frequently raided by the Society for the Suppression of Vice] might blush to sell if he only knew what they meant."[96] In like fashion, the conservative and Pre-Raphaelite-despising Robert Buchanan wrote in the *Athenaeum* that *Poems and Ballads* "bears some evidence of having been inspired in Holywell Street."[97] Morley made the aesthetic association between the poet's verse and pornography clear in his comment that "Mr. Swinburne's hunting of letters, his hunting of the same word, to death is ceaseless," later implying that he used repetition and the sensuality of words to replace rational thought.[98]

What both reviewers missed in Swinburne's poetry is a sense of the beautiful as it was understood by thinkers such as Shaftesbury, Ruskin, and Hegel to coexist with the good. Morley complained that "The lurid clouds of dust and fiery despair and defiance never lift to let us see the pure and peaceful and bounteous kindly aspects of the great landscape of human life. Of enlarged *meditation*, the note of the highest poetry, there is not a trace."[99] In a similar vein Buchanan claimed that "the glory of our modern poetry is its transcendent purity . . . More or less unavailing have been all the efforts of insincere writers to stain the current of our literature with impure thought; and those who have made the attempt have invariably done so with a view to conceal their own literary inferiority." [100] The two reviewers concur with the goal of ethical aesthetics to unite the social body through moral uplift and "purity." Swinburne's poetry, in its provocative display of bodies with the potential to incite individual viewers' senses, threatens to disrupt this ideology.

Swinburne's poems were aesthetically condemned because they address the

senses. Kathy Alexis Psomiades has explained that Swinburne's poems proble-
matically "require from their readers embodied responses, and in doing so they
implicate their viewers . . . in the celebration of aberrant sexuality. They stand
for an art that takes you over, that gets under your skin, that comes to you on a
level beyond the visually appealing ."[101] As Morley said, "most of the poems, in
his [Swinburne's] wearisomely iterated phrase, are meant 'to sting the senses like
wine.' "[102] They are sensational and sensual, and as such, evade the requisite disinterest of the aesthetic in their provocation of the reader's body. The tendency
of the aesthetic in the tradition of Shaftesbury and Kant is to limit art's sensuous
appeal, shifting the measure of a work's value from its pleasurable effects on an
audience, or affect, to the intrinsic considerations of the "perfection" and
"harmony" of the work itself.[103] This aesthetic holds that true art does not set
the body into motion by an appeal to the senses, but rather sets the mind into
contemplation through a finality of form (Buchanan notes the poems' "utter
worthlessness in form"). The aesthetic object becomes for its viewer or reader a
substitute body. Through its objectification, the physical and the irrational are
safely transubstantiated into the reflective reason of the aesthetic moment. Good
art, according this hegemonic cultural ideal, should invoke a sense of rational
harmony in the viewer by reifying the viewer's sense of its purpose.[104] In order
to induce aesthetic contemplation and understanding, art must sublimate or
transform its sensual appeals. Conversely, pornography's primary aim is to excite
the sexual drives of its viewers, often by a specular representation of sexual desire.
In high art, for instance, the female nude must act as a function of the pure, disinterested gaze, the body transubstantiated. In pornography, the naked female
represents the realm of mass culture where sensual desires are stimulated and
gratified in a scenario perceived as chaotic and regressive, beyond the control of
civilized society (Freud's letter to Martha Bernays exemplifies this perspective).

Swinburne's poetic narratives fail to suspend or transform the sexual desire
implicit in the speaker's gaze and naming of parts. Tannhauser, for instance,
dwells sensuously on Venus's charms in "Laus Veneris" until "his blood and body
so / Shake as the flame shakes" (lines 50–51). The speaker in "Fragoletta"
observes "The maiden's mouth is cold, / Her breast blossoms are simply red,"
and, after further naming of parts, pitches himself into such a frenzy that he begs,
"Cleave to me, love me, kiss mine eyes, / Satiate thy lips with loving me" (lines
41–42, 56–57). His poetic speakers are sexual enumerators, fervently speaking
the woman's body.[105] The speakers describe their own experiences of embodiment, inducing a specular desire in their readers. As is typical of pornography's
self-reflexive narratives, Swinburne's poetic narrators are all voyeurs who

recount their own sensations and reactions in order to reproduce the pleasure of the seen and felt. By preventing a reader's ability to remain disinterested, the poems turn readers away from the objectifying reason upon which the imaginary public sphere is based. As Psomiades has suggested, "Instead of marking the moment when beauty becomes public, it [Swinburne's poetry] marks the moment at which public man is privatized, drawn into the aesthetic-erotic realm, and at which he gives up his public power for private pleasure."[106] Such an impulse is seen to destroy the possibility of a shared, rational public sphere.

William Michael Rossetti tried to set up a defense of Swinburne's poems by arguing a traditionally elitist point of view that the verses should not be broadcast to all, but rather to a select few "qualified readers":

> His writings exercise a great fascination over qualified readers, and excite very real enthusiasm in them: but these readers are not that wide, popular, indiscriminate class who come to a poet to be moved by the subject matter, the affectingly told story, the sympathetic interpreting words which, in giving voice to the poet's own emotion or perception, find utterance also for those of the universal and inarticulate heart. Mr. Swinburne's readers are of another and a more restricted order. They are persons who, taking delight in the art of poetry, rejoicing when they find a poet master of his materials and the employment of them, kindle to watch so signal a manifestation of poetic gifts and poetic workmanship, and tender him an admiration which, if less than that of an adept, is more than that of a dilettante.[107]

Much of Rossetti's defense works with the idea that Swinburne truly preserves the "antique" spirit that subserves, to some extent, his "passionate sensuousness" while remaining in itself formally pure. He works within the domain of the educated-elite – classical language and culture – to preserve Swinburne's integrity as one of the privileged, for whom the pure space of Greek antiquity remains proprietary, with the mild chastisement that as "a mighty intoxication of poetic diction mounts to his head, and pours in an unruly torrent through his lips . . . he forgets the often still nobler office of self-mastery and reticence."[108] Rossetti claimed a space for Swinburne in the aristocratic-libertine heritage, while perhaps wishing that via "self-mastery and reticence" he might take on a more characteristically middle-class stance. Importantly, however, his claims were based on the formal qualities of the poetry, Swinburne's materials, and his mastery of them. In the late nineteenth and early twentieth centuries, form became the aesthetic defense under which sexual representations made their way into publicly accepted visibility.

While both the defense and attack of Swinburne's verse were based on classical notions of the aesthetic, the territory of that aesthetic and its function were up for debate. The newspaper critics wanted the poems purged of the sexual body and made safe for the middle classes. Swinburne and his defenders claimed the sexual body as the privileged domain of an artistic aristocracy, made pure by a formal treatment that only a masculine and publicly educated few could appreciate. Swinburne's own blistering attack upon his reviewers extended Rossetti's implied defense of elite privilege, and made his disdain for the new reading public clear. He began by differentiating the credentials of his reviewers from his own. First proclaiming "I have not studied in those schools whence the full-fledged phoenix, the 'virtue of professional pressmen,' rises chuckling and crowing from the dunghill," he then proudly admitted, "I have never worked for praise or pay, but simply by impulse, and to please myself."[109] Having established his own aristocratic superiority (and through his impulsive self-pleasuring aesthetic, suggested the pornographic), he attacked the standards for literature as prescribed by the new reading class:

> I have overlooked the evidence which every day makes clearer, that our time has room only for such as are content to write for children and girls . . . It would seem indeed as though to publish a book were equivalent to thrusting it with violence into the hands of every mother and nurse in the kingdom as fit and necessary food for female infancy.[110]

Swinburne's response to the new reading public, here hyperbolically feminized and infantilized to make his point more clear, was to reject the self-policing urges so evident in the critical writing of Matthew Arnold and the middle-class reviewers in favor of a social policing that excluded entire segments of the population.

Aesthetically, Swinburne tried to make a case for the spiritualization of the body in art. In his individual readings of "Anactoria" and "Dolores" he used phrases like "that transient state of spirit," and "the spirit of a poem" to empty the poetry of its guilty materiality. In defense of representing the body he said, "I knew that modern moralities and recent religions were, if possible, more averse and alien to this purely physical and pagan art [of sculpture] than to the others; but how far averse I did not know."[111] He wanted it both ways: to validate bodily experience in and of itself, and yet also to imbue the body with the spirit. In his disdain for his middle-class critics, Swinburne claimed the sexual body for his aristocratic art. Yet his emphasis on spirit shows that even he bowed to middle-class pressure to idealize the body, to reduce its materiality (and hence its threat).

Swinburne was one of the last British artists to attempt an aristocratic, sensual art.[112] But as can be seen here, the pressure from the dominant middle class was so great as to cause him to succumb, at moments, to its pressure. In his final burst of castrating rhetoric, he argued for a new mode of art that makes room for the body and sexual representation in a masculine territory (fully engorged no less) he thought he had pioneered:

> The office of adult art is neither puerile nor feminine, but virile . . . its purity is not that of the cloister or the harem . . . the press will be as impotent as the pulpit to dictate the laws and remove the landmarks of art; and those will be laughed at who demand from one thing the qualities of another – who seek for sermons in sonnets and morality in music. Then all accepted work will be noble and chaste in the wider masculine sense, not truncated and curtailed, but outspoken and full-grown.[113]

Like a lawyer arguing for a more pure form of the law, Swinburne can be seen here delineating the difference between a pure Kantian aesthetic and the Ruskinian–Hegelian one that intermixes the good and the beautiful. His "virile" art is pure in form; it does not stoop to moral prescription, an impotent form of beauty.

In his insistence on a purely formal art, Swinburne blazed the path for modernist critics and writers who relied on seeing aesthetic beauty as a purely formal quality in order to avoid the moral conundrums of ethically questionable and sensational subject matter. While remaining a peculiar transitional figure as a result of his insistence on the aristocratic tradition of writing and enjoying the body, Swinburne ushered in two important elements of modernist art: representation of the sexual body under the rubric of "disinterested" art and a concentration on formal rather than moral beauty. The two impulses together represent the only way of reconciling material representations to an ideally acculturated sensibility that insisted on concretizing the symbolic realm of the public sphere through the mutual understanding of rational individuals.

By stressing form as an idealizing, pure form of art, as Swinburne did, the body is purged of its unrestrained and threatening materiality (ironically in a gesture of reading that focuses on the materially manifest work of art). It is a subtle manipulation, but one that resolves the tension between the idealistic heritage of the elite-educated classes and the encroaching reading practices of the masses that allowed for material, sensual reactions to art. Form, by controlling the sexual representations and therefore the bodily reactions of its readers, fosters the objectification of the body which accompanies disinterestedness and allows the middle class to retain a sense of its cultural hegemony. As becomes more clear in the work of Aubrey Beardsley and James Joyce, the Kantian privileging of aesthetic form allows for an appropriation of pornographic tropes and images into art while simultaneously maintaining its claims to high-art, aesthetic status. Such a gesture colonizes both the pornographic genre and a portion of the market share upon which pornography has a hold.

Pornography, one of nineteenth-century England's most overlooked mass-cultural products, played a significant role in bringing lower-class bodies to the written page and exposing them to the discursive control of writers of all classes. It is with this in mind that we should look to its appropriation by modern artists as involving more than simply an effort *pour épater le bourgeois*, for in the hands of modern artists the body of pornography is transubstantiated into high art, where its potentially subversive bodies and bodily readers, the working classes, are made safe for middle-class consumption.

3 The mastery of form: Beardsley and Joyce

Denominations

Aubrey Beardsley and James Joyce may at first glance seem unlikely partners in any aesthetic project. Beardsley was a pen-and-ink artist of small-scale drawings that reached their peak of popularity between 1895 and 1930, but have continued to enjoy a small, appreciative audience since, and Joyce was a writer of large-scale novels that have dominated literary thought throughout much of the twentieth century. Both, however, have enjoyed a particular success with the academy, the institution which in the twentieth century best represents upper-middle-class, high aesthetic tastes. Equally, both artists had a penchant for depicting explicit sexuality in their works. With these two connections in mind, this chapter will focus on the similarities between these two artists that ushered in an era of explicit sexual representation in the arts.

In his 1925 book *The Beardsley Period*, art critic Osbert Burdett recognized the affinity between Joyce and Beardsley, and, after praising the "technical accomplishment" of Beardsley's works, reflected:

> It seems, too, hardly more than an accident of time that *Ulysses* was not published in the nineties. Its vast experiment would have interested them. They would have recognized the learning, and been beguiled by the effects, of its immense vocabulary. Even the absence of punctuation in the last chapter would have seemed to Beardsley, if not to Johnson, a legitimate experiment.[1]

In Burdett's eyes the two artists are linked together not by the sexual content of their art, but by the technical experimentalism and cultural capital of their work. While Burdett may have tried to buttress his own scholarly seriousness by purposefully avoiding discussion of the content of the last chapter of *Ulysses* – Molly Bloom's soliloquy in "Penelope" was often labeled and censored as pornography in the 1920s and 1930s – his evasion is symptomatic of a larger movement to disavow the sexual content of art even as it was pressing more thoroughly against traditional aesthetic conventions. To him, and to many who legitimated Beardsley's and Joyce's work in the *fin-de-siècle* and the first decades of the twentieth century, their artistic competence is based on the formal qualities of the works and the cultural capital expressed in them; in other words, their ability to represent the codes of artistic integrity as defined by the high culture of their time.

Beardsley and Joyce were masters of aesthetic form. Each introduced into his works sexually explicit images and tropes that until their time could only be found in pornography.[2] It is my contention that Beardsley and Joyce successfully incorporated the explicitly sexual tropes and images of pornography into their works even while cultivating reputations for these works as high art precisely because of their formal mastery over the material introduced. Critics were able to focus on form as enabling the aesthetic because Kant's reification of the art object as autonomous expression through form dominated aesthetic thought in the final decades of the nineteenth and the first decades of the twentieth centuries. As I suggested in chapter one, Kant's *Critique of Judgment* concretized a high-cultural shift in the eighteenth century from viewing the art object as having an instrumental value (e.g., to delight and instruct) to viewing the art object as having an autonomous value, existing for the sake of its own internal perfection. As Kant's aesthetic philosophy became culturally dominant in Britain in the latter half of the nineteenth century, form became the primary signifier of that which was considered beautiful, and hence high art.[3] Form, as opposed to any "charm" that might induce a necessarily subjective and particular sensation or emotion in the viewer/reader, is according to Kant that which is capable of constituting a delight of reason that, apart from any concept, is universally communicable and so capable of forming a judgment of taste.[4] Form in this sense should be understood as that which gives reality and objectivity to the thing known and which Kant regarded as due to mind. Form as conceptualized in post-Renaissance aesthetics is always aligned with the shaping powers of the mind, those of the artist as well as the viewer. Shaftesbury, in considering form, asked, "What is it you admire but mind, or the effect of mind? 'Tis mind alone which forms."[5] In Kant, form cannot be based on either the material or conceptual structure of the aesthetic object. Instead, as Samuel Weber has suggested, form in Kant "amounts to something like a *silhouette*, that is, the minimal trait required to individualize

The mastery of form: Beardsley and Joyce

a perception and to distinguish it from its surroundings."[6] Form becomes something like a unified temporal and spatial moment distinguishing shape from shapeless elements.

For the purposes of this chapter, form should be considered as bearing a doublefold valence, empirical and metaphysical. Empirically, form is realized as style, the shaping of figures, the line or touch of Beardsley's drawings, the punctuation and syntax that Joyce employed so deliberately. Metaphysically, form is realized as an effect of mind that can be realized as having some reference outside oneself. The metaphysical manifestation of form should be conceived as responsible, in part, for the distancing effect of the aesthetic, that which marks fixity from movement or dislocation, the individual from the mass, uniqueness from multiplicity. The assertion of form, the effects of mind, holds off a collapse into the pornographic.

In the 1890s, British artists took their lead from the French Art for-Art's Sake movement (which in turn had followed Kant), and in addition to repeating Gautier's rallying cry for aesthetic autonomy, followed his practice of asserting a beautiful form upon a subject seemingly inharmonious. Perfection of form was in itself seen as an aesthetic virtue. Subjects that heretofore had remained outside of art were allowed into art under the pretense that a beautiful form purified an ugly, sinful, or sensuous content. Thus in Arthur Symons's elegiac commentary on Beardsley's work he noted that the "spiritual corruption" represented in Beardsley's work is "revealed in beautiful form," and that beauty "transfigures" the evil depicted.[7] Similarly, Osbert Burdett remarked that "in an age when beauty had been pushed to its extreme, he [Beardsley] took this degradation for his subject and proved how beautifully degradation itself could be depicted."[8] While neither commentator was comfortable embracing the decadent, sinful subjects of Beardsley's works, they both were quite ready to qualify the treatment as artistic, beautiful.

Treatment became the defining narrative of Beardsley's work according to the critics of the early twentieth century. The importance of Beardsley's works was not in the represented, but rather the representing – his transfiguring touch. Focusing on form, critics maintained a pretense to disinterest, and thus perpetuated the high-cultural vantage point begun in the late eighteenth century with the division of high and low arts by intrinsic or instrumental value. By foregrounding their own form, Beardsley's works, portraying images that in another context would clearly be considered pornographic, deny, in Peter Michelson's words "the necessary connection between pornography and vulgarity, or immorality and ugliness."[9] Drawing on the empirical resonance of form to reconfigure the pornographic into the aesthetic, Beardsley relied on a vast technical vocabulary to assert classical lines against sexually moved subjects. Joyce also adopted this technique. As Stephen Dedalus says in *Stephen Hero*, "A classical style is the symbolism of art, the only legitimate process from one world to another."[10] Beardsley's elegant and controlling line was the key to his aesthetic reception and perpetuation by the high-culture institutions that value autonomy, control, and disinterest as conveyed through form.

The aesthetic criteria by which Joyce's works were judged were similar to Beardsley's. T. S. Eliot's classic 1923 essay "*Ulysses*, Order and Myth" privileged formal considerations over those of content by imposing the "mythical method" onto Joyce's novel. In Eliot's conception the myth itself serves as the ordering principle by which *Ulysses* is given form. Eliot argued that, "manipulating a continuous parallel between contemporaneity and antiquity . . . is simply a way of controlling, of ordering, of giving a shape and significance to the immense panorama of futility and anarchy which is contemporary history."[11] The keywords in Eliot's analysis, "manipulating," "ordering," and "controlling," joined later by a compliment to Joyce's formal "discipline," each suggest a politicized mode of dealing with the "anarchy" of modern culture. To Eliot, aesthetic technique effects a social and physical ordering, and that ordering is intentionally imposed. The mythical method serves as a signifier of artistic intention not just through the imposition of form, but also through its drawing upon that proprietary reserve of high culture: classical literature.

The emphasis on formal concerns arose and was perpetuated by middle-class anxiety about the increased access to art and literature enjoyed by the working classes in the late nineteenth and early twentieth centuries. The boom of print journalism in the 1890s, which catered largely to the newly educated working classes and the *petit bourgeois*, created alarm in the high-cultural sphere about the spread of certain forms of literacy that it troped in images of contagion. Words in the mass-cultural sphere became "promiscuous" words. "The printed word," Osbert Burdett commented in 1925, "is beginning to lose all distinction in newspapers and books that do no more than reflect the illiteracy of the mass of readers."[12] "Words," as Stephen remarks in *Stephen Hero* (mimicking the high-cultural viewpoint, as he does so often in regard to aesthetic taste), "have a certain value in the literary tradition and a certain value in the marketplace – a debased value" (*SH* 33). Words are debased because they take on meanings beyond the pure sphere of the literary; they are contaminated by meanings imposed by the crowd, by interest, personal and financial.

The debased value of art in the commercial, public sphere, catalyzed artists, beginning with the artists of the 1890s, to discover more abstruse ways of expressing their art. Burdett claimed that the "extravagance" of artistic assertion in the 1890s was a "protest against a commercial society, in which the pressure of numbers had become so great that the needs and standard of the multitude necessarily dominated everything."[13] John Rothenstein, a contemporary of Burdett's who also wrote on the artists of the 1890s, argued that "Machinery [and its attendant commercialism] destroyed within the space of a few years the instinctive good taste" of the people of England. Artists such as Aubrey Beardsley, he contended, were forced to create "a fantastic and exotic refuge from the present."[14] There was a defensive, high-cultural consensus around the turn of the century that "true" art was a project set in opposition to mass culture and mass-cultural forms.

Given modernism's purported high-cultural bias against mass culture, it is interesting to note how frequently mass-cultural forms made their way into art that aspired to high-cultural status. The emergence of a mass market for cultural commodities created by the expanding wealth and literacy of the lower classes freed artists at the same time that it constrained them. For while, on the one hand, increasing numbers of the working and lower middle classes beginning to purchase art and literature expanded the market, on the other hand, the proliferation of literary products tended to erode a cultural consensus that had for most of the nineteenth century been based on shared upper-middle-class patterns of consumption.[15] Artists were forced to find new means of expression that, while acknowledging and often exploiting this new market, continued to play upon the traditional signifiers of high art in order to perpetuate their place within high culture, to maintain an artistic aristocracy.

Inheriting the prevalent tenets of aesthetic philosophy developed in the tradition of Shaftesbury and Kant, the dominant high-culture view was that low- and mass-cultural media, like pornography, moved their subjects in their individual particularity, provoking through their appeal to the senses a physical, often sexual, response. The high arts were perceived as those which invoked a disinterested stasis, suspending their subjects in moments of (the idea of) universal intellectual apprehension. A stunning recapitulation of these values can be found in the oft-cited scene in Joyce's *A Portrait of the Artist as a Young Man* in which Stephen Dedalus distinguishes between the kinetic emotions, those excited by what he calls the improper arts – pornographic or didactic – and the aesthetic emotions, those characterized by stasis and elicited from art proper.[16] High art, as the domain of a certain segment of the middle class, was predicated on a censorship of the body as self-constituting subject. While art appreciation is a subject-centering activity, in Kantian and post-Kantian aesthetic philosophy it is based on the removal or suppression of the body from the aesthetic interaction in place of the more outwardly, community oriented understanding, or reason. Francis Barker, writing about the bourgeois disavowal of the material body, suggests that in post-Renaissance middle-class discourses, "The body and its passions are at work in and around the portions of discourse in which the subject is present to itself, but only as the effects of a guilty evasion, a turning aside uttered by the subject but in an important sense unknown to it."[17] As I showed in chapter two with regard to the *chronique scandaleuse* in the nineteenth century, the body was other to the bourgeois subject.[18]

If the body was other, increasingly distinctions had to be made between the bourgeois culture that operated under a "self-disciplinary fixation predicated on the outlawing of the body and its passions as the absolute outside," and the uncultivated masses that were not ideologically predisposed to differentiate between aesthetic disinterest and the interests of the senses.[19] Adorno has classified this latter group as those that exhibit, "an animal-like attitude toward the object, say, a desire to devour it or otherwise subjugate it to one's body."[20] As I suggested in chapter two, the middle classes associated the working classes with disease, consumption, the bestial, the feminine, and the uncivilized. To the middle classes the working classes represented the body, and as such were outside the culturally hegemonic bourgeois realm (while simultaneously functioning as a necessary other, as necessary as one's own body). In his 1896 work *The Crowd*, Gustave Le Bon inscribed the masses in a narrative of degeneration, assessing them as "belonging to inferior forms of evolution . . . women, savages, and children, for instance."[21] Le Bon's work is a testament to the fact that by the end of the nineteenth century, the working classes were formed symbolically into a new, externalized and abstract phenomenon enabled by the rapid production of mass media forms: the mass or crowd. The crowd was seen as impetuous, physically oriented, and mentally inferior.[22] Beyond any realistic conception, it should be clear, the mass was a construct of *haut bourgeois* self-assertion, a perpetual metaphor of an other that enabled self definition. The symbolic constituents of the abstract mass did not adhere to actual individuals, but functioned as an imaginary category for organizing class relationships.

The symbolic construction of the mass represented a distinctly separate construction of the citizenry than the eighteenth-century conception of the public sphere. The public sphere, developed after the Glorious Revolution when the powers of parliament began to supersede those of the monarchy, implied active, rational participation in government. The mass, or crowd, implied a separation between rational government and the body of the people. The public sphere of middle-class citizens that engendered high culture in the eighteenth century was predicated on a denial of the body. Inheriting those biases two hundred years later, the mass was all body. If high-culture art appreciation rested on a denial of an interest of the senses, the masses were seen as subjugating art to their bodies in a mode of conspicuous consumption antithetical to the repressed pleasures of disinterested contemplation.

Though a difference between modes of aesthetic consumption marked the occasion of the philosophies of taste and the aesthetic in England and Germany in the eighteenth century, the early twentieth century observed a more complete rupture between high and low modes of consumption. Importantly, the Oxford English Dictionary first published a distinction between literature and popular literature in 1904, associating the popular with mass-cultural modes of consumption.[23] While the low, or popular, arts were allied with profits and "interest," the high arts were associated with disinterest, symbolic capital over economic capital. With its priority on profit, consumption, and sensual enjoyment, mass culture was demonized by the defenders of high culture.

Walter Benjamin outlines this distinction in his essay "The Work of Art in the Age of Mechanical Reproduction," where he sets up a paradigm of high and low modes of consumption. He describes phenomena much like those I have been describing as distance and immediacy as "distraction" and "concentration." "Distraction and concentration," he says, "form polar opposites which may be stated as follows: A man who concentrates before a work of art is absorbed by it. He enters into this work of art . . . In contrast, the distracted mass absorbs the work of art."[24] As in the Kantian model, the aesthetic experience is authenticated by an attitude that disavows consumption in commercial or appetitive terms, aiming instead to remove the subject from himself and from an economy of endless personal interests. Aesthetic form is that which accommodates, perhaps even forces, distance. "The desire of the contemporary masses," Benjamin writes, is "to bring things 'closer' spatially and humanly, which is just as ardent as their bent toward overcoming the uniqueness of every reality by accepting its reproduction."[25] The bent towards bringing things closer is explained by Adorno in Aesthetic Theory in his claim that "As art became more and more similar to physical subjectivity, it moved more and more away from objectivity, ingratiating itself with the public."[26] That mass (re)production has facilitated the perception of a universal equality of things is to Benjamin simply the result of "The adjustment of reality to the masses and the masses to reality."[27]

Both Benjamin and Adorno indicate that changes in the social structure and the accessibility of the arts in the early decades of the twentieth century fundamentally challenged the ideal of an achieved objectivity in aesthetic contemplation/consumption. Before there was mass-cultural consumption, Benjamin proposes, art was characterized by its "aura," which he defines loosely as "the unique phenomenon of a *distance*"(my italics) however close an object may be.[28] While temporally Benjamin places the art of aura as having preceded the art of exhibition (of which mass-reproduced works form a part), I would argue, as I have throughout this work, that the notion of art as defined by a distance, or in associative Kantian terms, disinterest, arose and was further concretized in direct response to the perceived threat of marginalization by the arts of interest, the commercial arts.

Pornography, sexual literature written for profit with the specific purpose of identifying with and/or creating a physical subjectivity and a bodily reading/consumption, is the antithesis of the art of aura, for distance is anathema to a bodily reading. Reaching its zenith in an age of mass reproduction, pornography, especially in its visual forms, represents mass-culture and its physical repudiation of distance (even if its solipsistic pleasures are enabled by that very distance).

Verbal distinctions between mass and high culture resonated throughout the reviews of Aubrey Beardsley's art and James Joyce's literature, and while they had their high-cultural defenders, their introduction of pornographic representational techniques exposed them to the critics of mass culture. When the *Yellow Book* first hit the stands, there was a critical outcry over its affront to tradition. After the periodical had proclaimed that it intended to be "beautiful as a piece of bookmaking, modern and distinguished in its letterpress and pictures, and popular in the best sense of the word," a reviewer for *The National Observer* wondered "how they imagine that anything concerned with letters can be at once popular (in the ordinary sense of the word) and distinguished."[29] The reviewer then mockingly identified the *Yellow Book*'s readership as the *petit bourgeois*, a new readership whose patterns of consumption were supposedly but an imitation of the more studied ones of the reviewer's ilk:

> Now we have it: you can see men going home from their labour in the city, bearing the work deferentially in their arms: it flames from the forehead of many an "occasional table" in Brixton and Bayswater. For the great world likes to be told what it is to admire, especially when it is to admire something new. It stands to reason that a quarterly, which boasted its intention of throwing aside the "traditions of periodical literature" as "old" and "bad" was assured of a welcome from the obedient suburban populace, which since it cannot be the apostle of The Newness is content to be its acolyte.[30]

The mastery of form: Beardsley and Joyce

More explicitly, the *Pall Mall Gazette* belittled the *Yellow Book*'s constituency: "The lower middle class is in the movement. Highbury and Brixton are arrayed in yellow, and Mr. Aubrey Beardsley is already the patron-saint of the back parlour."[31] The gleeful disdain with which each reviewer comments on the interior decor of the *petit bourgeois* home, its "occasional table" and "back parlour," reveals a contempt for lower-middle-class assimilation (and perceived imitation) of upper-middle-class patterns of consumption, aesthetic or decorative. That the lower middle class would proudly display Beardsley's works on their tables or in their parlors is an indication of a conspicuous consumption (equivalent to Leopold Bloom hanging the picture of the nymph from *Photo-Bits* in his bedroom) that exposes their pretension to class and their "false" aesthetic consciousness. The *Yellow Book* in Bayswater and Brixton can be nothing but kitsch.

Just as popularity was perceived as a fault with Beardsley's periodical, the association with the populace was likewise a burden to *Ulysses*. The most often cited critique of Joyce's work when it first appeared in 1922 was its similarity in appearance to a telephone directory. The reviewer for *The Sporting Times* declared that "As the volume is about the size of the *London Directory*, I do not envy anyone who reads it for pleasure."[32] The *Daily Herald* noted that the book was "As large as a telephone directory or a family Bible, and with many of the literary and social characteristics of each."[33] Shane Leslie of the *Quarterly Review* worried that *Ulysses*, resembling "in size and colour . . . the London Telephone Book," was "a danger to the unsuspecting."[34] Surely its resemblance in the minds of its reviewers to a telephone book reflects nothing so much as their fear that such a "dangerous work" might create a "direct-dial" connection with the masses, who in turn might read a sexually explicit work like *Ulysses* with their bodies rather than employ the cultivated stance of intellectual distance. Equally dangerous, a telephone book is read only for certain passages, those items one "looks up"; in *Ulysses*'s case, its sex scenes.

That those under-educated in the techniques of cultured reading might have access to *Ulysses* was a fear repeatedly recognized in the reviews. A reviewer for the European edition of the *Chicago Tribune* worried:

> What it will mean to the reader is a question. Too many are the possibilities of this human flesh when finally in contact with the crude, disgusting and unpalatable facts of our short existence. One thing to be thankful for is that the volume is in a limited edition, therefore suppressed to the stenographer or high school boy.[35]

The *Dublin Review* was relieved that "As for the general reader, it is, as it were, so much rotten caviare [a high-cultural signifier if ever there was one, though in this case working to suggest the degenerate], and the public is in no particular danger of understanding or being corrupted thereby."[36] Thus extracted, these reviews all share an abhorrence of the general, the popular, and the new class of clerks and typists that emerged with their small disposable incomes after late-nineteenth-century educational reforms took hold. Where the works of Beardsley or Joyce seemed to cater to the mass's sensuous tastes through sexualized representations, the middle-class defenders of high culture trembled. Yet where the works provided difficulty, reserve, or elegance of form – all signifiers of a higher aesthetic that enforces distance – the reviewers delighted.

Despite the tenuous reception of Joyce and Beardsley's works by solid middle-class reviewers and their significantly documented battles with censorship, one needs hardly to be reminded that, especially in Joyce's case, the works were almost instantly canonized. Their canonization was dependent on their ability to assert a high-cultural aesthetic, even while appropriating – even flaunting – the pornographic. By discursively controlling the potentially revolutionary material(ism) of the masses, and by checking a sensuous reaction to their works through a disjunctive style that disrupts the normative flow of a pornographic pleasure, Joyce and Beardsley effectively rendered the sensuous and low in their works impotent while maintaining the hegemony of form, the high-art signifier of culture. To be sure, the pornographic in these works asserts its immediacy and constantly threatens to destabilize the aesthetic. But by prioritizing form in its empirical and metaphysical manifestations, these works foster the disinterestedness that is the supposed guarantee of the aesthetic quality of contemplation.

One manifestation of the form by which Joyce and Beardsley gain aesthetic distance from the pornographic tropes they use is through employing parody or ironic distance. The pragmatic function of irony, as Linda Hutcheon has noted, is to signal evaluation, a critical distance.[37] The deployment of the pornographic in Beardsley and Joyce is almost always accompanied by an ironic distancing that focuses not on the sexual representation itself, but on how that representation is mediated and received. This technique serves to set the text itself apart from the representations of the pornographic in order to signal a critical distance from them by repeating and reproducing them in a sociologically incongruent context. This has the effect of rendering the pornographic representations incongruous or even absurd, simply by making them perceptible as arbitrary conventions.[38] Once recognized as a system of tropes, pornographic images lose their performative effect.

If a reader is not complicitous with the parodic attitude, unable to understand the tropes as deconstructed, such technique may work against the agent of parody, for parody equally highlights its own artifices in such a way that the parodic text becomes a site of contestation, despite the mutually constitutive nature of such parody. It may seem the intention of the parodic text to control and indicate a difference from the parodied text, but a failure to appeal to an audience through a normative system of recognizable codes or "ideolects" through which one can ridicule marginalized languages or styles may result in what Frederic Jameson has described as pastiche:

> Pastiche is, like parody, the imitation of a peculiar or unique style, the wearing of a stylistic mask, speech in a dead language: but it is a neutral practice of such mimicry, without parody's ulterior motive, without satirical impulse, without laughter, without that still latent feeling that there exists something *normal* compared to which what is being imitated is rather comic. Pastiche is blank parody.[39]

Parody, then, is a local and temporal phenomenon. It can only exist for a specific group of people within a specific time frame, after which it fades, like all cultural memories, into mere pastiche.

The question remains whether what Joyce or Beardsley did with the pornographic in their texts should be read in the modernist way as parodic, or in the postmodernist way as pastiche. Surely one can rigorously read their works both ways. But an investigation into the marriage of the pornographic and the aesthetic in high art at the turn of the twentieth century needs to be mindful of the audiences to whom these works were aimed and the critics who guided these audiences into modes of reception, for the works' contemporary critics were the ones who, as the reviews above make clear, would have harbored a keener sensitivity to the pornographic as antithetical to the aesthetic. Representing the represented, the parodic text must perform the cultural labor of transformation. As readings of their works will show, Beardsley and Joyce assumed this labor.

Though Joyce and Beardsley incorporated seemingly subversive tropes, Bakhtin's theory of the carnival helps to remind us of the nature of parodic inversion. In transgressing norms, the very norms that are transgressed are also posited in their notable absence.[40] Parody's transgressions are ultimately authorized by the norms it seeks to subvert.[41] A high-art work that incorporates the pornographic transgresses high-art norms, but in doing so it foregrounds the very norms violated. In this sense, as Barthes has pointed out, parody can suggest "complicity with high culture . . . which is merely a deceptively off-hand way of showing a profound respect for classical-national values."[42] However, because parody is a dialogue between two texts, as this chapter will show, it can cut both ways, each text deconstructing the conventions of the other. The pornographic tropes and images incorporated often work to subvert their high-cultural context. "A parody of pornography," Susan Sontag has written, "so far as it has any real competence, always remains pornography."[43] But in Joyce and Beardsley, the parodying of pornographic texts functions primarily as a conservative and appropriating force for high art. Though foregrounding the constructedness of both pornography and aesthetics, Joyce and Beardsley's works relied on a complicity with their audiences to recognize the ironic distance from the pornographic tropes employed as subversive of both pornography and aesthetics, but formally in compliance with the aesthetic in the tradition of Shaftesbury and Kant. By resignifying and recontextualizing pornography, Joyce and Beardsley are frequently successful at limiting and dominating it. They appropriated pornography for high art, making sexual representation safe for the middle classes.

Appropriations

Beardsley's and Joyce's interest in and familiarity with a variety of pornography has been well documented by numerous scholars.[44] Both artists incorporated pornographic images and narratives in their works in such a way that allowed them to use, control, and limit the literature of and for the body to maintain high-art hegemony. While it should be clarified that such manipulations cannot be said to have been conscious decisions on the part of Beardsley or Joyce, who frequently demonstrated the will *pour épater le bourgeois*, such a power was effected through them by the very techniques they articulated. As Laura Kipnis suggests, "A class becomes hegemonic not through its capacity for sheer domination, but through its ability to appropriate visions of the world and diverse cultural elements of its subordinated classes, but in forms that carefully neutralize any inherent or potential antagonism and transform these antagonisms into simple *difference*."[45] The appropriation of the pornographic into high art resulted in neutralizing the potentially subversive effects of the increasing demand for underground sexual literature and pictures (market share) while exposing and therefore perpetuating the *haute bourgeoisie* control over/denial of the body as self-constituting subject (symbolic capital). The discursive exposure of the body as controlled form in high art is but a continuation of its distancing and objectification.

Modern art has been noted for its appropriating impulse (appropriations made possible by the expansion of cultural spheres, a form of aesthetic imperialism), and *Ulysses* is its classic example. But Joyce's acquisitiveness, like Beardsley's, can never be solely one-sided. As much as the images and tropes of pornographic texts are subverted from their primary aims when displaced into these artists' works, so they subvert their high-cultural surroundings, cutting at their contexts in often unforeseen irony. In the political analogy I have drawn throughout this work, the entrance of lower-class forms, or the body (politic), into high art enacts a social reintegration of representational types on the page. Put simply, mind meets body, whether this discourse is controlled by the high-cultural aesthetic techniques that deploy it, or if it indeed enacts a pluralist mode of representation. Regardless of the interpretations a late twentieth-century reader might put on these discursive appropriations, it is significant that these works were and have since been taken seriously as art (as opposed to pornography). As I will show below, their success is due to their treatment of such pornographic tropes.

The voyeur

Visual consumption is pornography's primary mode. It is not a passive act of watching, but rather a consumption, a taking in of an image for personal use, a subjection of the image to the body. All who enjoy visual pornography are, logically, voyeurs. Likewise, written pornography, which invariably contains scenes of voyeurism in order to mimic and incite the action intended for its readers, is a form of literature intended for the bodily consumer, one who will subject the written images to his or her body's passions. Seen as such, pornography is an inversion of the anti-materialist high-culture norms of aesthetic reception. It epitomizes the commercial, as Jennifer Wicke has commented, by foregrounding "the ease and rapidity of mass-cultural consumptive visual strategies" that are "appallingly emblematized by pornography itself, where the languor and voluptuousness of consumption in general gets raised to its apotheosis."[46]

Developed in the last decades of the nineteenth century, erotic postcards and photographs served as a cheap mass medium for the transmittal of erotic fantasies. By 1899, over 14 million postcards had been produced and distributed in Great Britain alone.[47] The erotic postcard, most typically featuring a nude or semi-nude woman gazing playfully at the camera or wistfully into the unknown (though the variety of poses is not limited and sometimes features a male partner), represents the organization into visibility of the sexual fantasy.[48] Prepackaged into an inexpensive, mass-produced commodity, erotic postcards create the voyeur as much as they are created by voyeurs. That is, they teach a method of looking and reacting to their subjects by creating a set of expectations of what can be found and seen. They set into practice a technique of consumption that is simultaneously a sexual practice.

Stephen Dedalus proves himself inculcated into the voyeuristic practice in *A Portrait of the Artist as a Young Man*, where in thinking of his lust for Emma he is ashamed to recall "the sootcoated packet of pictures which he had hidden in the flue of the fireplace and in the presence of whose shameless or bashful wantonness he lay for hours sinning in thought and deed."[49] Trained by erotic pictures to engage the sexual imagination upon the visible image, Stephen translates this practice into everyday experience: "He bore cynically with the shameful details of his secret riots in which he exulted to defile with patience whatever image had attracted his eyes."[50] The practice of pornography teaches its subjects to desublimate the sensuous apprehension. In this instance, the practice of pornography teaches its subjects to desublimate the sensuous apprehension of the image to effect an immediacy. Living beings are turned into images, photographic or cinematic displays to set into motion the bodily reader, the voyeur.

Leopold Bloom is likewise inculcated into the voyeur's mentality. It is not, *per se*, by nature that he is sexually stimulated by watching Gerty MacDowell reveal herself on the beach, but rather he has been readied for this experience (and knows how to exploit it) by a deep familiarity with pornographic, voyeuristic practice. The voyeuristic practice in its most troped pornographic form surfaces in the "Circe" episode where Blazes Boylan suggests to Bloom that he watch while Boylan and Molly have adulterous sex: "You can apply your eye to the keyhole and play with yourself while I just go through her a few times."[51] The keyhole/spyhole trope figures throughout pornography, a typical example being found in *My Secret Life* (*c.*1880) where Walter, having arranged with a prostitute to watch unseen while she engages with another man, gloats that through the slightly opened door, "I heard every sigh and murmer, saw every thrust and heave, a delicious sight . . . I seemed to have almost had the pleasure of fucking her as I witnessed him."[52] The voyeuristic practice is focused on a solipsistic engagement with the visual, a bodily incitation to reproduce the pleasure of the seen. In the self-reflexive moment of voyeuristic pleasure, Bloom "clasps himself," according to the stage directions, and shouts, "Show! Hide! Show! Plough her! More! Shoot!" (*Ulysses* 567). In so doing, Bloom exhibits a keenly pornographic, voyeuristic sensibility.

Bloom is, in fact, a high-cultural stereotype of the lower-class bodily reader/voyeur. Untrained in bourgeois sublimation, Bloom seeks to subjugate the majority of his experience to the interests of his senses. Whereas Stephen, displaying a more typically middle-class and Catholic sensibility, separates sexual experience, discursive, pictorial, or real, into a realm apart from the high-cultural sphere he seeks to identify with himself, Bloom makes no differentiation, no sublimation of his bodily interests. Where Stephen's sexuality is constructed around shame at his sexual subjection, Bloom exhibits relatively little shame (the "Circe" episode must be taken as an exhibition of an emotion quite different from Bloom's conscious shame). Though he is sexually dysfunctional with his wife, Bloom has no difficulty identifying himself as a sexual subject, and thus is able to bring that with him to all of his interactions. Bloom's sexuality is in part constructed around early nineteenth-century stereotypes of the perversely sexualized Jew, which, as Sander Gilman has argued, originated from the Jewish relationship to money in early modern Europe:

> The historical background to this is clear. Canon law forbade the taking of interest. The taking of interest, according to Thomas Acquinas, was impossible, for money, not being alive, could not reproduce. Jews, in taking money, treated money as if it were alive, as if it were a sexualized object. The Jew takes money as does the prostitute, as a substitute for higher values, for love and beauty. And thus the Jew becomes the representative of the deviant genitalia, the genitalia not under the control of the moral, rational conscience.[53]

In this way Bloom's subject position in relationship to his use and production of pornography is in keeping with Christian European ideals of rational citizenry. Both the pornographic and the Jew are always "interested," always commercial in relationship to the separate, symbolic economy of the aesthetic.

Bloom's interest in the classical statuary of the Dublin library is, in contrast to its presumed high-cultural function as a symbol of metaphysical harmony, that he may see the mesial groove of the Venus of Praxiteles's buttocks. He hangs the *Bath of the Nymph* over his bed in a gesture that, by displaying a mass-produced, pseudo-classical work in his home, demonstrates his complicity with lower-middle-class aspirations to imitate high-cultural patterns of consumption. While reverencing the "Splendid masterpiece in art colours" as a signifier of a tradition he hasn't the vocabulary to relate to, "Greece: and for instance all the people that lived then"(*Ulysses* 65), he relates to the work in the only way he knows how, with the pornographic, voyeuristic mentality. We learn in "Circe" that Bloom has kissed the nymph of the poster in "four places," and that with "loving pencil" has shaded her eyes, breasts, and pudendum (*Ulysses* 546). When accused of doing so by the nymph, Bloom ironically responds in high-cultural discourse. "Your classic curves, beautiful immortal," he pleads, "I was glad to look on you, to praise you, a thing of beauty, almost to pray" (*Ulysses* 546). Yet the nymph reveals Bloom's reverential "praise" to be lewd incitations, his high-cultural discourse a false appropriation. In a lower-class subversion of high-cultural practices, the distinctions between high-art "aura" and pornographic voyeurism are lost on Bloom. The nymph's ritual value to Bloom is not in creating a meta-physical moment of universalized apprehension, but rather in experiencing a particular physical reaction to her visually organized eroticism.

Again and again in Joyce one sees the conflation of the aesthetic and the por-nographic, both in terms of the consumptive attitudes they are intended to provoke as well as the objects that manifest their supposedly different effects. *Ulysses* posits a series of sites of contestation between the two, a confrontation so aggressive that their dialectical relationship is both exposed and threatened. Molly Bloom's response to her kitsch, classical statue of Narcissus (which Bloom bought and "carried home in the rain for art for art's sake," *Ulysses* 543) is even more heated than her husband's to the classical nymph. Here Joyce is playing upon a pictorial tradition featuring women in sexual dalliance with classical cherubim. In one photograph taken around 1870, a woman attempts to pull a painted cherub closer to her, a gesture that plays out, in part, Molly's explicitly sexual fantasy (figure 1):[54]

> that lovely little statue he bought I could look at all day long curly head and his shoul-ders his finger up for you to listen theres real beauty and poetry for you I often felt I wanted to kiss him all over his lovely young cock there so simply I wouldn't mind taking him in my mouth if nobody was looking as if it was asking you to suck it so clean and white he looked with his boyish face I would too in ½ a minute even if some of it went down what its only like gruel or the dew theres no danger besides hed be so clean compared with those pigs of men   (*Ulysses* 775–776)

Such a scene, relayed in such sexually explicit language, was before 1922 unimag-inable in writing with literary pretenses. One of the striking features of Molly's soliloquy, however, that serves as a continual reminder of the force and presence of aesthetic form, is its absolute lack of punctuation. Performing a carnivalesque inversion, the passage relies on the very hegemonic form it denies. That is, its very formlessness is an assertion of aesthetic form (that simultaneously questions form itself), a perpetual reminder of the technical mastery controlling the desire on the page. The teleological pornographic narrative is here controlled by a syn-tactical confusion where modifiers subvert direct relationships. In grammatically mimicking the feature of pornographic novels whereby each protagonist "modifies" or has a sexual relation to every other protagonist and no direct rela-tionships are privileged, Joyce plays upon the very form he denies while dem-onstrating his formal mastery.

A more condensed version of the same technique can be found at the end of

The mastery of form: Beardsley and Joyce

88.

Figure 1. Photograph by Guglielmo Marconi, *c.*1870.

"Nausicaa" when Bloom enters upon a series of associations that function as sexually suggestive, but are nowhere pornographically representative. Recapping his
masturbatory encounter with Gerty he thinks,

> O sweety all your little girlwhite up I saw dirty bracegirdle made me do love sticky we
> two naughty Grace darling she him past the bed met him pike hoses frillies for Raoul
> to perfume your wife black hair heave under embon *señorita* young eyes Mulvey plump
> years dreams return tail end Agendath swoony lovey showed me her next year in
> drawers return next in her next her next.   (*Ulysses* 382)

This excerpt serves as a perfect example of Joyce's incorporation and defamiliarization of pornography. The quote is interlarded with references to the pornography Bloom himself has read or seen, "for Raoul," and "heave under embon"
being quotes from the pornographic novel *Sweets of Sin* Bloom has browsed for
Molly earlier in the day, and *señorita* referring to the erotic photocard he owns
of "buccal coition between nude señorita (rere presentation, superior position)
and nude torero (fore presentation, inferior position)" (*Ulysses* 721), itself a
parody of the technical language that attempts to control the subversive content
of the pornography within.[55] Each word in the passage is pared to its metonymic
function, suggesting the full pornographic fantasy while controlling that fantasy
from taking over the narrative. There are no verbs to connect actions. There is
no representative language to give the linear account that is pornography's discursive form. In a masterly display of modernist abstraction, predicates are
denied (fittingly enough) their copula, everything is modified by everything else
but full meaning in terms of a continuous and explicit representation is denied.
Joyce's avant-garde, modernist form necessarily violates the pornographic forms
used within, recoding such works for the high-brow reader.

Molly's perpetual drifting in and out of sexual narrative functions as a check
to a possible bodily reading. The potential pornographic pleasure is always dis-
rupted, held at bay by an intervening discourse. For example, when Molly is
recalling her afternoon with Blazes Boylan, the sexual narrative is interrupted by
a series of other related, but non-contributing, discourses. At length she says:

> then he goes and burns the bottom out of the pan all for his kidney this one not so
> much theres the mark of his teeth still where he tried to bite the nipple I had to scream
> out arent they fearful trying to hurt you I had a great breast of milk with Milly enough
> for two what was the reason of that he said I could have got a pound a week as a wet
> nurse all swelled out in the morning that delicate looking student that stopped in No
> 28 with the Citrons Penrose nearly caught me washing through the window only for
> I snapped up the towel to my face that was his studenting hurt me they used to weaning

her till he got doctor Brady to give me the Belladonna prescription I had to get him
to suck them they were so hard he said it was sweeter and thicker than cows then he
wanted to milk me into the tea well hes beyond everything I declare somebody ought
to put him in the budget if only I could remember the one half of the things and write
a book out of it the works of Master Poldy yes and its so much smoother the skin much
an hour he was at them Im sure by the clock like some kind of a big infant I had at me
they want everything in their mouth all the pleasure those men get out of a woman I
can feel his mouth O Lord I must stretch myself I wished he was here or somebody to
let myself go with and come again like that I feel all fire inside me or if I could dream
it when he made me spend the 2nd time tickling me behind with his fingers I was
coming for about 5 minutes with my legs round him I had to hug him O Lord I wanted
to shout out all sorts of things fuck or shit or anything at all only not to look ugly or
those lines from the strain   (*Ulysses* 754)

The pornographic in this text is imbricated within a larger network of discourses, medical, aesthetic, economic, mythological and culinary, each intervening upon the other. As Bakhtin has theorized, when heteroglossia, or diversified
social discourses, exists within a novel, it constitutes what he calls a "double-
voiced discourse." That is, at any given time a speaker may express the intentions
of his or her language while simultaneously that language is being refracted
through the authorial representation of that language. Incorporated forms are in
Bakhtin's words "indirect, conditional, distanced."[56] In the end, "all the forms
for dialogizing the transmission of another's speech are directly subordinated to
the task of artistically representing the speaker and his discourse as the *image of a
language*, in which case the others' words must undergo special artistic reformu-
lation."[57] By creating the image of a pornographic language (and, arguably, the
image of all languages) Joyce emphasizes his formal stylization, the aestheticiza-
tion that at all moments signifies his high-cultural aspirations. Form masters the
language parodied therein in order to distance itself from the representation. It
creates a distance from the reader by disavowing a complete pornographic pleasure in the narrative. Though gaining ground in terms of its public visibility, the
sensuous content of *Ulysses*'s narrative is rendered impotent by form.

The corrupted reader

If images and statues offer themselves for voyeuristic consumption, books, especially in the *fin-de-siècle*, come equally in the eyes of hegemonic culture to represent a potential corruption. For, while in the late nineteenth and the early
twentieth centuries the middle and upper classes continued to be trained in

reading techniques that foregrounded an ideal disinterest, the large new reading population, including women and the working classes, was still being trained in a more rudimentary fashion that, in trying to prepare them for their stations in life, failed to pass on high-cultural ideals. Left to their own devices, it was believed, works of a questionable nature might "deprave and corrupt" the working classes who, in the middle-class imagination, were likely to subject such works to an interest of the senses because of their own more base, sensuous constructions.

Women of all classes were viewed as particularly susceptible to the influences of literature and the sway of their senses. As a majority of women in the second half of the nineteenth and early twentieth centuries were new readers, and as they infrequently received the classical education rendered in public schools (and as, Le Bon's quote above shows, they were frequently viewed as less evolved), they were just as liable as a working-class male to succumb to an interest of the senses. It is in this context that John Middleton Murray says of Joyce's book, "The head that is strong enough to read *Ulysses* will not be turned by it."[58] It is indeed the difficulty of *Ulysses* that rescues it from censorship and that, in an age shaped in part by T. S. Eliot's dictum to modern writers to cultivate "difficulty," privileges it as a work of art (and in formal terms as an effect of mind). For while *Ulysses* features, and in some ways celebrates, mass man in the form of Leopold Bloom, it is, as John Carey has suggested, also true that Bloom himself would never and could never have read *Ulysses* or a book like it.[59]

A drawing that reinforces the notion of the corrupted or corruptible reader is Beardsley's *The Toilet of Salome*, second version (figure 2). His initial drawing of Salome's toilette having been rejected for its blatant display of masturbation, Beardsley was forced to try to convey the same ideas in a more conventionally acceptable manner. He chose to do so by providing Salome with a bookshelf filled with books that would have raised an eyebrow had they sat upon any middle-class woman's shelf. Salome has been reading such works of decadence and overt sexuality as *Nana*, Zola's story of a Parisian prostitute; *Manon Lescaut*, the story of another great courtesan by Abbé Prévost; the works of the Marquis de Sade; Verlaine's *Les Fêtes galantes*; and Apuleius's *The Golden Ass*. Rather than show his characters in the act of masturbating, Beardsley makes the more indirect suggestion that such works as lie on her shelf incite the voracious sensual appetite Salome displays later in the play. Salome here represents the corrupted bodily reader who, having learned a mode of bodily subjection through her reading, forces it upon her daily experience.

It is interesting that in this drawing Salome is featured in modern dress and

Figure 2. *The Toilet of Salome*, second version, 1894.

Modernism, Mass Culture, and the Aesthetics of Obscenity

fashion. As opposed to the rest of the Salome drawings (save "The Black Cape") where she is featured in exotic garb, here she resembles many of the "New Women" Beardsley drew during his *Yellow Book* phase, women Holbrook Jackson once described as "sardonic" creatures who looked as if they "were always hungering for the sensation after next."[60] The association is important, for so many of the drawings that upset reviewers of the *Yellow Book* were not only evocative of the New Woman, but featured a New-Womanish figure looking at or choosing books. Contemporaneous reviewers frequently saw in the "Beardsley Woman" "disturbing signs of corruption, sexual deviance, and emancipation."[61] The cover designs for the *Yellow Book's* first and second volumes (1894) each featured a New Woman glancing over a selection of untitled books. Representing their modernity and independence, these pictures play upon the bourgeois fear of the corrupted reader, the reader as bodily consumer. In these images, mass culture becomes aligned with the feminine reader as sensuous consumer, "hungering for the sensation after next."

An unused cover design for the *Yellow Book* plays upon the theme of the New Woman and her books, but goes further in combining the ethos of the bodily reader with that of the voyeur (figure 3). As in many of his drawings, Beardsley uses a mediating figure to poke fun at, subvert, and expose the eroticism embedded within the voyeur's gaze. In this particular drawing, a pierrot figure holds up a table filled with books and returns the viewer's gaze. A woman stands above the table picking out a book, one hand symbolically placed in her muff, a traditional symbol for a woman's genitals. Poised atop of the stack of high-cultural books (Shakespeare and Dickens; authors reputed to have enjoyed mass audiences, thereby blurring the distinctions between high and low) is Beardsley's own explicitly pornographic work, *The Story of Venus and Tannhauser*. The pierrot figure, as if in anticipation of the woman's perusal of the pornographic pleasures described in *The Story of Venus and Tannhauser*, has an erection. Beardsley has anticipated the voyeuristic process of the reader.

The voyeur figure, however, also functions as a typical pornographic trope. The narrator/mediator digests the sexually exciting material in advance of a reader/viewer in order to stimulate a similar response in him or her. Beardsley has managed to portray an entire pornographic scenario without appearing to abandon the aesthetic to the pornographic. By using the traditional English bawdy symbology of the lady's muff, he merely refers to a possible interpretation.[62] Likewise, the pierrot's erection is but one in a series of suggestive, graceful lines. The pornographic book, *The Story of Venus and Tannhauser*, is also a

The mastery of form: Beardsley and Joyce

94.

Figure 3. Unused cover design for the *Yellow Book*,
1894–1895.

classical tale, a culturally sanctioned myth also used by Swinburne in "Laus Veneris" that operates as a signifier of high culture. All of the pornographic signifiers in the picture – a lady's muff, a sweeping line, and a classic tale – function doubly as signifiers of bourgeois culture and high art. As with so much of Beardsley's work, meaning is indeterminate and the erotic content cannot be fixed.

Like Joyce, there are remarkable moments in Beardsley's works that draw off and imitate the pornographic to such a degree that they challenge the ability of the aesthetic to posit the viewer in a relation of distance and disinterest with them. As also with Joyce, it is Beardsley's technical skill, i.e., the formal elements of his art, that provides a remove from, or a hold upon, the sexual images portrayed. It is no accident, then, that the *Lysistrata* drawings, while being the most sexually explicit, are also the most consistently praised as, in Holbrook Jackson's words, "the most masterly of all his drawings."[63] Robert Ross found in the *Lysistrata* drawings a series of validating canonical correspondences, remarking, "Conceived in the spirit of the eighteenth century, the period of graceful indecency, there is here, however, an Olympian air, a statuesque beauty, only comparable to the antique vases."[64] Ross's comparison was no doubt led by the fact that the drawings are "illustrations" of Aristophanes' classical play. Indeed, as in the use of the *Ulysses* myth, there was a remarkable leniency granted to art conceived in the classical vein. Yet Ross's comments also reveal an anxious effort to classicize what was clearly perceived as "indecent." In aesthetic judgments at the turn of the century, the cultural capital of classical erudition continuously outweighed mass-cultural incursions. Indeed, the classical canonicity of Beardsley's work was dutifully cultivated by him and his corpus can be viewed as a perpetual search for validating authorities.[65] In his letters, Beardsley described his work as "severe in execution," and indeed the *Lysistrata* drawings are stark, simple, and balanced – all words which conjure up classical design.[66] Referring to the pornographic nature of the *Lysistrata* and *Juvenal* drawings, a reviewer for the *New Statesman* noted, "He is haunted by the male genitals, and . . . he exaggerates their proportions in a way normally associated with the vulgarest pornography; but they must be among the most refined, meticulous, decorative and reverential drawings of the male genitals ever devised."[67]

Cinesias Entreating Myrrhina to Coition demonstrates a unique balancing between the aesthetic and the pornographic (figure 4). That the image depicted was common to pornography can be demonstrated in its likeness to a photograph

Figure 4. *Cinesias Entreating Myrrhina to Coition*, 1896.

Modernism, Mass Culture, and the Aesthetics of Obscenity

Figure 5. Anonymous photograph, *c*.1880.

The mastery of form: Beardsley and Joyce

of a woman in similar garb taken around 1880 (figure 5). Each image presents a frontally exposed woman in stockings, loosely draped with a robe. The photograph, organized for the consumption of the voyeur, features the "bashful wantonness" Stephen Dedalus found in the pictures he used, leaving the viewer's gaze unchallenged. Myrrhina both complies with and disrupts this visual organization. For while her eyes are cast aside from the viewer's, it is not in a gesture of "bashful wantonness." She is all but laughing, seemingly unconcerned with the viewer.

As in the above unused cover for the *Yellow Book* where the voyeuristic pierrot figure stands diminutively aside while eyeing a sexually self-satisfied woman, Cinesias is in this picture marginalized to a grotesquely small shape at the drawing's edge, made comic by his overwhelmingly disproportionate, erect penis. As with the pierrot figure above, Cinesias is a deconstruction of and a commentary on the voyeuristic process. Cinesias's upturned and fierce eye (perfectly in harmony with his battle-ready organ) provides no contact with the laughing woman who refuses to provide sexual relief to her tumescent voyeur. This, of course, is a reversal of the pornographic process, a refusal of its pleasures. Cinesias's grand penis, however, is quite in keeping with the pornographic, where the prodigious size of male genitals is a continuous source of sublime wonder, especially to the women who encounter them.[68]

The Lacedaemonian Ambassadors is certainly a tribute to, and a poking fun of, the pornographic tradition of the sublime penis, particularly in the knowledge that these men will not find pornography's quintessential willing partner (figure 6). In a reversal of the pornographic fantasy, their massive endowments do not serve as a source of pleasure, but rather of frustration. Here Beardsley's images function as both an appropriation of and a commentary upon the pornographic image and ideal. Beardsley uses Aristophanes' play as a high-cultural validation to frustrate the pornographic pleasure of the penis. In *Cinesias Entreating Myrrhina to Coition* he further orders and distances the art from the pornographic by creating a visual focus apart from the bodies depicted. As Christopher Snodgrass has commented, the eye-catching focus of the drawing is, rather than the sexually displayed bodies, the decoratively designed clothing and headpieces.[69] The dark or shaded parts of the work, those that call attention to themselves, are indeed the decorative details, such as costume, headpiece, or hair. The physically exposed parts of bodies are left in white, the same as the background upon which they lie. In this way the bodies themselves are underemphasized even while they are in fact the occasion of the drawing.

Figure 6. *The Lacedaemonian Ambassadors,* 1896.

The mastery of form: Beardsley and Joyce

Masturbation

The corruption attributed to sexually overt pictures and books takes a material form in the temptation such works offer to "self-abuse," or masturbation. The term "self-abuse" serves as a reminder of the conflicted subject-formation implicated in the bourgeois denial of the body and its "spurious" pleasures. While certainly masturbation was the feared outcome of access to "dangerous" works, it was absolutely beyond the margins of the representable, for in representing masturbation one acknowledged the possibility of a selfishly physical and sexual subjectivity. Both Beardsley and Joyce represent the physically stimulating powers of books as well as representations of the act of masturbation itself.

When Bloom opens the *Sweets of Sin* in "Wandering Rocks" and begins to read the sexual body, "*Her mouth glued on his in a luscious voluptuous kiss while his hands felt for the opulent curves inside her deshabille*," (*Ulysses* 236) the narrative features the reaction of a bodily reader (the actual pornography is italicized, as in the text):

> Warmth showered over him, cowing his flesh. Flesh yielded amid rumpled clothes. Whites of eyes swooning up. His nostrils arched themselves for prey. Melting breast ointments (*for him! For Raoul!*). Armpits' oniony sweat. Fishgluey slime (*her heaving embonpoint!*). Feel! Press! Crushed! Sulpher dung of lions! (*Ulysses* 236)

Bloom surrenders to the technology of pornography and subjects his reading to the interests of his senses. He enters into a specific reading practice that is intended to engage the mind and body in a sexual interrogation or incitation. In the above passage Bloom exhibits a self-reflexivity about his bodily pleasure peculiar to the modern pornographic sensibility.

Equally peculiar to the modern pornographic sensibility is the admission and acceptance of masturbation. For while good Victorians like *My Secret Life*'s Walter denied the impulse to masturbate, moderns, beginning quite radically with Beardsley, acknowledged masturbation.[70] Two of Beardsley's toilet scenes, *The Toilete of Salome*, first version, and *The Toilet of Helen*, feature the act in notably similar ways (figures 7 and 8). After the 1893 Salome drawing was suppressed, the 1895 Helen drawing appeared as a reinterpretation of the same theme with an attempt to get the picture past his censors. In *The Toilete of Salome*, first version, carnal desire is quite simply represented. Salome sits in the center of the drawing before a mirror, a frequent trope in Beardsley for a woman's taking in of her own pleasure. Her hand is quite obviously placed in her crotch, just as is the pageboy's in the left corner of the drawing. The picture was reputedly suppressed because

Figure 7. *The Toilete of Salome*, first version, 1894.

The mastery of form: Beardsley and Joyce

of the pageboy's actions, not Salome's, and one must infer that the depiction of a barely disguised penis extending from a pubic tuft in the male crotch makes his gesture more overt, more anatomically representational and therefore similar to pornography. Snodgrass also points out that the pageboy "possesses the buckling spine traditionally associated in the Victorian mind with what results from seminal fluids being wasted in autoeroticism."[71] The page to the far left stands playing a bass viol; as noted by Freud this is yet another symbol for masturbation, one that passes uncensored through much of Beardsley's work.[72] The viol on which s/he "fiddles" (note the suggestive positioning of the right hand) bears vaginal hearts, both at the top and in the location of what are rather unfortunately called the viol's f-holes. This specific genital trope Beardsley may well have appropriated from the pornographic illustrations of Félicien Rops, whose hearts functioned as vaginal signifiers.[73] The page holding a tray of coffee has exposed genitals (noticeably in difference from the erect shape of the coffee pot spout he holds). The action is quite bare and – despite the sweeping harmonious lines, integrating symmetry, and the unity of theme – it is a dangerous theme that outweighed the few high-cultural signifiers to save this work from censorship. This is one instance where style does not invoke form. The pornographic, itself always stylized, asserts itself over the aesthetic.

In contrast, *The Toilet of Helen* features none of the blatant sexual exposure of the Salome drawing. Though sexuality and self-pleasuring are its themes, the drawing masks them successfully through ornate, rococo designs and eighteenth-century bawdy symbology. Helen/Venus appears at center and embodies a series of high-cultural and low-cultural contradictions. Dressed in refined, aristocratic undergarments, her breasts are exposed. The shaggy ribbing of her corset is set in contrast to the smooth simplicity of her breasts, a contrast evocative of a centaur or satyr, thus implicating her with the bestial. The implication is furthered by the juxtaposition of the cloven-hoofed leg of her dressing table against her own similarly shaped foot. Here the sexual is coimplicated with the bestial and Helen is shown to be both refined and aristocratic while at the same time bestial, sexual. Helen captures in miniature the paradoxical nature of Beardsley's sexual art. It is elegant, civilized, and aspires toward beauty (Beardsley's women at toilet are a frequent evocation of the artificial beauty to which he aspires) while containing within that form an untamed lust barely permissible by the society that seeks to control it. By placing Helen in the eighteenth century and positioning her as an aristocratic lady with attendants, Beardsley purposefully circumvents the bourgeois hegemony of his own century. Indeed, somewhat like Swinburne, he hearkens to an older tradition and alignment of the libertine aristocratic with the sexual in order to find high-cultural validation for his representations.

The mirror positioned between Helen's widely spread legs functions as a symbol of self inspection, i.e. masturbation. A picture drawn for a 1920s era pornographic "best-seller," *An Up-to-date Young Lady* by Helena Varley, featured a similar gesture on the part of its heroine (figure 9). To know oneself through the self-reflexive action of the mirror is to be sexually acquainted with oneself. This trope suggests a differentiated subjective sense from the bourgeois hegemonic one of body as other, and, as will be explored in chapter four, increasingly comes to represent the twentieth-century bourgeois subject. That is, with the deeper penetration of moral-medical health into bourgeois subjectivity, sexual subjecthood found its answer in the new fields of sexology which created sexual subjects in order to further establish health and morality. One can see in the illustration to *An Up-to-date Young Lady* that the young woman has on the floor with her a medical sexual manual of some sort that encourages her self-exploration. While the manual is on the one hand subversive in its incitement to sexual behavior, it is on the other a scientifically sanctioned validation of the sexual body, a bourgeois affirmation that recodifies what was once subversive. A sexual self becomes, in the twentieth-century, a healthy self, an integration of two previously separate categories. This is an attitude, however, that doesn't penetrate the cultural consciousness completely until well into the 1960s, and while D. H. Lawrence was an early advocate, Beardsley and Joyce remained equivocal about sexual self-knowledge and moral-medical health.

Equivocality functions as an important guise for the masturbatory incitements of many of Beardsley's representations. In *Lysistrata Shielding her Coynte*, Lysistrata has her hand ambiguously placed before her genitals (figure 10). The illustration's title directs a reading of the gesture, while the depiction itself is ambiguous. As Linda Gerstner Zatlin has commented, "the parting of her fingers in what might be construed as a caress instead of an attempt to shield her genitals reinforces her sexual knowledge even as it subverts the generally accepted public view against masturbation."[74] Accompanied by yet another sublime, pornographic penis, the gesture of her defensiveness looks more disingenuous when accorded with the dreamy heaviness of her eyelids, the dilation of her nostrils, and the general complacency of her visage. Hers is not the face of a woman in fear. The opened rosebuds in her hair, usually drawn much tighter in Beardsley's works, suggest a dilated opening below. This is further accentuated by the placement of her two fingers at her crotch, suggesting the labia that might be seen through her otherwise transparent dress. The hand both covers and uncovers,

Figure 8. *The Toilet of Helen*, 1896.

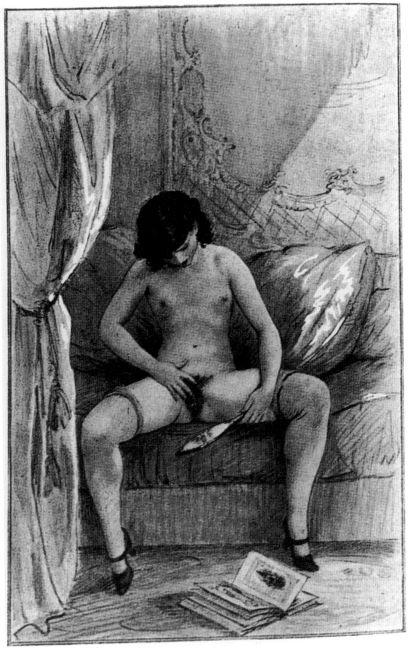

Figure 9. Anonymous illustration from *An Up-to-date Young Lady* by Helena Varley, *c*.1920.

The mastery of form: Beardsley and Joyce

Figure 10. *Lysistrata Shielding her Coynte*, 1896.

shields and displays. The erect terminal god at her right functions as a voyeur to her pleasure (and another mediating figure for the viewer's gaze) while simultaneously exposing, as in Joyce and a certain class of pornography, the latent sexuality of the classical figure.

Beardsley's publisher, Leonard Smithers, published a book, *Priapeia*, in 1888 that housed a series of epigrams on "terms" or statues of Priapus, phallic ornaments erected in the gardens of wealthy Romans. The short Latin verses of *Priapeia*, translated on opposing pages into English, were written mostly from the point of view of the sinister, proud Priapus who threatens all who trespass his garden with a spearing by his 12-inch grand pole. The term is flirtatious with women, boys, and men, and will pierce anything. One brief example can be found in verse forty-eight: "Altho' you see that part of me to be wet by which I'm signified to be Priapus; 'tis not dew, believe me, nor is it hoarfrost, but that which is wont to gush forth spontaneously when my mind recalls a wanton girl."[75] The term was featured prominently in pornographic illustrations of the eighteenth and nineteenth centuries. Beardsley's close access to Smithers's library makes it likely that he was familiar with *Priapeia* as well as many of the typically French pornographic novels in which such figures were celebrated. As in *Ulysses*, the *Lysistrata* series displays an apparent relish in exposing high culture's beloved classical culture for the sexually suggestive culture Beardsley read it to be. Beardsley favored representing periods predicated on order, symmetry, and harmony – the classical and neo-classical – in order to exploit their contradictions, to suggest that the formal, aesthetic qualities so typically associated with the classical were in fact bound up with the pornographic.

One of literature's most notorious masturbation scenes is the passage in "Nausicaa" where Bloom masturbates before a partially exposed Gerty MacDowell. Couched in the mass-produced language of sentimental romance, "Nausicaa" is the story of low culture's longing and attempt to assimilate, or be appropriated by, high culture (in a more radical sense it could be said to be the opposite – *Ulysses*'s longing to assimilate and be appropriated by low culture). It is also the story of its inevitable failure as a result of the false ideology perpetuated through mass man's inevitable interpellation by the commercialism of popular culture, which colonizes the high merely as a set of empty signifiers to promote desire. For in addition to Gerty's pretense to class through commercial products and ladies' magazines, Gerty vies for Bloom's attention by imitating high art rather than the "improper" ones. That is, as Margot Norris has pointed out, she gives a static rather than a kinetic performance, trying desperately to portray an idealized figure (of the sentimental sort she reads about).[76] Gerty's narrative, describing "The waxen pallor of her face was almost spiritual in its ivorylike purity though her rosebud mouth was a genuine cupid's bow, Greekly perfect" (*Ulysses* 348), reveals a longing in Gerty to assimilate herself to the cultural standards of high art, to become the reified manifestation of that metaphysical aura that can only exist for her as desire and the wish to be so desired. Bloom's bodily consumption of her high-art imitation becomes not just another instance of kitsch consumerism, but a poignant one in their mutual submission to a desire for a cultural validation from which they are both debarred.

Schematically, "Nausicaa" is another of Joyce's exercises in controlled figuration. It effects the formal sublimation associated with high art even while it exposes the "low" genres of affect: sentimental fiction and pornography. By displacing and metaphorically figuring rather than mimetically representing what happens, the text draws attention to the action, making it all the more ridiculous as it is filtered not through the language of pornography, but of sentimental romance. While Bloom's actions are those reserved for pornography, and he demonstrates the pornographic technique of consumptive voyeurism, it is not until he pulls the metaphors of Gerty's passage together with his anatomy, "My fireworks. Up like a rocket, down like a stick" (*Ulysses* 371), that any connection between Bloom and the carnivalesque masturbation scene is linguistically made. Obviously such a connection is quite insistently implied throughout, but the language itself is untainted. This is made clear in the climactic scene:

> and she let him and she saw that he saw and then it went up so high it went out of sight for a moment and she was trembling in every limb from being bent so far back he had a full view high up above her knee no-one ever not even on the swing or wading and she wasn't ashamed and he wasn't either to look in that immodest way like that because he couldn't resist the sight of that wondrous revealment half offered like those skirt-dancers behaving so immodest before gentlemen looking, and he kept on looking, looking. She would fain have cried to him chokingly, held out her slender, snowy arms to come to him, to feel his lips laid on her white brow the cry of a young girl's love, a little strangled cry, wrung from her, that cry that has wrung through the ages. And then a rocket sprang and bang shot blind and O! then the Roman candle burst and it was like a sign of O! and everyone cried O! O! in raptures and it gushed out of it a stream of rain gold hair threads and they shed and ah! they were all greeny dewy stars falling with golden, O so lively! O so soft, sweet, soft! (*Ulysses* 366–367)

Much in the style of Molly's soliloquy, the passage above is syntactically askew. It denies the very form typically used to express such actions, and in doing so foregrounds that form's absence. Relying on hegemonic pornographic form to produce its own inversion, the passage is but another example of the Bakhtinian carnivalesque. As in the carnival where high culture is inverted or suspended in order to celebrate the body of the people (the grotesque as opposed to the classical in Bakhtin's conception), so here the normative narrative form one would expect to depict such an action, pornography, is denied in order to subvert the body. The body is displaced; it evades narrative form. The body is at once everywhere and nowhere. Gerty and Bloom seek their private bodily pleasures while the beach itself is filled with the bodies of pleasure-seekers watching the fireworks. What is lost is the distance upon which the aesthetic form relies, uniqueness is lost to multiplicity. All pleasure is conflated into climactic "O!"s where individual pleasure is indistinguishable from the whole. Desire in the reader is controlled by a flow of intervening discourses and a denial of the mimetic. Pleasure is aesthetically controlled by decentering it from individual pleasure to carnivalesque pleasure. The ironic displacement of the pornographic in "Nausicaa" suggests a collusion with the fundamental pornographic impulse which insists that all stylized art, all polite life, is a travesty of a reality based on sexual appetite. Thus while *Ulysses* disdainfully mocks low-cultural pulp fiction, its high-cultural aspirations are simultaneously undermined by the pornographic discourse it denies only to highlight later.

After Gerty's narrative, Bloom makes the connections between his reaction to Gerty's exposure and his acquaintance with pornography clear. "Anyhow I got the best of that," he says, "Damned glad I didn't do it in the bath this morning over her silly I will punish you letter" (*Ulysses* 368). Bloom searches for representations that will approach the pornographic in order to subject them to his bodily pleasure, a practice he has learned from pornography. Fantasizing about the "shoals" of women typists and clerks (with whom he classes Gerty) who want sexual gratification, Bloom recalls "A dream of well-filled hose," a mutoscope series "for men only" that he has seen at Mutoscope pictures on Capel Street (*Ulysses* 368). Bloom continues to reinforce the turn-of-the-century stereotype of mass man and mass culture. Exposed to the debasing effects of mass culture (the mutoscope pictures, for instance), mass man becomes an effect of their technique, an expression of the urge to subjugate art and representations to the body.

The irony of the attempt to bring representations closer to the body is that the representations quickly become the mediation of the body. Bloom is a perfect example of one whose sexuality becomes mediated not through his own imagination, but rather through the discursive and representational practices set into motion through pornography. When Bloom hires a prostitute to say dirty words to him (*Ulysses* 370), the woman's own sexuality is displaced onto the words she can generate for him. What is exciting for him is not her body, but her own reproduction of discursive practice.

Sado-masochism

If masturbation was a sexual practice infrequently expressed in Victorian porno-graphic works, sado-masochism was a well-worn trope that Beardsley and Joyce made use of in their works. Steven Marcus has suggested that in the nineteenth century the literature of flagellation assumed in its audience an interest in and a connection with the higher gentry and aristocracy, those with the common experience of education at public school.[77] Indirectly, then, sado-masochism (in its most commonly expressed form, flagellation) is a signifier of high culture and/or high-cultural vice.

Beardsley plays on this notion of flagellation in his frontispiece for John Davidson's *Earl Lavendar* (1895) (figure 11). While there are myriad flagellation images in turn-of-the-century erotic postcards, it is more likely that Beardsley followed his literary predilections in his sado-masochistic portrayals. For while erotic postcards featured women being punished by women, or by men, it is more common in the literary tradition to see a man being punished by a woman or another man.[78] In that Beardsley depicts an aristocratic woman at flagellant play with a submissive man, he both associates his illustration with that tradition and removes it from either the bourgeois or mass-cultural realm where such a depiction would create an uproar. The drawing features a woman dressed in a gown of elegant Greek simplicity about to whip a kneeling man, semi-clad in a Greek, robe-like garment. Each of the characters approaches undress. The woman is just holding her dress from falling down her breasts, and the man is about to lower his robe to reveal his buttocks. If Beardsley had chosen to go a step further in undress, surely the picture would have been labeled obscene, for then it would have depicted an action overtly sexual, overtly in connection with the pornographic photographs that feature the same action. His restraint, however, is not simply a capitulation to censorship, but an important signifier of gentlemanly intention. The clothing, in its Greek resonances, assists in building up the picture's cultural capital. The accompanying book's title, *Earl Lavendar*, is a signal that this drawing refers to aristocratic vice. In being so, it both perpet-uates the stereotype of aristocratic lascivious depravity, and delimits such a representation from effecting bourgeois subjectivity. As other to itself, the representation is rendered safe for bourgeois consumption. The impotence of the picture's threat to bourgeois hegemony is reinforced in its depiction of impo-tent aristocratic male subjection. The three candles, typically a Beardsleyan phallic symbol, are superseded by the three prongs of the woman's switch. While there are pokers for the fire (another reference to the switch), there is no blaze

Figure 11. Frontispiece to John Davidson's *Earl Lavendar* by
Aubrey Beardsley, 1895.

in the fireplace (the eighteenth-century symbol for sexual activity). The impotence is quite finally rendered in the male subject's essential decapitation by the drawing's frame.

The cover design for the first issue of *The Savoy* uses the sexual implications of flagellation to create an atmosphere of barely suppressed sexuality (figure 12). In this instance, Beardsley uses the pornographic to unsettle the culturally staid (in a reversal that nevertheless depends on the culturally staid to preserve its place for art). The Beardsley New Woman is here depicted in staunch dignity, her heavy and severe buttoned coat cloaking any hint of her body (and in that sense drawing attention to it). Standing at attention with whip in hand, she oversees a frontally exposed, dancing amour who exposes the sexuality her clothing and stiff posture repress. Her whip, functioning as a display of control to restrain the amour, functions on the other hand to signify the loss of control that accompanies the sexual perversity for which the whip might be used. If the woman cannot control the amour, neither can she control the seething sexuality of the drawing as a whole. Behind her stands a terminal god, so frequently seen in Beardsley as the signal of lust, and below her sits a sundial decorated by three satyrs. A pagan temple balances the female figure and the whole is surrounded by what Christopher Snodgrass calls "distinctly pubic vegetation."[79] In this depiction then, the sexually liberated – the amour, the terminal god, and the satyrs – are each delimited by their high-cultural affiliation with classical culture and their modern status as mere garden decoration. The woman, in her repressive bourgeois clothing holding the whip, is the only figure of potential transgression. And again, it is Beardsley's equivocality about his figures that, while perhaps viewed as threatening by dominant culture, cannot be singled out for explicit violations of public admissibility.

Joyce was well acquainted with the literature of flagellation, and in addition to a full acquaintance with Sacher-Masoch's work (he had four of his works in his library),[80] Richard Brown has linked Joyce with other works of masochism, James Lovebirch's *The Flagellations of Suzette* and Jacques Descroix's *La Gynecocatrie*.[81] *La Gynecocatrie* contains many similarities to the "Circe" episode and Joyce may have taken several ideas from the work for his own.[82] In the French story, the protagonist Vicomte Julian Robinson is made, throughout his "education" to wear women's clothes. Just as Bloom becomes female in the "Circe" episode (*Ulysses* 535), Julian becomes Julia; and as Julia is forced to entertain a suitor called Lord Alfred Ridlington who later turns out to have been a woman, so Bloom is offered to Charles Alberta Marsh (*Ulysses* 539). Under the governess that Julia serves there are three female pupils – Maud, Beatrice, Agnes

Figure 12. Cover design for *The Savoy*, no. 1, by Aubrey Beardsley, 1896.

The mastery of form: Beardsley and Joyce

– who alternately help or hinder her. Bella Cohen also has three assistants: Kitty, Florry, and Zoe.

By featuring Bloom as the masochistic subject, Joyce transgresses the typical class boundaries of the literature of flagellation. He plays upon them interestingly, however, by showing Bloom take the part of the masochist to three upperclass women, Mrs. Yelverton Barry, Mrs. Bellingham, and Mrs. Mervyn Talboys. Bloom's actions are a commentary on class relations: he is submissive with these women whereas with the housemaid, Mary Driscoll, he is sexually aggressive, laying hold of her body and, when rebuked, commanding silence from her (*Ulysses* 460–461). With the Dublin society ladies, however, the tone changes from commanding to obsequious. While Bloom seeks to be the master of Mary Driscoll's working-class body, he seeks to be mastered by the ladies' upper-class bodies. (Interestingly, for Stephen in *Stephen Hero*, the middle-class body is antisexual. Thinking of Emma he imagines, "He would have liked nothing so well as an adventure with her now but he felt that even that warm ample body could hardly compensate him for her distressing pertness and middle class affectations," *SH* 72.)

Bloom sends each of the ladies pornographic letters describing his sexual fantasies that emphasize his socially inferior position. In Mrs. Yelverton Barry's letter, Bloom mentions that he has looked down on her box at the *Theatre Royal* from his seat in "the gods," i.e., the cheap seats, and gazed upon her "peerless globes" (*Ulysses* 465). Mrs. Bellingham's account emphasizes her personal wealth, her possession of a personal coachman and "hidden treasures in priceless lace" (*Ulysses* 466). Her position of domination is further emphasized in Bloom's denomination of her as "a Venus in furs" (*Ulysses* 466). Calling Bloom a "plebeian Don Juan," Mrs. Mervyn Talboys is urged by him to complete her social superiority via a masochistic fantasy where he urges her, "to chastise him as he richly deserves, to bestride and ride him, to give him a most vicious horsewhipping" (*Ulysses* 467).

In each of his confessions to the ladies, Bloom attempts to script a fantasy according to the pornographic traditions with which he is familiar. With Mrs. Yelverton Barry he signs his letter with the moniker of another known pornographic author, James Lovebirch (author of *The Flagellations of Suzette,* Paris: Librairie Artistique, 1915). He asks her, as he does with each of the ladies, to perform certain sexual acts, and tells her he wishes to send her a copy of Paul de Kock's *The Girl With the Three Stays* (Joyce's English translation of a real book entitled *La femme aux trois corsets* published in Paris, 1878) (*Ulysses* 465). Addressing Mrs. Bellingham in several letters as his "Venus in furs," Bloom writes her physical description in a mock pornographic encomium that she later describes:

> He lauded almost extravagantly my nether extremities, my swelling calves in silk hose drawn up to the limit, and eulogised glowingly my other hidden treasures in priceless lace which, he said, he could conjure up. He urged me, stating that he felt it his mission in life to urge me, to defile the marriage bed, to commit adultery at the earliest possible opportunity.
> (*Ulysses* 466)

Bloom creates or passes on a form of pornography to each of the ladies (a book, a picture, his own pornographic descriptions) in the attempt to fulfill his own erotic imagination, which in turn has been formed by these very pornographic media. The text shows that Bloom's sexuality is produced discursively or visually in the mass-produced sexual fantasies of pornography, the myriad of books and pictures produced in the late nineteenth and early twentieth centuries. If commercial capitalism mass-produces a particularly idealized sexuality as seen in Gerty's cosmetic longing, "Art thou real, my ideal?," it is equally busy mass-producing the hard-core materialist fantasies of a Bloom who seeks sexual satisfaction in reproducing for himself (and imprinting onto others) such pornographically mediated fantasies.

An interesting commentary on the mass-production of the sado-masochistic fantasy is suggested in Bloom's stashed away "press cutting from an English weekly periodical *Modern Society*, subject corporal chastisement in girls' schools" (*Ulysses* 721). The subject of wide public debate as well as pornographic novels and photographs, chastisement in girls' schools and reformatories marked a provocative intersection between bourgeois high-cultural denial of the body and mass culture's exploitation and subjugation of the body to its pleasures. Pornography, in works like John Carrington's *A Study in Flagellation* (1901), exposed bourgeois institutionalized flagellation of girls (or boys for that matter) as a veiled sexual pleasure, a pleasure permitted so long as it remained "veiled" within formal institutional protocol, a denial of the body's pleasures instead of an engagement with them.

Gender-bending and homoerotics

In a continuation of the masochistic theme, "Circe" plays out the social implications of the classed body in a gender-bending fantasy scenario that provides acerbic social commentary. In Bloom's submission to Bella/o (a parody of Sacher-Masoch), his transformation from man to woman, and from woman to prostitute, makes obvious the hegemonic cultural association between the working classes and the sexual body. The prostitute *is* the sexualized, working-class body. What's more, her body becomes the object of capitalist penetration: whoever will pay may subject it to his will. When Bloom becomes a whore in the masochistic fantasy, the tone shifts from the playful subjection of masochistic fantasy to the tough whore-house commercialism of Bello:

> My boys will be no end charmed to see you so ladylike, the colonel, above all. When they come here the night before the wedding to fondle my new attraction in gilded heels. First, I'll have a go at you myself. A man I know on the turf named Charles Alberta Marsh (I was in bed with him just now and another gentleman out of the Hanaper and Petty Bag office) is on the lookout for a maid of all work at a short knock. Swell the bust. Smile. Droop shoulders. What offers? (*He points.*) For that lot trained by owner to fetch and carry, basket in mouth. (*He bares his arm and plunges it elbowdeep in Bloom's vulva.*) There's fine depth for you! What boys? That give you a hardon? (*He shoves his arm in a bidder's face.*) Here, wet the deck and wipe it round! (*Ulysses* 539)

The association of the prostitute's body with an animal's is made clear not just in the above quote where Bloom's fee is compared to a dog's, but several lines later where Bello brands his initial C into his rump, marking possession and capital interest (*Ulysses* 540). The prostitute's body marks the intersection of the working-class body and the sexual body.

If the body of the prostitute was an accepted sexualized body, probably the least accepted of sexual bodies at the turn of the century was the homoerotic one, unless, that is, it formed part of a male fantasy about female eroticism. Beardsley's works are rife with images of homoeroticism and gender-bending, but as in most of his drawings, he is able to get past censorship of such representations by using bawdy symbology to complete his indeterminate inferences, and by presenting such inferences in a high-cultural surrounding. An interesting example of this is his cover design for *The Savoy*, no. 2 (1896) (figure 13). In the cover design, two women are shown hats by a midget salesman. Hats, hat-boxes, and clocks, as Linda Gerstner Zatlin has shown, were emblematic in eighteenth-century illustrative tradition of female genitalia; they continued to signify such things in the music hall of the early nineteenth century.[83] The drawing is filled with hats, hat-boxes, and clocks. The bed at right sits unmade and the inference is clear that the two women have recently left it.[84] In this home where the portrait hanging on the wall is of a woman, the man's diminutive stature suggests that the female lovers have no place for a full-grown male in their bedroom. Though all of the inferences in this picture are subtle and an observer not acquainted with the slang might see in the drawing two ladies of fashion picking out a hat, a photographic sequence of erotic postcards taken around 1910 makes the homoeroticism of women, hats, and hatboxes clear (figure 14). In this series a nude woman gives a hat in a hatbox to another nude woman. Gazing into a mirror in a moment of self-reflexive sexual knowledge, the two then go on to gaze into one another's eyes in an acknowledgment of their shared sexual knowledge. Such a photo sequence exposes the latent meaning of the Beardsley drawing, and equally suggests his dependence on the pornographic tradition to complete his meaning. In as much as he draws on pornography, however, he also depends on a vast bourgeois ignorance of the trope to keep his intentions more vaguely suggestive than overt.

The *Lysistrata* series provides an overt and interesting play on homoeroticism. In this series Beardsley utilizes the pornographic lesbian fantasy to suggest a female self-sufficiency both titillating and taunting to the male voyeur. *Lysistrata Haranguing the Athenian Women*, for instance, plays upon the multitude of erotic photographs featuring nude women in sexual flirtation (figures 15 and 16). There is little to differentiate Beardsley's representation from those of pornography save the notion that his is an artistic interpretation of a classical play. The bodies are not overly realistic, and there is a pleasant balance in the picture as a whole, but the technique does not seem to "master" the content. There is no distancing technique and the sexual body is highlighted rather than denied.

Beardsley attempts to cancel the potential homoerotic charge of *The Examination of the Herald* by suggesting that neither participant is particularly moved by their mutual exposure (figure 17). The herald reveals his pornographically grand penis to the orientalized old man who, penis adroop, finds the organ an object of curiosity, but, as the flaccid state of his penis attests, not especially stimulating. The herald's equipoise is demonstrated by his easy posture. Hands upon his hips, lips in a grin of complacency, he merely stands to allow the old man an inspection. A gesture with potentially powerful homoerotic content, a man fingering another's penis, is drained of its subversive charge in the apparent disinterest with which each undertakes the inspection. The penis is not a sexual subject, but rather a mere object of curiosity. The exoticism of the older man, whose symbolic earring renders him less overtly masculine, and the grotesque disproportion of the herald's organ to his body, distance the realistic portrayal of a pornographic pleasure. The defamiliarization of shapes insists not on a mimetic, bodily reading of the figures, but on an aesthetically distanced, contemplative one.

In *How King Mark Found Sir Tristram Sleeping*, the male genitalia are equally the object of a gaze, this time one that assimilates either shock or excitement (figure 18). As Snodgrass's reading of the drawing has suggested, each of the bodies in this illustration is gender-problematic. The sleeping Tristram is, with his long

Figure 13. Cover design for *The Savoy*, no. 2, by Aubrey Beardsley, 1896.

Figure 14. Anonymous photographic sequence of women with hats, *c.*1910.

The mastery of form: Beardsley and Joyce

AVBREY BEARDSLEY.

Figure 15. *Lysistrata Haranguing the Athenian Women*, 1896.

Modernism, Mass Culture, and the Aesthetics of Obscenity

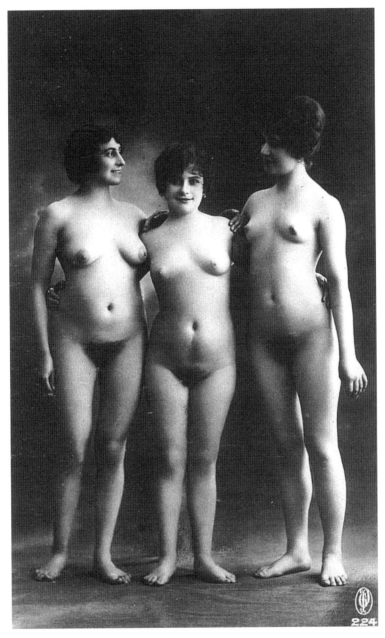

Figure 16. Anonymous photograph, *c.*1900.

The mastery of form: Beardsley and Joyce

Figure 17. *The Examination of the Herald*, by Aubrey
Beardsley, 1896.

Modernism, Mass Culture, and the Aesthetics of Obscenity

Figure 18. *How King Mark Found Sir Tristram Sleeping,* by
Aubrey Beardsley, 1893.

The mastery of form: Beardsley and Joyce

hair, accentuated chest, and oddly ambiguous genitalia, an androgynous figure. King Mark's tunic folds at his midriff in such a way as to emphasize a feminized opening and a phallic lack. In Mark's gaze upon Tristram's genitals there is a sense of a homoerotic shame, compounded by the heart-shaped leaves that form the illustration's border. Their insistence and directionality give phallic potency to the scene, as if to expose what isn't realized by the characters. In Snodgrass's words, "Predisposed to hide salacious details within the structure of other images, Beardsley compounds the illusion (characteristic of pornography generally) that he is taking the voyeuristic reader into his confidence, providing a surreptitious (and often projective) glimpse into the guilty secrets of the text and perhaps even of the author himself."[85] Through hidden details and bawdy symbology, Beardsley's works create an intimacy and therefore an immediacy with their viewers that is indicative of pornography in general. Yet the drawing itself appears representationally innocent, Tristram himself lacking one of pornography's prized features, a penis. Characteristic of modern incorporations of sexual representation into high art, the drawing foregrounds the body only to deny it.

Animals

An intimacy with the symbolic tradition of women and animals is necessary to understand Beardsley's continuation of and play upon these pornographic tropes. A long-standing pictorial tradition, women have frequently been paired with animals, typically dogs or monkeys, as functional male substitutes. Depicting a male touching a naked female infrequently occurs in any post-Baroque representation, and thus animals are frequently featured in eighteenth- and nineteenth-century art as women's intimates. When in the nineteenth century scientific discoveries led to an entire discourse associating women with the "less evolved" sensuousness of beasts, late nineteenth-century representations of women with animals began to take on a different overtone, a practical assimilation of erotic interests. Playing upon these associations, there was an entire sub-genre of Victorian pornography featuring women in erotic poses with animals. One illustration from Alfred de Musset's *The Gamiani, or a Night of Excess* – a pornographic work from the first half of the nineteenth century that Beardsley specifically mentions having received from Smithers in a letter in 1896 – features a woman about to receive an ape from the rear (figure 19).[86] Knowing of Beardsley's likely familiarity with the drawing, his illustration for the cover of Edgar Allan Poe's *The Murders in the Rue Morgue* takes on a more sinister and pornographic tone than what is implied by the drawing alone (figure 20). His depiction appears more sinister because, as opposed to the pornographic representation where the woman shows herself to be an initiating partner, in the *Rue Morgue*, as in *The Burial of Salome* (figure 21), a bestial figure appears ready to take advantage of an unconscious, if not dead, female corpse. In *The Burial of Salome*, for instance, the satyr figure appears fully aroused as he lowers Salome's legs into her powder casket. His ears phallically alert, eyes locked into a gaze, and mouth wearing a salacious grin, the growth from his pubic tuft is masked by Salome's angularly located, phallic leg. His hands are notably hidden between her legs and he seems poised for sexual action, if not already partially engaged. While the ape figure of the *Rue Morgue* cover is less sexually overt, its association with a tradition of male substitutes makes the intention clear. Beardsley suppresses the directly pornographic depiction of sexual action or genitalia, using its tropes to signify a similar intent. While *The Burial of Salome* depends on the grotesque disfiguration of the three characters to defamiliarize the viewer from the sexual content (and therefore check a pornographic pleasure), the *Rue Morgue* suppresses the sexual content entirely, distancing itself from the very implications it makes.

In a passage in *Ulysses* that conflates bestiality with voyeurism, Bloom recalls how he and Molly conceived their son Rudy:

> Must have been that morning in Raymond terrace she was at the window, the two dogs at it by the wall of cease to do evil. And the sergeant grinning up. She had that cream gown on with the rip she never stitched. Give us a touch, Poldy. God, I'm dying for it. How life begins. (*Ulysses* 89)

In a typical pornographic translation of the visual, Molly demonstrates a desire to set into practice what she has seen. The desire is made more illicit, more "dirty," in that she has seen animals have sexual intercourse. By turning to Bloom she acknowledges her desire to "do it like an animal," an assimilation that perpetuates the stereotype of the lower-class (and feminine) body as the bestial, sexualized body. While the sexualized intent of the passage is obvious, the narrative, a series of fleeting, semi-formed thoughts, briefly touches upon the pornographic moment. The moment is distanced from a representational realism by the use of slang terms for sexual intercourse, "at it," and "give us a touch." Metonymizing the full acts, Joyce effectively delimits and controls the pornographic, bodily content contained within the narrative.

The exotic other

Nineteenth- and early twentieth-century pornography capitalizes on imperialistic fantasy in countless ways, playing upon the Western idealization of the

Figure 19. Anonymous illustration from one of at least seven known versions of *Gamiani, ou Deux nuits d'excès* (Paris: Barraud, *c.*1864).

Figure 20. Cover design by Aubrey Beardsley for *The Murders in the Rue Morgue* by Edgar Allen Poe, 1896.

The mastery of form: Beardsley and Joyce

Figure 21. *The Burial of Salome* by Aubrey Beardsley, 1894.

Orient (considered in the nineteenth and early twentieth centuries to be what is now called the Near East and North Africa) as a locale seemingly unfixed by the more rigid social and institutional codification of sexuality in the West, and therefore open to its fantasies. As a subject for art, the exotic lies outside the restrictive operations of classical rules and opens up an entirely unexplored imaginative region. Pornographic notions of the Orient, just as hegemonic cultural notions, do not necessarily reflect any specific reality of the Orient, but, as Edward Said has suggested, do reflect a particular European definition of itself as contrasting image, idea, and experience to its exoticized other.[87] Reflecting Western thought at large, the exotic other was in the nineteenth and early twentieth centuries a fixed trope in pornography (just as it was in the art of dominant culture), a license for portraying untiring sensuality and unlimited desire as well

Modernism, Mass Culture, and the Aesthetics of Obscenity

as mysterious, licentious and inventive sex. The metaphor of the harem, for instance, was a particularly rich male power fantasy in its endless supply of exotic, submissive women to fulfill the limitless pornographic pleasures imaginable. Many a pornographic novel played upon this – *The Lustful Turk* (1828), *Scenes in the Seraglio* (*c*.1860), and *A Night in a Moorish Harem* (*c*.1906) being but a few examples of the exotic's lasting hold on the British imagination. Buck Mulligan expressed his own version of the harem fantasy in "Oxen of the Sun," where he proposed "to set up . . . a national fertilising farm to be named *Omphalos* with an obelisk hewn and erected after the fashion of Egypt" where he would "offer his dutiful yeoman services for the fecundation of any female of what grade of life soever who should there direct to him with the desire of fulfilling the functions of her natural" (*Ulysses* 402).

Joyce shows travel writing to be an important "empirical" source feeding the abstractions of Bloom's vaguely pornographic fascination with all things Turkish. While attending Dignam's funeral Bloom imagines the cemetery caretaker luring a woman back to his home for a sexual encounter. The association recalls for him "Whores in Turkish graveyards" (*Ulysses* 108), the Turkish custom of prostitution in graveyards frequently noted by nineteenth-century travel writers (Bloom possesses several books of travel writing in his library). The lugubrious practice looms large in Bloom's imagination, and, in combination with the other commonly encountered expressions of Oriental sexuality played up in the pantomime or music-hall songs, exposes how Oriental sexuality was a mass-produced cultural fantasy of exotic, sexualized otherness.

Intermittently throughout the day Bloom imagines Molly in Turkish pants, and in "Circe" has a vision of her in Turkish costume:

> Opulent curves fill out her scarlet trousers and jacket slashed with gold. A wide yellow cummerbund girdles her. A white yashmak violet in the night, covers her face, leaving free only her large dark eyes and raven hair. (*Ulysses* 439)

Prepared for a pantomime performance, Molly's costume conflates the sexual description of the *Sweets of Sin* (her "opulent curves") with the eroticism of the theater (a public, bodily performer) and the mysterious, exotic Orient (her face but half revealed by the yashmak).[88] The transgressiveness is further compounded by the fact that Molly is dressed as a man. She is in this image an exotic other, an image for pornographic fantasy.

Bloom claims in "Circe" that Molly also harbors exotic sexual fantasies. Explaining his appearance in nighttown to Mrs. Breen as a participation in or extension of Molly's fantasies, he says:

The mastery of form: Beardsley and Joyce

> She often said she'd like to visit. Slumming. The exotic, you see. Negro servants too in livery if she had money. Othello black brute. Eugene stratton. Even the bones and cornerman at the Livermore christies. Bohee brothers. Sweep for that matter.
>
> (*Ulysses* 443)

Each of the above references is to black performers or their impersonators, personalities of the music-hall stage. The exotic is again shown to be a by-product of mass culture, a mass-produced, commodified fantasy perpetuated in culture through its representations. The commodification of the exotic as sexual fantasy is made startlingly clear in the multiplicity of turn-of-the-century French postcards featuring exotic women.

The myth of the exotic other is the enabling myth of Beardsley's illustrations to Wilde's *Salome*. That is, based on cultural assumptions of the Orient as sexually fecund, licentious, and libidinally voracious, other to the bourgeois Anglo-Saxon self, Beardsley is given greater freedom with Wilde's already suggestive play than might otherwise have been the case if he had been representing, say, the Arthurian legend (which equally features a woman-as-temptress in the figure of Guinevere). Pornographic details abound in the *Salome* drawings, and perhaps for the first time in a work of art with such obvious high-cultural aspirations, tumescent penises make their way into public visibility.

Enter Herodias is an amalgamation of exotic others, each figure representing Beardsley's penchant for the grotesque (figure 22). The bizarre form of Herodias at center, with her huge balloon-like breasts and her pillar-like posture, would seem to be the illustration's focus, and yet none of the characters in the drawing directs their gaze at her. To her right, an undressed, effeminate page boy stands, genitals exposed (though Beardsley was forced to impose a fig-leaf over his genitals in the published version) and notably flaccid in Herodias's attendance. While his genitals betray him as male, his face and hair suggest the female. He is holding a mask, as if to suggest that his sexuality is itself a performance. He is in every sense a sexual other, denying not only a heteronormative response to Herodias's sexualized presence, but sexual classification itself. The figure on Herodias's left, a grotesque combination of Beardsley's foetus and old man figures, displays a rather large erection protruding through his clothing. Though again, oddly, he gazes not at the presumed sexual focus of the drawing, Herodias, but offstage. To emphasize the figure's erection, three candles burn in the lower left portion of the frame, two held up by erect-penis candlesticks. There is sexual excitement in the frame, but, unlike a pornographic representation, it is an undirected excitement. In a pornographic representation, energy is focused on the sexualized object of the gaze, often directed there through a mediating voyeur figure

Figure 22. *Enter Herodias* by Aubrey Beardsley, 1894.

The mastery of form: Beardsley and Joyce

whose own excitement in gazing at the sexual object is intended to function as a model to the viewer's. While Herodias would seem to be the intended object of the gaze, the mediating figures of the drawing offer the viewer no assistance, and in fact distract attention from her rather than reinforce it. What is overtly sexual in this picture, exposed breasts, protruding erections, and upright penis candlesticks, is juxtaposed and circumvented in the style of a Joycean narrative. While sexual details are provocatively laid out for the viewer, there is no obvious narratological relationship between them to complete the pornographic fantasy. The visual organization of a pornographic image relies on a narrative telos to engage the reader in completing that telos in his or her imagination, and, by extension, on his or her body. By evading pornographic completion, Beardsley shows a canny ability for incorporating the elements of the pornographic in such a way that does not assimilate the pornographic. Form here is the master of content.

In a similar depiction of the exotic other, *The Stomach Dance*, Beardsley is able to present a more accessible pornographic pleasure while still maintaining the hegemony of form. In *The Stomach Dance* the implied gyrations of Salome's body provoke an erection from the grotesque musician accompanying her, but the swollen penis is skillfully drawn to blend in with the folded design of his costume (figure 23). While the picture exaggerates and plays upon the sexual jurisdiction of exotic otherness, it is that very otherness that, in its presumed decadence, accords with hegemonic cultural belief. A painting of almost identical subject, Jean-Léon Gérôme's *La Danse de l'almée* (1863), created a controversy when it was first exhibited at the Salon of 1864, but was a major success with the public and certain critics who, not surprisingly, found high-art, classical validations for it in the qualities of stasis and universality (figure 24). The painting was noted by one critic for the "universal combination of the frenetic movement of the arms and the torso set upon 'legs of marble'."[89] Beardsley masters the pornographic incorporations in *The Stomach Dance* by exploiting dominant cultural belief in both the sexual decadence of the Orient and the mastery of form over content as a signifier of artistic integrity.

It is nowhere more clear than in the *Salome* drawings that Beardsley fully exploited high-cultural beliefs and signals in order to introduce into his works the potentially subversive. That subversive material, however, points out the merely stylized quality of the art that attempts to contain it, and by doing so travesties, or parodies, the very nature of high art. Though Beardsley successfully appropriated the pornographic for high-cultural consumption, importantly, the pornographic, unlike Gerty MacDowell's attempt to be "Greekly perfect," suc-

Figure 23. *The Stomach Dance* by Aubrey Beardsley, 1893.

The mastery of form: Beardsley and Joyce

Figure 24. *La Danse de l'almée* by Jean-Léon Gérôme, 1863.

cessfully embodied high art. Inasmuch as the formal techniques of Joyce and Beardsley limit the pornographic tropes and images that they employ, those tropes still speak the body, and render a more diverse form of discursive representation than offered in post-Renaissance art.

In a previous chapter, I called the incorporation of pornographic tropes and images into art an "aesthetic of the obscene," a paradoxical phrase that captures the tenuous nature of representing the unrepresentable. Beardsley and Joyce were masters of the aesthetic of the obscene in that they were foremost masters of the distancing techniques of a formal aesthetic. As critical focus moved in their time from the represented to the representing, a mode of aesthetic reception was privileged that served once again to de-emphasize the body, ironically in a move that made way for the representation of bodies. Bodies could be portrayed so long as readers or viewers could be taught to concern themselves not with the bodies themselves, but with how those bodies were portrayed, in what form they were manifest. The idealization of the body continued with the privileging of form.

There were plenty of people, however, who remained unschooled in this aesthetic understanding, and, in their affiliation with the body, were labeled "the mass." While the masses were seen as bodily consumers of art in an oppositional mode to bourgeois reception, a mode of aesthetic reception gradually developed throughout the twentieth century that was more akin to a sensuous subjugation.

This, ironically, can be attributed in part to the increased visibility of sensuality on the pages and canvases of the works of writers and artists such as Joyce and Beardsley. For while it is possible to read their incorporation of pornographic tropes and images into high art as an aesthetic appropriation or domination of the pornographic, such domination lasts only as long as the techniques with which they were conceived can be interpreted; that is, the distancing techniques of parody soon turned to simple pastiche as sexual representation in art became itself normative. We in the late twentieth century can no longer discern the parodic edge accompanying pornographic representations in modern artworks because they no longer bear the shock of the pornographic. The genre as it existed then is lost to us except as we are able to recover it through historical investigation. The acute sense of separation by which art and pornography existed previous to these artists has been mitigated by them and the artists that followed. Though to be sure pornography as a genre still exists today, it has, as a category, been altered by the emergence of explicit sexuality in works considered art. More obviously, art has been colonized by pornography. What is considered pornographic persistently pushes at the periphery of art. Through the agency of modern artists, the boundaries between art and pornography shifted dramatically. As I will explore in chapter four, this also came about as the result of a subject-formation based upon the moral-medical conflation of sex and health. As chapter four will show, D. H. Lawrence was one of the first proponents of this bodily mode of being.

4 Being disinterested: D. H. Lawrence

Lady Chatterley's Lover's utopic impulse is not, as previous critics have asserted, located in its assimilation of the gratifying sexual fantasies of pornography, but rather in its search to find in the sexually engaged body a moment and place beyond or outside of discourse, a moment that I want to characterize as an idyllic reinterpretation of the Kantian aesthetic and its disinterested free play of cognition. In this reinscription, the text works against cognition, indeed against all epistemological modes, in order to assert what Lawrence might have described as "pure being," an ontological framework. It will be the concern of the first section of this chapter to show that *Lady Chatterley's Lover*, like much of the turn-of-the-century sexology and psychology that enabled it, proposes the body as a bulwark, almost a pure space, against cultural codification and sees in its actions and motivations a disinterested mode of being. The disinterest that in the aesthetic tradition of Shaftesbury and Kant was fostered through aesthetic form is in Lawrence's work already located within one's body.

In viewing the body as the site of disinterest, *Lady Chatterley's Lover* offers a direct challenge to aesthetics in the tradition of Shaftesbury and Kant, which relies on an objectification of the body and senses in order to realize them within, or transfer them to, the cognitive faculties. Aesthetic realization of the beautiful in this tradition is always a "wresting away" from the selfish, private interests of the body in order to achieve the supposed distancing and disinterested effects of the mind. Lawrence's text identifies these distancing effects as belonging to *both* aesthetics and pornography. Pornography and aesthetics are equally characterized in Lawrence's texts as mental representations of experience as feeling, each solipsistic and selfish in its own way. Lawrence sought to overcome the mental objectification of sensation through his reinscription of the body in sexual union as more reliably disinterested than the mind because of its "unknowingness." All consciousness and knowing is, in Lawrence, interested. Therefore Lawrence looked to "being," whatever that may entail, to escape the selfishness that it was, ironically, the project of aesthetics in the tradition of Shaftesbury and Kant to circumvent.

What remains problematic in Lawrence's literary claim for the disinterestedness of physical being is the attempt to disavow the enabling discourses upon which he bases and articulates his conclusions. Lawrence strove to situate the body as outside of cultural relativism and the interests that are the necessary components of discourse. As a writer, however, his medium necessarily propagated what, in light of the ambitions of his project, amounted to a failure. By writing the body as against culture he was still writing the body, by necessity of the medium he used, into culture. This did not stop Lawrence from trying to convey his ideas. In the *Lady Chatterley* novels the body is constructed in positive differentiation from civilization, primarily on the basis of its seeming opposition to individual and economic interest (the two realms of personal will that Sir Clifford embodies).[1] The body, specifically in sexual union, is portrayed in Lawrence as a disinterested being of desire and fulfillment, a moment/place of transcendence that is simultaneously purely physical. Moments of coition are described as moments of unknowing where consciousness (for the texts insist on representing consciousness even in the very moments they strive to achieve the loss of consciousness) ebbs and flows, simulating oceanic movement. The ocean as trope describes something which, while inanimate itself, contains animation, an entity which is and does not know.

The loss of consciousness described in the love scenes can be said to decenter the subjects in a way similar to the Kantian sublime, where that which excites the feeling of the sublime may be, as Kant says, "ill-adapted to our faculty of presentation," challenging the limits of cognition and imagination and setting the mind in motion, if only to seek the solacing gratification of tracing its own limit.[2] The loss of consciousness and the subsequent awe of Connie Chatterley during and after her love-making with Mellors is paradigmatic of the sublime. If the sublime is, as Jean-Luc Nancy has suggested, "the unlimited removal of the beautiful," or all form as such, it is tempting to see in Lawrence's sexual depictions an attempt to invoke the sublime as an evacuation of taste and all culturally derived modes of cognition.[3] For, as I have established in previous chapters, form is the most significant signifier of beauty and taste in the aesthetic tradition of Shaftesbury and Kant. Yet if this is so, the sublime rendered in the *Lady Chatterley* novels cannot adhere to the Kantian sublime in which all fades into insignificance before the ideas of reason, the mind's own representation of itself which makes "intuitable the supremacy of our cognitive faculties on the rational side over the greatest faculty of sensibility."[4] The supremacy of cognition that Kant championed is what Lawrence fought against most. The supremacy Lawrence attempted to realize in his representation of moments of ecstatic union is not that of the cognitive faculties, nor of the senses. Rather, it is the supremacy of an achieved ontological awareness that can only be described in the language of knowing, but is in fact an unknowing.

This chapter will show that, in setting his texts in opposition to the mental abstractions of idealist philosophy, Lawrence borrowed from the very forms he wanted to deny. Language imparts consciousness and knowing, it bears the traces of its forms. Writing provides no escape from the rational, epistemological orientation so reviled in *Lady Chatterley's Lover*. This dynamic becomes especially visible in Lawrence's attempt to correct the idealized sensation of pornographic discourse. In declaring his writing in opposition to, or a correction of, pornography, Lawrence necessarily appropriated those very forms. In trying to avoid idealized sensation, Lawrence's work is vexed with the relationship between the sensible and the supersensible that both aesthetics and pornography engage. As I explore in the second section of this chapter, this leads Lawrence to question the disembodiment propagated through various forms of mass media. A political tract as much as a work of art, *Lady Chatterley's Lover* works on multiple levels to disavow interest and disembodiment in the economic, textual, and aesthetico-cognitive realms. Through this, it champions a class leveling which erodes the former social hierarchies embedded into the conception of the aesthetic in the tradition of Shaftesbury and Kant. Lawrence champions not merely the body, but the body politic, the body of the masses. While Lawrence replaced the disciplined freedom of aesthetic cognitive free play with bodily free play, his attempt to secure the body, indeed his text, for disinterest, is continually threatened by the very discursive techniques of pornography that the text appropriated in order to correct. The pornographic, a discourse characterized aesthetically and economically by its interest, poses a perpetual challenge to the disinterested impulses of *Lady Chatterley's Lover*.

Sexology and aesthetic disinterest

Lady Chatterley's Lover proposes the body in sexual congress as a utopic time and place of disinterest. The text recreates the ideal aesthetic moment, the moment described in Kantian aesthetics as a metaphysical unity of sensuousness without desire, as a moment of being rather than knowing. Lawrence's effort both to represent sexuality and to define that very sexuality as disinterested marks a unique, if troubled, solution to the problem of reconciling sexually explicit representations to middle-class aesthetic sensibilities that since the eighteenth century had manifest themselves as profoundly interested in disinterest, disinterest functioning as an internalized mode of social control and self representation.

Lawrence's solution was enabled by the fields of sexology and psychology as developed at the turn of the century. Continuing the long-held Western tradition of separating the mind from the body, and viewing the body as a mute expression of resistance to a culture rendered civil through the agency of mind, sexologists began in the nineteenth century to study the interplay between the body and culture, and in doing so to make the body speak, as Foucault has pointed out in volume one of *The History of Sexuality*, "the truth."[5] Flowing from the conclusions of Darwin, who posited the desiring body as the ground of human existence, sexologists saw the body as the node of one's being, that which revealed an "original" state of being, and consequently exposed the forces of culture upon that state.[6] In a sexological frame of reference that is now recognized as Freudian, the mind was perceived as too decentered and self-deceiving, simply too interested, to be held accountable for the truth of one's being. Instead, the body was constructed as the space of accountability. The sexual body became a site of knowing (pornography is indeed an offshoot of this attitude, a hyper-knowing)[7] and sexologists such as Krafft-Ebing began to make rather generalized pronouncements such as "Sexual feeling is really the root of all ethics, and no doubt aestheticism and religion."[8]

The body, while perceived as the outside or limit of culture, was simultaneously inscribed as its organic root, the foundation upon which all culture is built. As I discussed in chapter one, Freud conceived of the body as the logical instrument of the irrational effects of mind. In representing reason as the always already destabilized tool of the irrational faculty of desire, Freud identified the body as that which conveys "the truth." Desire, that which had been viewed in German idealist aesthetics as generating from individual needs or wishes, personal interest, was conceived by the post-Darwinian sexologists, and especially by Freud, as an anonymous system of rules, an impersonal, disinterested force at work both inside and outside of the body.[9] The body reveals these desires in the form of symptoms. Sexologists were eager to claim that, though sometimes circuitously, the body always manifests the truth.

As this conception of desire became dominant, sexology conflated the signifiers of the German aesthetic tradition of the beautiful with those of the sexual, loosening the divisions Kant had set up one-hundred years before between the agreeable, that which is sensually pleasing, and the beautiful, that which is cognitively pleasing with only itself as an end. This conflation of the sexual with the beautiful can be traced to the post-Darwinian creation of the field of natural history in the latter half of the nineteenth century. Grant Allen's *Physiological Aesthetics* (1877) forms an important part of this trajectory in its attempt "to elucidate physiologically the nature of our Aesthetic Feelings."[10] Allen's work, deeply influenced by Herbert Spencer's *The Principles of Psychology* (1866), situates all aesthetic response in the bodily senses. Allen carefully catalogues the various levels of aesthetic response afforded through the senses – sight, hearing, touch, taste, smell and "organic sensibility generally" – and repeatedly attempts to establish that "Aesthetic Feelings are the cumulative effect of many infinitesimal physiological factors."[11] Following Spencer's lead, he is at pains to point out that sexual feeling itself, because it denies disinterestedness, cannot be considered aesthetic.[12] For this reason Spencer and Allen point toward but do not complete the assumptions of sexological aesthetics. For while Spencer and Allen made it possible to conceive of aesthetic response as rooted in the body, a body that had developed increasingly fine levels of response through the evolutionary process, the sexologists that followed in the decades after them focused on the role that sexual response played in aesthetic reactions.

Seeing the sexual impulse as the key to the survival of the species, sexologists began to translate this impulse to all aspects of life, including aesthetics. Havelock Ellis, for instance, sought to find an anthropological explanation of the beautiful in the following claim from the second volume of *Studies in the Psychology of Sex* (1899):

> It would be out of place here to discuss comparatively the origins of our idea of beauty. That is a question which belongs to aesthetics, not to sexual psychology, and it is a question on which aestheticians are not altogether in agreement . . . Practically, so far as man and his immediate ancestors are concerned, the sexual and the extra-sexual factors of beauty have been interwoven from the first. The sexually beautiful object must have appealed to fundamental physiological attitudes of reaction; the generally beautiful object must have shared in the thrill which the specifically sexual object imparted.[13]

Ellis's language highlights how sexology privileges the higher law of "fundamental physiological attitudes of reaction" over cognitive response. The beautiful is no longer encountered as an effect of the cognitive faculties, but rather an effect of the body, which is essentialized as manifesting a predictable set of attitudes and reactions. Through this lens it is possible to see how the empirical science of the body vied for precedence over the philosophy of the mind.

Freud conceptualized the beautiful along the same lines as Ellis in *Three Essays on the Theory of Sexuality* where he said "There is to my mind no doubt that the concept of 'beautiful' has its roots in sexual excitation and that its original meaning was 'sexually stimulating'."[14] Sexual psychology embraced the idea that that which is sexually desirable to the body is beautiful. The sexological aesthetic constitutes a challenge to the aesthetic tradition of Shaftesbury and Kant in that it posits *interest* as the root of the beautiful. Intriguingly, sexologists were aware of the problems their ideas posed to the concept of disinterest and attempted to ameliorate their threat to the aesthetic as a philosophical category. While Freud offered the idea of sublimation as a mechanism for controlling conscious desires (interests), Ellis as aesthetician created a supplemental category for the sexual, equal in value to the sublime:[15]

> Not only is the general fact of sexual attraction an essential element of aesthetic contemplation . . . but we have to recognize also that specific sexual emotion properly comes within the aesthetic field. It is quite erroneous, as Groos well points out, to assert that sexual emotion has no aesthetic value. On the contrary, it has quite as much value as the emotion of terror and pity. Such emotion must, however, be duly subordinated to the total aesthetic effect.[16]

Terror and pity, of course, comprise part of the list of emotional responses produced by the sublime according to Edmund Burke's *A Philosophical Enquiry into the Origin of our Ideas of the Sublime and the Beautiful* (1757). Ellis's appeal to such recognizable signifiers, and his positioning of sexual emotion as equal in value, effectively posits "sexual emotion" as a valid, indeed essential, component of aesthetic contemplation. The sexual is seen as a subset of a larger aesthetic field, but that field is intimately bound with "the idea of carnal pleasure."[17] According to sexology at the turn of the century, the aesthetic is materially grounded, a property of body and "sexual emotion" rather than mind.

The sexological aesthetic marks a significant reversal of the aesthetic as expressed in Kant's *Critique of Judgment*, which asserts that "A pure judgement of taste has, then, for its determining ground neither charm nor emotion, in a word, no sensation as matter of the aesthetic judgement."[18] What differentiated this aestheticized-sexual-feeling/sexual-feeling-for-the-aesthetic from purely personal interest for Ellis is its "fundamentally objective element" throughout the animated world, the fact that, by virtue of Darwinian biology, all animated beings share a life impulse, a sexual drive.[19] This perspective is a precursor to a widely held twentieth-century view, shared by Lawrence, that the law of sexual desire is the Law, a field of forces with a series of aims that conflict with their own cultural construction. This view maintains that the body locates a truth forever perverted by mind and culture.

Though continuing the long-held Western configuration of the body as at odds with its culture, sexology reversed the negative valence of such difference. Where much eighteenth- and nineteenth-century philosophy held the body suspiciously at bay as the potentially disruptive source of irrational interests, forcing its instinctual approbations and aversions upon social practice, sexology reconfigured the body as in many ways a disinterested victim, a pure space denatured by the interests of society.[20] This shift toward privileging the body had its counterpart in a changing political attitude toward the working classes in the nineteenth century in which the middle class sentimentalized the working classes and began to see in them a source of value. This value was epitomized in Marx's insistence on accounting for the material means of production – human bodies. Just as the body was reinscribed as the unknowing victim of social restraint, so the body politic, the working classes, were written in the latter half of the nineteenth and the early twentieth centuries, especially within the Marxist-socialist tradition, as the unknowing victims of social exploitation, subject to the controlling interests of a middle-class dominated society. Such a reinscription made way for an analogous sentimentalizing of the lower classes, those perceived to live a life more closely in connection with their bodies, as themselves embodying the truth.

D. H. Lawrence's writing, with its sensualized lower-class males, from *Sons and Lovers'* Walter Morel to *Lady Chatterley's Lover's* Oliver Mellors, epitomizes this attitude. Lawrence's emphasis on the experience and "voice" of the body is in part an extension of sexological theory's privileging of the body as the space of truth. It is also in part an extension of this bodily truth to the body politic, the working classes. Throughout his novels, as the critic Nigel Kelsey has pointed out, Lawrence presents "class conflict at a personal level embodied in the textual opposition between body and mind."[21] Through this textual positioning of the body, Lawrence attempts to challenge both the aesthetic and the pornographic as mental representations of sensation and feeling that perpetuate the interests of the upper-middle class.

The modern concept of the aesthetic, as I have elaborated in previous chapters, is formulated around a social and political model of disciplined freedom. In the discourse of aesthetics in the tradition of Shaftesbury and Kant, the work of art is, like the bourgeois subject, autonomous and self-determining. The subject and the work of art each acknowledge, in Terry Eagleton's words, "no merely intrinsic law but instead, [each] in some mysterious fashion, gives the law to itself."[22] The free play of the imagination functions as a symbol of the morally good which acts according to duty (autonomously) rather than uncontrolled desire (heteronomously), freely rather than according to necessity. With such a mandate, the aesthetic must continue to foster disinterest, an indifference not to others' interests but to one's own, the disavowal of one's own personal prejudices in favor of the common humanity.[23] The aesthetic is formulated around this specific notion of the rational, articulate subject acting autonomously, but in the interests of the whole.

Under such communally oriented notions of the aesthetic, D. H. Lawrence reinscribed the body as the disinterested space of aesthetic free play, permitting, as Peter Brooks says in another context, "the illusion of a freedom from materiality," even while most deeply materially engaged.[24] Perhaps a source for such thinking, Edward Carpenter was in 1896 already advocating the sexual act as both disinterested and social, very much in the mode of the aesthetic:[25]

> Sex to-day throughout the domains of civilisation is thoroughly unclean. Everywhere it is slimed over with the thought of pleasure. Not for joy, not for mere delight in and excess of life, not for pride in generation of children, not for a symbol and expression of deepest soul-union does it exist – but for our own gratification. Hence we disown it in our thoughts, and cover it up with false shame and unbelief – knowing well that to seek a social act for a private end is a falsehood.[26]

Sex here takes the place of an aesthetic interaction between subject and object. It de-prioritizes individual, sensual gratification in favor of a more socially amenable form of disciplined freedom. Carpenter's concepts of joy and excess conjure for the sex act the late twentieth-century aestheticized concept of *jouissance*, Barthes' notion of that which fissures paradigms and moves beyond words in its very excess, the unspeakable.[27] It is in the spirit of this *jouissance* that Lawrence replaces the aesthetic moment of apprehension, "free play," with the sexual union, hoping in turn to find in coition an aesthetic-like space for excess, that which is beyond consciousness.

Part of the effort to move beyond personal interest in *Lady Chatterley's Lover* is manifest in descriptions of Connie and Mellors that efface their individual personalities. When Mellors thinks of Connie, she is referred to simply as "the woman." His disinterested mode of loving transcends boundaries of class and personality and so when he loves her he loves "the female in her" rather than the "person," and takes "no notice of Constance or Lady Chatterley; he just softly" strokes "her loins or her breasts."[28] The sexual body, in its profound disinterest, erases class difference, indeed erases individual difference. While the novel features the sexual body as class leveler, Mellors proudly speaks of being in "physical touch" with his soldiers (*LCL* 301), and the text frequently alludes to the army and soldiering in order to level class differences between men.

To be unnamed is to remain unknown as an individual, simply to be. The namelessness of Connie and Mellors with regard to one another signifies their ability to reach a higher state of ontological awareness through their relationship. When Hilda and Connie arrive in Mansfield, Hilda tires of hearing Connie speak of Mellors's history and says, "*He! He!* What name do you call him by? You only say *he*" (*LCL* 260). Connie replies, "I've never called him by any name; nor he me; which is curious when you come to think of it. Unless we say Lady Jane and John Thomas," the ironically class-specific names of their respective genitals (*LCL* 260). The personality invested in the naming of the genitals operates as an opening to an alternate self which then allows their primary, "named," selves to move into a disinterested state beyond consciousness. When Mellors introduces his penis to Connie he becomes "helpless," his consciousness draining away, while his penis "fills" and "surges" and "rises up," entering Connie and "melting" her mind (*LCL* 227). The sexualized body becomes the active, free space of disinterested being. The phrase "disinterested being" is itself redundant in the Lawrencean lexicon, for being is inscribed as the opposite of knowing, that which is always already interested. Sexual intercourse is an act of freedom based democratically on the body, yet circumscribed by the passage of time. It is only in these moments of union where individuality is lost to unity that – like the Kantian subject arrested and raised through a momentary interaction with the beautiful, though on a physical plane – the disciplined "free play" of aesthetic disinterest is realized in a mode that Lawrence would have classified as anti-aesthetic because anti-consciousness.

In propagating disinterest, Lawrence's project was set at odds with cognition as itself a tool of what Lawrence called "will," a rigidified form of personal interest. In this way, *Lady Chatterley's Lover* inhabits a complicated relationship with Kantian and German idealist aesthetics; rejecting their emphasis on mind, the text nevertheless embraces the project of selfless disinterest upon which they are grounded. The youthful love affairs of Connie and Hilda in Germany (their location contributing to the attack on German idealism) are described in terms that make clear the text's intention to set up an alternative to the kind of loving it describes as wholly cognitive. Of the two sisters' romantic choices, the narrator says, "Neither was ever in love with a young man unless he and she were verbally very near: that is unless they were profoundly *interested*, TALKING to one another" (italics mine)(*LCL* 4). To be "verbally very near" is to displace physical intimacy with linguistic, and therefore cognitive, loving. The girls engage in an epistemological rather than ontological form of love. The text makes clear here its view that language is necessarily *interested*, an ideal rather than material system that distorts the truth of being as manifest in the body. Lawrence's equation of language to consciousness reflects Marx's statement in *German Ideology* that "Language is as old as consciousness, language *is* practical consciousness, as it exists for other men, and thus as it exists for myself as well."[29] Language, like cognition, is bound in the process of knowing, and knowing, in *Lady Chatterley's Lover*, is a form of death.

Thus all sex scenes work to undo knowing. In the first love scene between Mellors and Connie, Mellors approaches Connie "Without knowing" (*LCL* 122). Wondering what Mellors is thinking and feeling, Connie is stultified, "She did now know" (*LCL* 124). When Connie first experiences orgasm, she lies "unconscious of the wild little cries she uttered at the last" enjoying the "unspeakable motion" (*LCL* 142). Mellors too lies "unknowing" and together they lie "and know nothing, not even of each other" (*LCL* 142). If speaking is knowing, this too is banished from the sexual moment. Lying together after coition, Mellors "said nothing. He would never say anything" (*LCL* 188). Connie is "utterly still, utterly unknowing" and as they lie together "in an unfathomable silence" the narrative asserts that "of this, they would never speak" (*LCL* 188). After a while Mellors is rendered into an aesthetic object that defies translation into (Connie's) language with "dark, wide eyes, his face a little flushed and his hair ruffled, curiously warm and still and beautiful in the dim light of the lantern, so beautiful, she would never tell him how beautiful" (*LCL* 189). Lawrence here denies the communication of aesthetic experience that is a necessary component to the Kantian judgment of the beautiful. Knowledge gained here can never be objectively known. It is the knowledge of being, an inarticulable beauty.

Interestingly, while the narrative seems aware of the difficulty of translating being into knowing, the text asserts itself as though unaware, as though its own verbal descriptions of this unknowing and being are themselves not a form of knowing. This paradox leads to the deeply fissured reactions, critical and popular, the novel has endured throughout the century. More commonly the problem is spoken of as one of bringing sex to the page. Graham Hough, writing in the early stages of Lawrence criticism, assessed the problem as such:

How has fiction got on at all in the past, if such a large part of life [sex] has been kept behind the curtain? Of course by presenting the subsequent emotional effects of sexual activity, its consequences in character and action, without attempting to present the sexual activity itself. It may well be that this is the right procedure. Not only are intimate sexual experiences not talked about in the novel, they are not commonly talked about at all. No one ordinarily puts such experiences into words . . . The crucial question, therefore, is whether what is ordinarily never put into words at all can be put into words without altering and deforming the experience. It is a purely empirical question, and I think the unprejudiced answer must be that it can . . . The experience of reading this part of the book is less of shock than of recognition. We can say of it what Dr. Johnson said of wit – it is at once natural and new.[30]

Hough begins the passage acknowledging that previously sex has been presented as a form of knowledge subsequent to the event. Hough's assessment as to the success of the presentation of sexual matter, however, represents the difficulty that the text negotiates, for he has to resort to assessing the representations "empirically," a mode that already reduces the representations to no more than representations, and as such makes them instruments of knowledge. The sexual body as ontological entity must be translated into an epistemological mode before being written or talked about. While Hough as critic makes a valid space for the sexual representations under the perhaps surprising legitimizing agency of Johnsonian wit, his critique fails in a larger sense to understand the project of the sexual scenes in themselves. For empiricism, idealism, and their combined form, aestheticism, are each attacked in *Lady Chatterley's Lover*.

Clifford Chatterley, the embodiment of rational empiricism, idealism, and aestheticism, is criticized at one point when Connie realizes that "he didn't mind whether she were *demi-vierge* or *demi-monde*, so long as he didn't absolutely know, and wasn't made to see. What the eye doesn't see and the mind doesn't know, doesn't exist" (*LCL* 16). Clifford's knowing, as characterized by the empirical and ideal modes, is depicted as entirely limited. His association with aestheticism, a mode the text displays as a cognitive, or idealized, sensuality, is made clear in a scene with Mrs. Bolton where he asks her for a yellow book, signifier of the hedonistic, self-conscious school of Aestheticism, and then, in a manner that parodies the best of Wildean aesthetes, complains about the scent of the hyacinths; "it's a little funereal," he says, impressing Mrs. Bolton with his "higher fastidiousness" (*LCL* 102).

Set in counterpose to the empirically realized Clifford is Oliver Mellors, whose thin, white body is at one point described in Connie's thoughts as "like a lonely pistil of an invisible flower," or, in other words, that which defies empirical understanding (*LCL* 88). When Connie actually does see Mellors washing himself outside of his house, the text works hard to move the experience beyond the empirical, calling it a "visionary" moment rather than a vision. The incomplete sentences that describe Connie's assessment of the body show the text attempting to create the body not as an active instrument, but as a being, almost an object. Note the lack of active verbs in the following passage:

> Perfect, white, solitary nudity of a creature that lives alone, and inwardly alone. And beyond that, a certain beauty of a pure creature. Not the stuff of beauty, not even the body of beauty, but the lambency, the warm white flame of a single life, revealing itself in contours that one might touch: a body! (*LCL* 68)

Each of these sentences forms a predicate without a subject, and by doing so strives to mimic the body-as-being as opposed to the body-as-instrument-of-knowing, either Connie's or Mellors's (with the exception of Connie's thought that she might touch the body, an acceptable form of knowledge in the text in that it coincides with being). The passage moves progressively away from beauty toward the body. What Connie sees is "Not the stuff of beauty, not even the body of beauty." She transcends that form of apprehension that involves mind – the apprehension of beauty – and moves straight into sensual being. She apprehends a body, a body one might touch.

Lawrence's attempt to create through this scene an alternative basis of aesthetic judgment for beauty is made more clear in the second version of the novel, *John Thomas and Lady Jane*, where Connie sees the body and experiences a moment of transcendence akin to the Kantian aesthetic, but then rejects the kinds of experiences normally associated with that aesthetic. After having revealed to her a new self the text relates:

> It was a self which had seen powerful beauty, seen it alive, and in motion, seen it as the greatest vision of her life. She was well accustomed to the beauty in the world of art, and from this she had derived, truly, the deepest satisfaction of her life: from beauty and from knowledge. Human contact, love, sex, marriage had all meant little to her, strictly, compared to the curious rapture and fulfillment she had got from certain Beethoven symphonies, or from a book like *Les Liasons Dangereuses*, from some poetry, from some pictures, from the sight of Florence in the sunshine: or even from a course of philosophy lectures. Life! they talked about life! But what was life, except experiencing the beautiful experience of works of art or works of nature, or acquiring the never ending gleaming bits of knowledge that come to one?[31]

Art, the site of the beautiful to Connie's cultured set, is devalued by the experience of the body which is somehow more "real," more true to life.

Being disinterested: D. H. Lawrence

Though more overtly against art in *John Thomas and Lady Jane*, all of the *Lady Chatterley* texts work to remove the materially grounded, transcendent moment of free play from its traditional association with the aesthetic text, song, or artwork, in order to reinscribe the experience of the body as a higher form of disciplined freedom, a superior social model. Where aesthetics in the tradition of Shaftesbury and Kant located the selfishness disruptive to social order in the body, Lawrence locates selfish, personal interest in the cognitive will and its instrument, language. The sexual body, Lawrence claims, is beyond sensuality, a last refuge for the disinterest which is a necessary factor in a social model based on collective interests, as *The First Lady Chatterley* makes clear: "It is the sex warmth alone that makes men and women possible to one another. Reduce them to simple individuality, to the assertive personal egoism of the modern individual, and each sees in the other the enemy" (*FLC* 272). If aesthetics in the tradition of Shaftesbury and Kant lifted the individual out of himself at the expense of his body, Lawrence's aesthetico-ontologics attempt to show how connecting more deeply with one's own body can be more effectively self-effacing. Lawrence raised the body to the unique level of social community that Kant found possible through the aesthetic, but in doing so he attacked the aesthetic itself as a specifically upper- and middle-class mode of cognition. This is expressed in *The First Lady Chatterley* when Connie visits the depressed mining town of Tevershall and thinks to herself, "If one could have a sense of *life*-beauty with them . . . The beauty of a live thing! If one could waken them to that! Not art and aesthetics, which somehow is always snobbery."[32] When Connie thinks to herself that "these people are cut off from their own beauty" she is really restating the notion that they are cut off from their own bodies. "Life beauty" is an aesthetic-like utopia found only in the body.

As Connie herself learns about her own body through her lover, she also learns about the working classes. The *Lady Chatterley* texts participate in a larger social movement to transfer the site of accountability and of disciplined freedom from the mind to the body, and, by extension, to the body politic. Their incorporation of pornography is in this sense the disciplining of pornographic form within a social model that relies on the dialogization of sexuality to balance its interests.

Disinterest and the body politic

It is often remarked that *The First Lady Chatterley* is a decidedly more political text than *Lady Chatterley's Lover*, the first text stressing the social differences between the two lovers and the near impossibility of surmounting the difficulties those differences impose. Progressively through each text, Lawrence can be seen to be deleting the implacable problems raised by the differences between a more definitely lower-class Parkin (as he is called in the first two versions) and Lady Chatterley, while simultaneously elaborating the sexual connections between the lovers. *The First Lady Chatterley* contains relatively little sexually explicit material, even obscene words appear with dashes in them in order to avoid actually spelling them out. By finding in the sexual body a space of class disinterest, the final text seeks to erase the class differences that vexed the previous versions, while maintaining the concept enunciated in the first version, that "Parkin was beyond class in passion" (*FLC* 168).

By the third version, Mellors is beyond class in most arenas. "Almost a gentleman" but of no specific class, he has a "native breeding" rather than a "cut-to-pattern class thing" (*LCL* 70 297). The "native" aspect of Mellors's personality comprises Lawrence's longing to do what he reviles in Sir Clifford: to negate the means of production. Not a product of class or society, Mellors is conceived in the final version as a product of nature, the natural result of his body's own propriety.

The text reveals a binary desire both to erase class difference and to exploit the perennial British *frisson* created by staging cross-class desire. Not surprisingly, however, the impulse to level class differences caused greater uproar in England than the novel's representations of explicit sex. When a series of parodies of and fake sequels to *Lady Chatterley's Lover* were produced in the 1930s after Lawrence's death, only one parody was published in England, *Sadie Catterly's Cover* by Robert Leicester (London: Cranley & Day, 1933). The humor of the parody centers not around the sex (as with all of the other parodies) but instead around the novel's class consciousness. In this story, Sadie Catterly, a very upper-middle-class woman, is seduced not by her "fourth-under-gardener's" sexual magnetism, but by his dialect, which she learns to speak so that the under-gardener can exclaim, "Tha's got the nicest, nicest dialect as is."[33] On the level of plot, the obvious demonstration of leveling in the *Lady Chatterley* novels occurs in the simple fact of a love affair between a Lady and her servant. Their forthcoming child is the actual embodiment of such leveling, as is foreshadowed when Connie visits the Flint's baby at Marehay who gazes "cheekily" at Connie because "Ladyships were still all the same to her" (*LCL* 138).

It is interesting to note that E. M. Forster's *Maurice*, written twelve years prior to *The First Lady Chatterley*, though not published until 1971, works like the *Lady Chatterley* novels toward leveling the classes through sexuality, an idea Forster probably gained from Carpenter's work.[34] *Maurice,* like the *Lady Chatterley* novels, privileges the body over "the soul" – abstract idealism – and stages cross-class desire through a near-impossible love affair between a Cambridge-educated gentleman of the rising middle class and his friend's gamekeeper. In a line that might have been penned by Lawrence, the narrator asserts, "The body is deeper than the soul, and its secrets inscrutable."[35] Working in many ways, as Lawrence's texts do, to establish a "natural" space beyond class and conventions, homosexual love is defined in *Maurice* as an idyllic, more "true" love because not already conventionalized by language or society:

> And their love scene drew out, having the inestimable gain of a new language. No tradition overawed the boys. No convention settled what was poetic, what absurd. They were concerned with a passion few English minds have admitted, and so created untrammelled. Something of exquisite beauty arose in the mind of each at last, something unforgettable and eternal, and built of the humblest scraps of speech and from the simplest emotions. (M 93)

That the class barriers between Maurice and Scudder, the gamekeeper, are eventually surmountable can only be resolved in the end when they decide "They must live outside class, without relations or money," setting themselves apart from "the timorous millions who own stuffy little boxes, but never their own souls" (M 239). Just as in Lawrence and the mainstream of sexological thinking, Forster describes the body as at odds with the economic and social order. Both Lawrence and Forster identify the selfishness of class interests and the rigidity of their conventions as problematic for society as a whole. Each proposes cross-class coupling as the solution to this problem. However, the difficulty of bringing the disinterested body of being into an already classed order is manifest in the utopic and truncated endings of each novel. Both *Maurice* and *Lady Chatterley's Lover* can only suggest that their lovers will live happily ever after. Neither novel can realize the future it proposes.

In their efforts to assert class leveling, both *Maurice* and *Lady Chatterley's Lover* represent the crumbling of the English aristocracy. Maurice's friend and ex-lover (of a sort, their relationship included the body but not its gratification), Clive Durham, lives in a crumbling grand estate, Penge, and marries a Miss Woods who "Brought no money to Penge. She was accomplished and delightful, but belonged to the same class as the Durhams, and every year England grew less inclined to pay her highly" (M 167). While Penge is depicted as physically crumbling, Wragby, Sir Clifford's family estate, is shown as a deteriorating stronghold against the encroaching industrial working classes. When Mellors walks in the woods of Wragby, he experiences a seclusion that he knows is illusory. The industrial noises and lights creep into the woods, blurring the difference between park and town (*LCL* 126). When Mrs. Bolton moves into Wragby to care for Clifford, it is noted as "curious how much closer the servants' quarters seemed to have come; right up to the doors of Clifford's study, when before they were so remote" (*LCL* 86). The absorption, or erasure, of the old England by the new is chronicled in detail in Connie's visit to Sir Winter, another gentleman-owner of collieries:

> New mining villages crowded on the park, and the squire felt somehow that the pop-ulation was alien. He used to feel, in a good-natured but quite grand way, lord of his own domain and of his own colliers. Now, by a subtle pervasion of the new spirit, he had somehow been pushed out. It was he who did not belong anymore. There was no mistaking it. The mines, the industry had a will of its own, and this will was against the gentleman owner. (*LCL* 169)

The industrial and working classes are shown in these texts pressing up against the former spaces of aristocratic privilege. The sexual relationships between the privileged and the working classes in these novels function as both the symptom and the solution to the erasure of older class hierarchies. In that the aesthetic in the tradition of Shaftesbury and Kant was developed within this older social order, its disavowal in these novels further signals their participation in ushering in an emergent social and aesthetic order. In *John Thomas and Lady Jane* Connie realizes "that there was no real class-distinction any more" (*JTLJ* 288), class having died with the war in 1914. In *Lady Chatterley's Lover* she thinks, "There was only one class nowadays: moneyboys" (*LCL* 110), all defined by their relationship to money and their desire for more, their interest in interest, as it were.

While traditional thought had ascribed this encroaching classlessness to popular culture as a movement of the lower classes, the *Lady Chatterley* texts are quick to point out that all classes were participating in the "humanlessness" perceived to be "killing the world" (*JTLJ* 289). Mass culture as a state of mental evacuation aimed at all classes is a much chronicled factor in the *Lady Chatterley* texts. Lawrence attacks the new mass culture on the very same points that he attacks aesthetic idealism, for its disembodiment and its interest, personal and financial. As with most of the perceived evils in *Lady Chatterley's Lover*, it is Clifford Chatterley who is associated with the rise of mass culture. Clifford's desire to achieve popularity with his writing, with "the vast amorphous world he did not himself know," is achieved not through the traditional channels that Connie's father, a member of the Royal Academy, used, but rather through "new channels of publicity, all kinds" which include entertaining "all kinds of people at Wragby, without exactly lowering himself" (*LCL* 19–20). Mass culture penetrates class boundaries without "exactly" being noticeable as such. Instead, Clifford sells himself to nothing in particular, to the vast amorphous mass.

Clifford's fascination with the radio, the apotheosis of disembodiment, is portrayed as a form of individual evacuation: "he would sit for hours listening to the loudspeaker bellowing forth . . . with a blank entranced expression on his face, like a person losing his mind, and listen, or seem to listen, to the unspeakable thing" (*LCL* 116). The radio is seen as a site of social leveling, even in its attempt to address a sophisticated audience. Connie hears, "the loudspeaker begin to bellow, in an idiotically velveteen-genteel sort of voice, something about a series of street-cries, the very cream of genteel affectation imitating old criers" (*LCL* 130). This scene enacts the reversal of kitsch in its high-cultural imitation of low culture. There is a disjunction between the crier's call and its affectation, its mimicry is seen as an imperfect blending, even a parody, of class for the sake of entertainment. Importantly, the *Lady Chatterley* texts distinguish between two kinds of social leveling; a positive leveling, or breaking of barriers, that is achieved on an individual basis through human contact, and a negative leveling that is achieved through abstracting the humanity of individuals and diffusing them through mass-cultural media. Real equalizing cannot occur at a disembodied level.

Mass culture is the death of "reality" as physical contact in what Connie experiences as "the simulacrum of reality" (*LCL* 16). Helping Clifford to write his modern, "personal" – i.e., interested – stories, Connie herself becomes assimilated to the stories and lives the life of the simulacrum:

> The oak-leaves were to her like oak-leaves seen ruffling in a mirror, she herself was a figure somebody had read about, picking primroses that were only shadows or memories, or words. No substance to her or anything . . . no touch, no contact! Only this life with Clifford, this endless spinning of webs of yarn, of the minutiae of consciousness, these stories Sir Malcolm said there was nothing in . . . Sufficient unto the moment is the *appearance* of reality. (*LCL* 16)

Perhaps the ultimate irony of *Lady Chatterley's Lover* is that the simulacrum is figured so specifically in writing. What the narrative implies is that the members of Connie and Clifford's set become themselves discursive effects.

The tone of the modern, personal stories that Clifford and Connie might write is parodied in the opening chapter of *Lady Chatterley's Lover*, implying that their cognitive processes are informed by the kinds of literature they read and write. The self-confirming process of culture is manifest in the ideologically charged sentences which are stylistically short and clipped, mimicking the stiff-upper-lip verbal style of the British middle and upper classes. If the classic stoic acceptance of the "tragic age" issued by the novel's opening shows a determined will, more ironically stated is Connie's position as a modern female. In the following passage, presumably a reflection of Connie's thoughts, Lawrence satirizes the attitude of the modern woman, one of the primary ideological targets of the novel:

> And however one might sentimentalise it, this sex business was one of the most ancient, sordid connections and subjections. Poets who glorified it were mostly men. Women had always known there was something better, something higher . . . The beautiful pure freedom of a woman was definitely more wonderful than any sexual love. The only unfortunate thing was that men lagged so far behind women in the matter. They insisted on the sex thing like dogs . . . But a woman could yield to a man without yielding her inner free self . . . she could use this sex thing to have power over him. (*LCL* 3–4)

Presented in a matter-of-fact, "knowing" tone, the text parodies the mind-set of the free-thinking modern female whose will combats and makes "tools" of men.

That Connie's youthful mind-set is meant to evoke literary consciousness itself is established when Connie discusses "the sex thing" which is roused after "enlightened discussion" and marks "the end of a chapter" (*LCL* 4). The sexual liaison, the narrative asserts, "had a queer thrill of its own too: a queer vibrating thrill inside the body, a final spasm of self-assertion, like the last word, exciting, and very like the row of asterisks that can be put to show the end of a paragraph, and a break in the theme" (*LCL* 4). Connie's thoughts are those of a self-conscious author, writing and willing her sexuality into consciousness. The text satirizes this form of sexual/textual knowing as an inferior mode of being. The sex described in the first chapter by Connie is a sex "in the head," roused by words and conceived by the participants as if part of a story. Connie and her set write themselves into being, mentally as well as sexually. The men that Connie marvels over are those that "just went off from the top of their heads as if they were squibs and expected you to be carried heavenwards along with their own thin sticks" (*LCL* 53). These men are so identified with the linguistic or literary consciousness as to lose the distinction between their penises and their pencils. They become writing tools, as it were.

Textual interests

Attacking the literary frame of mind from a work that is itself literary poses the central irony, indeed the central fissure, in the text's own logic. Believing that he could escape the traps of language himself, Lawrence tried to escape the "knowing" text in order to assert disinterested being. The greatest challenge to disinterested being comes in the form of the pornographic signifiers that in their very interest and knowingness threaten at each sexual turn to corrupt the disinterested bodies. The descriptions of disinterested being in *Lady Chatterley's Lover* are by their very nature colored by the linguistic associations used to describe them. The pornographic images and tropes recalled by the love relationship of Connie and Mellors undermine and threaten the attempt to create a space of disinterested free play. The text itself is always already interested.

One of the most telling revelations of this threat comes in the form of a parodic sequel to *Lady Chatterley's Lover*, *Lady Chatterley's Husbands*, one of two sequels commissioned by the American publisher Samuel Roth for his "Ardent Classics" erotic series. *Lady Chatterley's Husbands*, written in 1931 by Anton Gud, though published, in pornographic style, anonymously, features a sexually adventurous and persistently upper-class Connie who pursues a life of enlightened promiscuity, seeing her own sexual fulfillment as the *sine qua non* of human experience.[36] While it is not clear whether the author intended his sequel to be parodic, the stylistic imitation necessarily works that way, and exposes how *Lady Chatterley's Lover* was received by contemporary minds, exploiting its sensational elements in order to create a popular readership. The sequel sends up Lawrence's novel specifically for its literary qualities. The opening paragraph mocks Lawrence's symbolic natural description, his gendered metaphors, and his prolix tendencies:

> Thousands of sea gulls flapped white wings against the grey cliffs of Dunoon, swooping and skimming restively over the waters of the bay. Teasing blue waves advanced wickedly on the adamant shore; like La Romba dancers in the maddening curves of their quivering approach. The wantons threw themselves at the rocks and slipped away, elusive, laughing, to let the ever-replenishing rear guard have its fling. This derisive, co-operatively feminine onslaught of the waves against the stiff dignity of the cliffs, tickled Connie in some obscure strata of her female vindictiveness . . . Waves – provocative as La Romba dancers. It was a good metaphor.[37]

Connie is forever pausing in *Lady Chatterley's Husbands* to appreciate a literary turn. When she expresses her pregnant state as of one "expecting" she thinks "Yes that was a good word. She had never before realized its aptness."[38] Yet even while Connie is herself fabricating her reality through words, she disdains it in others as a poor substitute for sensation:

> The careful transfer of scenery into crosstitch samplers of words was well enough for people who had no depth of honest sensation to provide a third dimension to this matter that transpired between your own eyes and the external world. If you had no

155.

excitement inside of you, you attempted to fix up the sky and trees and seas with fascinating words as though sky and trees and seas could be a *raison d'etre* [sic].[39]

Thus the sequel points out one of the fundamental paradoxes of Lawrence's
writing. His effort to go beyond words into a "third dimension," as this text calls
it, makes him more wordy than ever.

Lady Chatterley's Lover's verbosity with regard to the sexual body renders it
pornographic. This point is established by the fake sequel's exploitation of such
mannerisms in its own text for the purpose of titillating its readers. Marketed by
mail order along with other erotic books, *Lady Chatterley's Husbands* clearly
intended to exploit the sexuality of Lawrence's novel while studiously avoiding
the pornographic. Anti-obscenity laws in the 1930s worked primarily through
what could or could not be sent through the US Post Office. So while this fake
sequel plays up the erotic aspects of *Lady Chatterley's Lover*, especially in its black-
and-white print illustrations of a naked, swooning Connie, it complicates the
line Lawrence tried to draw between the sexual body as disinterested space of
free play, and the sexual body as a site of interest, personal, physical, and – in the
case of Roth's publishing through mail order just as Lawrence did with *Lady
Chatterley's Lover* – economic.[40]

Linguistically representing the sexual body necessarily conjured its contemporary and historical associations with pornography. Though Lawrence, with his
seemingly earnest hatred of pornography, may well have desired to rewrite the
sexual body in order to correct the very consciousness he saw arising from mediated sexuality, he could not help but draw upon the linguistic conventions produced by that increasingly popular genre. While the sequel maintains a
semblance of Lawrence's philosophy, it does so only to highlight what is already
present in Lawrence's writing itself: a specific sexual vocabulary almost solely
associated with the pornographic.

It is well known that Lawrence was disgusted by James Joyce's *Ulysses*, and that
Lady Chatterley's Lover is in part an attempt to show that "it can be done without
the muck."[41] If *Ulysses* imitates pornographic consciousness in order to expose it
in a formally stylish way as one of myriad competing discourses composing the
thoughts of the novel's characters, Lawrence tries to counter that consciousness
in *Lady Chatterley's Lover* by disconnecting it from its "mob-meaning," vilifying
formal aesthetics, and insisting on "true" sexual experience as that which moves
beyond consciousness. Still, Lawrence's only tool was language. With the exception of *Ulysses*, representations of sexualized bodies had not by this time established high-cultural associations or conventions. In 1928, sexually explicit
representation was embedded within the pornographic, one of the only discourses

Being disinterested: D. H. Lawrence

(medicine being another) to address sexuality in explicit, physically descriptive language. An entire vocabulary of sexual interactions was developed and expanded through pornographic language practices in the eighteenth and nineteenth centuries, and that language primarily remained proprietary to pornography until co-opted by "serious," or high-cultural, modern artists.

Lawrence tried to distance himself from that vocabulary and its empirical detail by both satirizing it and offering an alternative. An instance of this is shown when, after several previous encounters, Connie and Mellors make love one day in the hut. Connie experiences their first sexual encounter with a degree of detachment. In order to analyze the scene I will quote at length:

> And he lifted her dress right back, till he came even to her breasts. He kissed them softly, taking the nipples in his lips in tiny caresses.
>
> "Eh, but tha'rt nice, tha'rt nice!" he said, suddenly rubbing his face with a snuggling movement against her warm belly.
>
> And she put her arms round him under his shirt, but she was afraid, afraid of his thin, smooth, naked body, that seemed so powerful, afraid of the violent muscles. She shrank, afraid.
>
> And when he said, with a sort of little sigh: "Eh, tha'rt nice!" something in her quivered, and something in her spirit stiffened in resistance: stiffened from the terribly physical intimacy, and from the peculiar haste of his possession. And this time the sharp ecstasy of her own passion did not overcome her; she lay with her hands inert on his striving body, and do what she might, her spirit seemed to look on from the top of her head, and the butting of his haunches seemed ridiculous to her, and the sort of anxiety of his penis to come to its little evacuating crisis seemed farcical. Yes this was love, this ridiculous bouncing of the buttocks, and wilting of the poor insignificant, moist little penis. This was the divine love! After all the moderns were right when they felt contempt for the performance; for it was a performance.   (LCL 184)

In its metonymic description of sexualized body parts and actions, the scene begins with the explicit kissing of the breasts. In that pornography receives its charge from enumerating body parts in sexualized variations, the impulse of the scene above is pornographic. Typically in a pornographic narrative, Connie would function as the voyeur figure whose sensations operate as a verbal cue for the reader of the text to engage his own sensations imaginatively in similar fashion. Yet Connie's "modern self-consciousness" deviates from a tone that would encourage a bodily incitation on the part of a reader in that it does not enhance the mimetic attraction of the action, but rather satirizes it. The descriptively sexual is made "ridiculous" (a word associated with Clifford and the disengaged modern mind in the first chapter of the novel where his mind-set is characterized by the repetition of the word nine times in one page) by the adjectives that modify it: anxiety, little, ridiculous, farcical, wilting. The scene enacts a deflation of the pornographic impulse, a belittling of that which in pornography is the unsurpassed moment. Even the penis, always large beyond imagination in pornography, is here small and insignificant.

But of course all of this is a prelude to the reinscription of the sexual moment in Lawrence. The pornographic impulse has first to be destroyed in order for Lawrence to demonstrate what he wants to sanctify in sexuality and its literary representations.[42] The irony is that he reinscribes literary sexuality with many of the same tropes of the pornography he wants to eschew. On the level of plot he perpetuates pornography in that Connie's orgasms occur when she is in one way or another forcibly taken by Mellors. Her first orgasm occurs when Mellors apprehends her in the woods and takes her by force. In *John Thomas and Lady Jane* Connie actually tries to push him away while he overpowers her (127). Once she succumbs she becomes sexually ravenous. In typical pornographic tropes, the text relates that "she wanted him, with wild and rapacious desire," she "was like a volcano. At moments she surged with desire, with passion, like a stream of white-hot lava" (*JTLJ* 129). The woman-as-volcano is a classic pornographic trope, used, for example, in *Autobiography of a Flea* (c.1887) to describe its young heroine Bella as "a person of infinite freshness and beauty – a mind of flaming sensuality fanned by the accidental course of events into an active volcano of lust."[43] In *Lady Chatterley's Lover* Connie's pornographic desires have been cut from the text, but her submission to Mellors is still stressed; "His body was urgent against her and she hadn't the heart to fight anymore" (*LCL* 141). Mellors breaks the band of her underclothes in his aggressive haste (*LCL* 141).

Just as conventional pornography of the eighteenth, nineteenth, and twentieth centuries repeatedly features a sexual aggressor who wears down a woman's resistance until she submits, often by force, and then is converted into passion, so *Lady Chatterley's Lover*, in its war against the modern will, features Connie at her most passionate when she is sexually overcome by Mellors. The sexual aggressor turned adored lover, or the pleasurable rape, is central to the topography of pornography in the eighteenth, nineteenth, and twentieth centuries. To cite a few examples, in Cleland's *Fanny Hill* (1749) a young London prostitute, Harriet, tells the story of losing her virginity to a gentleman while she is herself passed out, coming to consciousness only to find him inside of her: "I had neither the power to cry out, nor the strength to disengage myself from his strenuous embraces, before, urging his point, he had forced his way completely and triumphed over my virginity." Afterwards Harriet describes herself as "melted into a softness that could refuse him nothing" and explains that she met her "young ravisher" frequently afterward.⁴⁴ The entire plot of *The Way of a Man With a Maid* (1908) revolves around the sexual aggressor turned adored lover. Jack abducts the woman who has scorned his attentions, Alice, and proceeds to violate her in all possible ways. She eventually succumbs to the physical passions he is able to rouse in her and they become paramours. Looking over the contraptions for her restraint in his apartment Jack "suddenly remembered that its assistance was no longer needed; it had done its duty faithfully; with its help I had stripped, tortured, and violated Alice – and today she was coming of her own free will to be fucked!"⁴⁵

In a more subdued fashion, *Lady Chatterley's Lover* mimics the initiation and conversion theme that is a staple of the pornographic genre. If Connie's "modern" will produces the disengaged sexual moment as seen above, her subsequent loss of will as provoked by her union with Mellors produces the scene that follows immediately after, where, having confessed that she cannot love Mellors, he takes her into his arms, and "She felt his penis risen against her with silent amazing force and assertion, and she let herself go to him" (*LCL* 186). Against her conscious will she succumbs to the sublime penis, a truly pornographic trope if ever there was one,⁴⁶ and is transported to a sexual scene representationally quite different from the former:

> And it seemed she was like the sea, nothing but dark waves rising and heaving, heaving with a great swell, so that slowly her whole darkness was in motion, and she was ocean rolling its dark dumb mass. Oh, and far down inside her the deeps parted and rolled asunder, in long, far-traveling billows, and ever, at the quick of her, the depths parted and rolled asunder, from the centre of soft plunging, as the plunger went deeper and deeper, touching lower, and she was deeper and deeper disclosed, and heavier the billows of her rolled away to some shore, uncovering her, and closer and closer plunged the palpable unknown, and further and further rolled the waves of herself away from herself, leaving her till suddenly, in a soft, shuddering convulsion, the quick of all her plasm was touched, she knew herself touched, the consummation was upon her, and she was gone. (*LCL* 187)

The sexual body is here disembodied in a metaphorical movement that seeks to move away from, rather than across, the body. Lawrence idealizes the sex act into unconscious essence, already a paradox by the impossibility of making something unconscious into an idea. As Anne Fernilough has noted, though he "never ceases to denounce idealism and 'the ideal', Lawrence constantly risks reifying the body into what is merely another transcendental category."⁴⁷

The orgasmic passage from *Lady Chatterley's Lover* ironically approximates the masturbation scene in the "Nausicaa" chapter of Joyce's *Ulysses*, the book Lawrence set out to "correct." Where Gerty MacDowell experiences an ascendance, "And she saw a long Roman candle going up over the trees, up, up . . . it went higher and higher . . . high, high, almost out of sight, and her face was suffused with a divine, entrancing blush," Connie simply goes down, deeper and deeper.[48] Lawrence's depiction of Connie's orgasm can be read as a correction of the cognitive solipsism of Gerty's and Bloom's sexual pleasures in Joyce's representation. Lawrence presents a "true" self located within the unconscious sexual body. What each scene shares, and where their link with pornography can be found, is in their stylistic repetition of words, whether up or down, in a mimetic drawing out of the body's movement toward climax. Yet clearly Lawrence associates Joyce's work with pornography, and in *John Thomas and Lady Jane* encodes the reading of *Ulysses* with the nineteenth-century discourse of masturbation. When Clifford asserts his pleasure in reading *Ulysses*, Connie remarks, "You said you were stimulated by *Ulysses*. But you were so drab and irritable later on, and it took all the work of the mines to get you out of it" (*JTLJ* 217). Coding Clifford's reaction with Victorian stereotypes of masturbation, the text suggests that reading *Ulysses* is akin to a physical and spiritual enervation.

Part of what Lawrence recoiled from in Joyce was the very formalism by which *Ulysses* promoted Kantian disinterest. As Fernilough puts it, "Lawrence never subscribed to the Kantian legacy of Romanticism which survived in the theory of significant form."[49] In *Lady Chatterley's Lover* Duncan Forbes's tubular art achieves a "certain kind of purity of form and tone," but "Mellors thought it was cruel and repellent" (*LCL* 310). Mellors sees in Forbes's art "self-pity and an awful lot of nervous self-opinion" (*LCL* 311) which characterizes Forbes's own self-serving interests. The aesthetic formalism privileged by Kant and manipulated in Joyce is in *Lady Chatterley's Lover* revealed as a form that thinly disguises the interests of the upper-middle classes.

Lady Chatterley's Lover tries to avoid the pornographic and the incitation of interested bodily readers through a demonstration of bodies that are themselves disinterested (their desire is not mentally generated). To do so, as I have argued, he must represent bodies in sexual play, necessarily approaching the images and tropes found in pornography. The similarities between Lawrence's novel and pornography are such that a reader acquainted with the pornographic genre would have seen in the novel many coded gestures identical to those of pornography.

Perhaps the most obvious assimilation to pornography comes in the form of the final novel's name. *Lady Chatterley's Lover* sounds like many a pornographic title. From *The Adventures of Lady Harpur* (1907) to *Lady Gay Spanker's Tales of Fun and Flagellation* (*c.* 1896) to *Lady Bumtickler's Revels* (*c.* 1890),[50] the eroticization of aristocratic ladies in pornography surged in the late nineteenth century and reached a peak around the turn of the century. Such adventures were often cross-class affairs where the ladies made liberal use of their servants, as in *Eveline* (1904), where the upper-class heroine returns from boarding school to seduce her footman, John. In a similar vein, the playful naming by Connie and Mellors of their genitals as the "Knight of the Burning Pestle" and the "Lady of the Red-Hot Mortar" (*LCL* 245) not only enacts a class leveling through the body, but re-enacts a tradition of bawdy literature that revels in sexually punning names, *Harlequin Prince Cherrytop and the Good Fairy Fairfuck* (1905) being one example.

One of the central scenes of *Lady Chatterley's Lover* that shares ground with the pornographic is Connie's initiation into anal sex. It is a final maidenhead which pornographic protagonists, male and female, at first feel shame and difficulty in having penetrated, but then grow to love.[51] In pornography, anal penetration is typically troped as a final frontier, the ultimate achievement in carnal sensation. Though Lawrence may have invoked this pornographic trope in order, like pornography, to violate cultural taboos for his own moral ends, the assimilation of pornography makes his success tentative. Tellingly, the text invokes colonialist discourse to describe Connie's experience; "she came to the very heart of the jungle of herself" (*LCL* 268). Colonialist discourse is an overdetermined system of tropes in pornography, highlighting a teleology of conquer-and-submit power struggles. When the text says that in allowing Mellors to "have his way and his will of her" Connie "had to be a passive, consenting thing, like a slave, a physical slave" (*LCL* 267), it evokes typical pornographic imagery in the power dynamic that is buttressed by colonial imagery, that of a slave. Much late nineteenth- and early twentieth-century pornography centers around a kind of physical slavery in its fascination with harems, rapes, and upper-class exploitation of the servant class. One of the ironies of the sodomy scene in *Lady Chatterley's Lover* is the list of validating sources Lawrence invokes to privilege anal sex, from Abélard and Héloïse to Greek vases. While throughout the novel the text has continued to strive to differentiate itself from pornography and that which is purely interested in sensual gratification or associated with high-cultural titillation, here the novel glamorizes all of the above. Reveling in "The refinements of passion and the extravagances of sensuality" the text exclaims, "What liars poets and everybody were! They made one think one wanted sentiment. When what one really wanted was this piercing, consuming, rather awful sensuality" (*LCL* 268). Lady Chatterley awakes rather gleefully to find that in her night of physical slavery her nightie has been split in two. At this point the novel most closely identifies itself with the pornographic, not necessarily by detail of description, indeed it is fairly discreet here, but rather in its delight in phallic power and its impulse toward sexual knowing. Connie is said to "learn" through the "phallic hunt of the man" (*LCL* 268).

As with almost all pornography, the phallus is the supreme instrument, the prized visual and sexual object nonpareil. Connie's reaction to Mellors's penis is in every way in keeping with those of pornography:

> "So proud!" she murmured, uneasy. "And so lordly! Now I know why men are so overbearing! But he's lovely, *really*. Like another being! A bit terrifying! But lovely really! And he comes to *me*! —" She caught her lower lip between her teeth in fear and excitement. (*LCL* 226)

> I could not, without pleasure, behold, and even venture to feel such a length, such a breadth of animated ivory! . . . [it was] perfectly well-turned and fashioned, the proud stiffness of which distended its skin . . . In short, it stood an object of terror and delight![52]   *Fanny Hill* (1748)

Surely Lawrence's description of Connie's response to the penis assimilates the pornographic. Indeed, so much of the text, even while morally setting itself as against the pornographic as a vehicle for mentally objectifying sensation, necessarily collapses into the pornographic because the language of the text itself contains always a trace of interest, the interests of the discourses from which it is derived. *Lady Chatterley's Lover*'s approximation of the pornographic raises again the question, what differentiates Lawrence's novel from other pornographic novels?

The answer resides in the reception of *Lady Chatterley's Lover*. To those inclined toward the formalist school, believing in form as itself the embodiment of disinterest and therefore that which disavows the interests of pornography, the novel is pornographic. For those who follow post-Darwinian sexological thought and see the body as itself disinterested, pursuing the representation of sexual bodies within a larger literary and moral discourse represents a "healthy realism" which points the way toward an aesthetic self-actualizing. Such a subject-formation reconciles the supposedly conflicting impulses of body and culture by aestheticizing and therefore bringing the body into the realm of culture.

One of Lawrence's earlier critics, Eliseo Vivas, wrote his critical study, *D. H. Lawrence: The Failure and Triumph of Art* (1960), from the formalist viewpoint. In the work, Vivas set out to distinguish which of Lawrence's novels successfully fall under the category of art. Reiterating a classical aesthetic notion he says, "What the poet gives us is what he brings up from the depths of his creative imagination, in the ideal isolation of his perfected form and informed substance."[53] A work "fails to function in the aesthetic mode when it arouses emotion or insinuates questions concerning matter of fact or value that prevent the intransitive contemplation that is the proper reaction to art as art."[54] For Vivas, there can be no overlap between a sexually explicit representation and art, and so he quibbles, "as for Lawrence's intention, he cannot claim that *Lady Chatterley* is intended to stimulate the reader erotically and claim also that the book is not obscene in the aesthetic sense," defining the obscene as "an aesthetic category" that "refers to the fact or alleged fact that the book cannot be read by a person in an attitude of intransitive attention, or in Bullough's terms, with proper aesthetic distance." [55] Vivas finds fault with Lawrence's attitude that he wants his novel to stimulate the "natural sex flow."

For Lawrence, however, and the readers who shared his ideas, the "desublimation" of the sexual impulse in art was thought necessary in order to tap dimensions of experience lying beyond the reach of conventional, epistemologically oriented society. Representing explicit sexuality participated in a dialectical process in which sexual ecstasy fulfilled the word's etymology and transported one outside or beyond culture. This ecstatic being-ness was then reconciled with the intellectual and moral – "cultural" – imperatives of the text in which it was inscribed. As the authors of *On Pornography* have suggested, Lawrence's "erotic writing is offered as a means of becoming open to the sensuous potentiality of the self, but the senses must in turn be brought into revitalising relation with the whole of one's experience."[56]

Lawrence's process is one of unknowing that demands a "bodily" knowing. This ideology is especially adhered to in the work of his contemporaries, who frequently translated what I am calling Lawrence's representations of being, or aesthetico-ontological awareness, into a form of self-knowledge. Frederick Carter, an acquaintance of Lawrence's who went on to write *D. H. Lawrence and the Body Mystical* (1932), was a fervent advocate of bodily knowing. Carter suggested that in looking for a "technique and a definite process whereby man might know himself" Lawrence had "to plunge the mind beneath the surface of conscious reactions and feel the responses of the lower organs."[57] That Lawrence was speaking to a newly formed field of subjects who themselves were ready to create in sex a reifying process of self-actualization can be seen in the number of people who responded positively to the text. Another contemporary of Lawrence's, Horace Gregory, makes the claim that "Just as the earlier book [*Sons and Lovers*] was to represent the case history of thousands of inarticulate young men, so *Lady C.* was to state a cause for millions who searched a solution of the world's problem through normal sex."[58]

Lawrence's most sympathetic critic in the twentieth century, F. R. Leavis, exposed his own self-regulating, post-sexological bias toward the writer in his assertion that "the insight, the wisdom, the revived and re-educated feeling for health that Lawrence brings are what, as our civilization goes, we desperately need."[59] Leavis's praise for Lawrence's "organic wholeness and vitality,"[60] while reflecting a formalist discourse, actually adhered to the school of self-knowledge tied to bodily health, "organic" suggesting that which is from the body. While Leavis fought Lawrence's battles on the field of form, seeking validation for him in Joyce's camp even as he decried Joyce as contrived, he persistently praised "that strong vital instinct of health"[61] as characteristic of Lawrence's work. Leavis's awareness of Lawrence's departure from traditional aesthetic form forced him to validate the novels as activating self-knowledge and therefore to be assessed only in so much as they performed a self-disciplining poetic introspection: "They are not always, everyone can see, achieved enough to be wholly impersonal works of art, containing within themselves the reasons why they are so and not otherwise, and leading one, for their significance, not back to the author, but into oneself and out into the world."[62] In Leavis's view, the literary public in the 1920s was emancipated from critical standards as the "educated public disintegrated."[63] Leavis's morally self-regulatory readings, as will be discussed at greater length in chapter five, provided a needed function in their didactic reconciliation of the sexual body with social-personal values. They marked a new era in aesthetic criticism, validating what the aesthetic in the tradition of Shaftesbury and Kant had tried to eliminate from the interaction more than a hundred years before: the body and its senses.

As Freudian theory became more commonly integrated into the field of academic criticism in the late 1950s, its concepts began to be taken as norms by which to judge the "realism" of writing. Graham Hough approved of *Lady Chatterley* on these grounds, and is one in a wave of critics who began to create a validating academic climate for sexual representation, noting "It is obvious that the nature and quality of sexual experience has a powerful influence on character and development. We cannot therefore deny that Lawrence has opened up a wide new territory to the novel by presenting openly what everyone knows in private and what everybody knows to be important."[64] It was that kind of judgment that not only authorized a space within bourgeois academia for Lawrence's sexual representations (however tenuous they may still be), but further allowed other writers such as Anaïs Nin, Henry Miller, Lawrence Durrell, and Norman Mailer, to name a few, to follow in Lawrence's wake and commit themselves to writing the sexual body into culture.[65]

Lawrence played a double game, writing the body into culture by attempting to write the body *against* culture. Lawrence expressed understanding that language functions as a medium of cultural consciousness, but nevertheless used language to try to create a new form of consciousness, one in which sexual representations and language could be assimilated to disinterest, community, health, and well-being. The language he used to do so, however, was tainted with the pornographic, that which was associated with interest, individualism, and social disruption. Lawrence effected the incorporation of pornographic vocabulary and actions into serious literature, high art, through attempting to reinscribe aesthetic disinterest as a mode of bodily being. He did this as an extension of the sexological project which equated such bodily being with health, origins, and truth. Rewritten into the bourgeois ideology of self-knowledge tempered with cultural value – the autonomously disciplined freedom of the social subject that was previously the aesthetic subject – sexual representations in the novel, high and low, have become in the twentieth century the norm.

5   Modernist criticism: the battle for
    culture and the accommodation of
    the obscene

In the late twentieth century, nobody is surprised
to encounter an explicit sex scene in a novel. Further, such a scene does not dis-
qualify the work in which it appears from being considered high art. The aesthetic legitimacy of explicit sexual representation that we in the late twentieth
century take for granted is a result not only of the appropriations of pornographic tropes and images by Beardsley, Joyce, and Lawrence into their works,
but, importantly, of modernist criticism's ability to shape our understanding of
art and literature such that its difference from pornography in both function and
form has been made less clear. As this chapter will explain, modernist literary
critics were pivotal in creating methods of approaching pornographic language
and images in high-art texts in such a way that mitigated and/or rationalized
those texts' ability to provoke the embodied response typical of pornography.

It has recently been claimed that modernist artists and critics defined themselves and the art they championed in opposition to mass culture.[1] In the wake of
these claims, a few scholars have attempted to show that central modernist figures
such as T. S. Eliot were in fact profoundly influenced by mass-cultural forms such
as jazz or the music hall.[2] The relationship between mass culture and modernist
criticism was more fluid and more complicated than has yet been recognized.
Though modernist critics I. A. Richards, F. R. Leavis, and T. S. Eliot publicly
disparaged the effects of the "sensational" media, this chapter will show that these
critics simultaneously appropriated the very techniques attributed to mass-
cultural consumption – shock and sensation – into their lexicon of high-cultural,
aesthetic values. In doing so, their modernist critique reversed the central project
of aesthetics in the tradition of Shaftesbury and Kant, the dominant aesthetic

practice of the late nineteenth and early twentieth centuries, to validate as fine arts only those that invoke disinterested contemplation rather than a sensuous interest on the part of a reader or viewer. Interestingly, however, modernist criticism furthered one aspect of this post-Renaissance aesthetic project: to bring the body and its senses more overtly into relation with the ethical and social realm. Modernist critics were concerned with educating bodies and the body politic into a state of "cultural health," the twentieth-century version of the civil society envisioned by the first theorists of aesthetic taste in the eighteenth century. The modernist criticism of Richards, Leavis, and Eliot advocated an aesthetic practice that made way for the representation of sensual bodies in art, in addition to a mode of aesthetic reception that included the sensual body as integral to forming aesthetic judgments. While making room for the body, modernist critics continued to promote the effort of the aesthetic in the tradition of Shaftesbury and Kant to objectify, rationalize, and make intelligible the body and its irrational sensuousness. Ironically, they did so by appropriating the very consumptive strategies that they accused mass culture of fostering.

Modernist criticism emerged in the early decades of the twentieth century as the first practical criticism of English literature produced from its new institutionalized status in the university. While the tradition of *belles-lettres* has been a long one, the professionalization of literary criticism as a discipline and its enfranchisement in the university is a relatively new development. Several universities developed programs in the late nineteenth century. Cambridge University's program, which dominated English literature studies through the middle decades of this century, did not truly gain momentum until after the First World War in the 1920s.[3] From this program, I. A. Richards, F. R. Leavis and William Empson, together with T. S. Eliot, established the intellectual basis that English literature studies followed in Britain (and its former colonies) throughout much of the twentieth century. Among these prominent critics, Leavis is generally recognized as the formative figure of the standards of university teaching in English.[4] Eliot, an honorary fellow of Magdalene College, was the only member of the group not to teach at Cambridge, having declined an offer from Richards to do so. He was, nevertheless, a celebrated force there, where he delivered the Clark lectures in 1926, and where his poetry and criticism were studied seriously with all the new zeal that Leavis's teaching could bring to it.[5] Leavis himself enjoyed a tenuous relationship with Cambridge, which for many years placed him on its fringes; while he characterized his own work as in opposition to the academic establishment, it is important to remember that by the 1950s, if not before, he was "the new establishment."[6]

The individual aims of Leavis, Richards, and Eliot, the three critics I will focus on in this chapter, were part of a larger project not only of making English literature a subject of serious study at university, but of making it the moral focus of a public debate about individual sensibility and the "health" of culture at large. The "problem" or "decline" of culture,[7] as they saw it, was imputed not just to the abundance of poor quality, mass-media entertainment which purportedly numbed its audiences into automatic response, but, more importantly, to the concomitant inability detected in the majority of the population to respond to the "real" works of culture. If mass culture was an encroaching illness that fostered "cheap mechanical responses"[8] and transformed its participants into senseless automatons, then "real" or "elite" or "minority" culture, as it was variously labeled by its champions, was mass culture's antidote.

Through the "direct shock of poetic intensity,"[9] in T. S. Eliot's words, "real" culture was thought to be able to revitalize not only the individual, but eventually the entire culture. Eliot's language is an important clue to the nature of the modernist critical agenda regarding mass culture. It reveals a rhetorical sleight of hand that makes possible the incorporation of certain mass-cultural forms into high art. By championing the "shock" to "sensibility" that could only be experienced by "true" or "high" culture, modernist critics appropriated the very labels that had been reserved previously for mass-cultural practices. Modernist criticism not only made a place for the bodily reader of cultural works in its notion of sensibility – by which it meant the connection between sensations, emotions, and cognition – but, in its use of the "invigorating shock" of real culture, it made a place for the very kind of aesthetic reception that had previously been attributed to readers of sensational thrillers or pornography.[10] Sensation and feeling, once the province of mass culture, became its antidote. Where in the aesthetic tradition of Shaftesbury and Kant physical sensation had no place in the "true" aesthetic interaction because of its particular appeal to an individual's own selfish interests, modernist criticism championed "organic sensation" as one of the most positive virtues of the sensitive reader. "Organic sensation" became a new sign of the authentic.

The acceptance of sensation under the rubric of the aesthetic opened the way for a positive revision of the place of a number of mass-cultural practices in high art, most notably the pornographic. The pornographic contains a set of assumptions about its own consumption which always involves an engagement or incitation of the body on the part of the reader or viewer. It explicitly advocates the mind–body connection that modernist critics championed through their notion of sensibility. Within dominant aesthetic practices, the shift from a disinterested

intellection, which rested on the removal of the body from the aesthetic interaction, to an aesthetic consumption, which included the body as an integral,
indeed foundational, part of the interaction, not only made way for pornographic representations in works that aspired to high-art status, but equally
informed the way in which those works would come to be read. Modernist critical reading practices began to incorporate mass-cultural patterns of response just
as modernist works themselves had appropriated the tropes and images of mass
culture, including pornography.

For Leavis, Richards, and even Eliot, the critical project of valuing and
responding to culture was one that promoted unity between citizens not on the
basis of certain class affiliations or external coincidences, but rather on the
understanding of their most intimate subjectivity, the emotions and thoughts
produced in response to aesthetic objects. To understand how these critics went
about trying to create this "unified sensibility" on the basis of appropriate
response to cultural phenomena, and how this in turn led to an accommodation
of the pornographic in literature, this chapter will examine their thoughts on
mass culture and aesthetic reception.

Mass culture

The defining impetus behind modernist criticism was that mass-produced forms
of cultural entertainment, such as fiction, radio and films, were destructive to
the quality of individual lives, and hence the fabric of society as a whole. In the
inherited tradition of Matthew Arnold's claims for the civilizing and spiritualiz-
ing effects of culture, the criticism of Richards, Eliot, and especially that of
Leavis, attempted to define a rationale for concretizing and preserving, as Pamela
McCallum has phrased it, "the ethical efficacy of cultural phenomena."[11] But in
order to claim that a specific body of cultural artifacts (e.g., the literary canon)
was central to the social whole, an argument had to be made against the forces
that appeared to endanger or work in opposition to this cultural body. Ethical
culture, as they saw it, was imperiled by mass culture in terms of both its production and consumption. The masses of printed novels, newspapers and magazines threatened to relegate "classic" English poetry and literature to the
margins of social interest, making relative the value of its production. In terms
of consumption, mass-cultural consumers were seen to demonstrate passive consumptive habits based on predictable sets of expectations. Defenders of high
culture saw that these patterns of consumption would have to be ameliorated in
order for high-cultural phenomena to be privileged.

Literary criticism of the 1920s and 1930s attempted to identify and attack mass-cultural incursions into the realm of culture through a rhetoric of high-cultural hysteria, punctuated quite clearly in the now famous *Scrutiny* manifesto of 1932, which not only declared that "the age is illiterate with periodicals" and that "the general dissolution of standards is commonplace," but indeed, in a mere empirical observation, noted "Many profess to believe (though fewer seem to care) that the end of Western civilization is in sight."[12] Part of the sky-is-falling frenzy was provoked by Eliot's influential notion of the "dissociation of sensibility" as expressed in his 1921 essay, "The Metaphysical Poets." Eliot's idea that "in the seventeenth century a dissociation of sensibility set in, from which we have never recovered" created a potent myth of the divided personality of both "the mind of England" and the individuals within it.[13] F. R. Leavis formed his own view of English literary and cultural history on Eliot's, and he supplemented Eliot's idea with his own notion that the Shakespearean era represented the last "organic society" England had known. Since then, according to Leavis, indus-trialized capitalism, or the "technologico-Benthamite society" as he called it, had begun to make irrevocable and regrettable changes to the previously whole fabric of English culture.

A striking factor in Eliot's chronological placement of the idea that thought and feeling, mind and body, had been rent asunder is, as other critics have noted, that he located the origin of this so-called modern crisis in the English Civil War period, thus associating it with the first articulations of opposed class-interest by popular revolt.[14] Part of the project of modernist criticism then, to reintegrate the body with the mind into one unified sensibility, should be read analogously as a desire for the reintegration of divided class sensibilities. Modernist works such as *Ulysses* or *Lady Chatterley's Lover,* which introduce sexually explicit bodies into their larger, multi-perspectived frameworks, enact this reintegration by setting the pornographic, or bodily, representations as incitations, into dialogue with the other discourses that enter the text. By allowing that which is perceived as a lower-class discourse into high art, a social reintegration of representational types occurs on the page, whether this bodily discourse is controlled by the "high-cultural" aesthetic techniques that deploy it, or it is subversive of the aesthetic it joins, or if it enacts a pluralist model of representation.

Eliot made the political function of this reintegration quite overt in his 1920 essay "Philip Massinger" where he wrote, "The Elizabethan morality was an important convention; important because it was not consciously of one social class alone, because it provided a framework for emotions to which all classes could respond, and it hindered no feeling. It was not hypocritical and it did not suppress."[15] The Elizabethan era provided a social and psychological model of "wholeness" and "integrated sensibility" for Eliot and Leavis, as well as for Q. D. Leavis, whose published thesis, *Fiction and the Reading Public* (1932), contributed to the hyperbolic tone of the mass-culture debate. Rhetorically maintaining the strict class boundaries that part of his project strove to overcome, F. R. Leavis remarked in an essay on Joyce that Shakespeare belonged "to a genuinely national culture, to a community in which it was possible for the theatre to appeal to the cultivated and the populace at the same time." Joyce's modernist literature, on the other hand, was "characteristic . . . of dissolution."[16]

Though Eliot's association of the body with this prelapsarian state of culture is only implicit, Leavis made his association more explicit through an appeal to philological authority. Describing the "popular basis of [Elizabethan] culture" as "agricultural," Leavis said that the philologist "Mr. Logan Pearsall Smith shows how much of the strength and subtlety of English idiom derives from an agricultural way of life." Quoting Smith he concluded that "when we examine these phrasal verbs, we find that by far the greater number of them also render their meanings in terms of bodily sensation. They are formed from simple verbs which express the act, notions, and attitudes of the body and its members."[17] To Leavis's mind a "whole" or "organic" society is one that expresses bodily sensation in language, or where language, body, and thought are so close as to be identical expressions of one another. Leavis equates language with culture, and therefore this ideal compression of body and language demonstrates not just a desire to integrate the stratified people of the social body into one culture, but also to experience one's own body more fully. The primary influence on Leavis's work was the author he championed throughout his life, D. H. Lawrence. Leavis advocated an aesthetic that validates Lawrence's writing, and ought to be recognized as having originated *in* Lawrence's work.

Eliot's and Leavis's paradigms of unified sensibility and the organic society worked toward creating a mode of aesthetic understanding that supports the works of modernist artists who incorporated mass-cultural tropes and images, most notably those of pornography, into their topoi. Though critical assessment of Eliot's and Leavis's concepts of a lost unity have tended to follow Raymond Williams's pronouncement of Leavis's version of history as "myth in the sense of conjecture . . . a surrender to a characteristically industrialist, or urban, nostalgia," these ideologies powerfully shaped a unified sense of loss and subsequently a purpose for culture, and especially for English literature studies.[18]

While the notion of the social and physical body's lost wholeness rallied conviction in the power of literature and culture to restore that loss, the degradations of mass culture were an equally potent galvanizing tool. Mass culture was framed as a contemporary enemy which, as a phenomenon, could not be defeated. Defense against this phenomenon, then, was devised as having to originate from within the subject, whose sophisticated reading and viewing practices could protect against mass culture's cheapening or deadening effects. Teaching readers how to respond appropriately to cultural material, or, in the context of the study of English literature, how to "read" poetry and novels, was believed to ensure that a specific kind of response toward the text in question would be formulated.

Modernist critics identified the problem of mass-cultural media as the low level of sensitivity and responsiveness required from its audience. In *Principles of Literary Criticism* (1925), Richards suggested that "At present, bad literature, bad art, the cinema, etc. are an influence of first importance in fixing immature and actually inapplicable attitudes to most things . . . Against these stock-responses the artist's internal and external conflicts are fought, and with them the popular writer's triumphs are made."[19] Q. D. Leavis, a pupil of Richards's at Cambridge who took his concepts as the foundational concepts of her own work, expanded his argument with the idea that writers of cheap, mass-produced fiction "work upon and solidify herd prejudice and . . . debase the emotional currency by touching grossly on fine issues." Further, they foster "cheap mechanical responses" to circumstances which ought, in her opinion, to be more finely discerned because "The training of the reader who spends his leisure in cinemas, looking through magazines and newspapers, [and] listening to jazz music, does not merely fail to help him, it prevents him from normal development partly by providing him with a set of habits inimical to mental effort."[20] To both Q. D. Leavis and Richards, mass culture was responsible for inculcating slothful patterns of aesthetic consumption.

These sentiments are echoed relentlessly throughout F. R. Leavis's critical writings. For example, in his pamphlet "Mass Civilisation and Minority Culture" he suggested that "When we consider, for instance, the processes of mass-production and standardisation in the form represented by the Press, it becomes obviously of sinister significance that they should be accompanied by a process of levelling-down." The concepts of mass-production and standardization apply "more disastrously" to films because, in Leavis's view, their influence is more potent; "they provide now the main form of recreation in the civilised world; and they involve surrender, under conditions of hypnotic receptivity, to the cheapest emotional appeals, appeals the more insidious because they are associated with a compellingly vivid illusion of actual life."[21] The characterizations above make clear that the typical consumer of mass culture in the 1920s and

1930s was understood to be an emotionally stunted, passive receptacle with an endless capacity to be filled with cheap, formulaic media. It was assumed that mass-cultural forms reproduced in their readers and viewers (in a mode thought non-dialogical) stock responses. According to modernist criticism, the mass-culture consumer was essentially the imprint of all he or she consumed.

Modernist critics located the class of the mass-culture consumer disparately, sometimes in the middle class, often in the working or lower classes. Factually, however, mass culture in its various forms was reaching into pockets of all classes. Eliot, in an essay on the music-hall entertainer Marie Lloyd, definitively placed the passive consumptive habits of mass culture within the middle class, which he saw as slowly absorbing all classes of society:

> With the decay of the music-hall, with the encroachment of the cheap and rapid-breeding cinema, the lower classes will tend to drop into the same state of protoplasm as the bourgeoisie. The working man who went to the music-hall and saw Marie Lloyd and joined in the chorus was himself performing part of the act; he was engaged in that collaboration of the audience with artist which is necessary in all art and most obviously in dramatic art. He will now go to the cinema, where his mind is lulled by continuous senseless music and continuous action too rapid for the brain to act upon, and will receive, without giving, in that same listless apathy with which the middle and upper classes regard any entertainment of the nature of art. He will also have lost some of his interest in life.[22]

What this essay and this passage show is that Eliot's notion of culture, unlike Leavis's and Richards's, is inclusive of a broad variety of social practices at every level of society. Indeed his later works, *The Idea of a Christian Society* and "Notes Toward the Definition of Culture," suggest that by culture he meant the spiritual fabric that pervades and motivates all social practices. Eliot's sentimentalizing of the working man's interactive aesthetic receptivity corroborates the notion of the Richardses and the Leavises that mass culture hypnotizes its audience into a state of pure receptivity.

Eliot's suggestion that all art is a necessary collaboration between audience and artist requiring mental effort contributed to the development of a dominant aesthetic mode in which "interest" is privileged. Q. D. Leavis shared Eliot's preference for aesthetic interactivity, even though her language coded a class bias which identified passive mass-cultural consumptive practices with the lower classes. As opposed to Eliot's, her concept of culture was more closely allied with literary culture and she romanticized a time when the majority of the population was illiterate and uneducated. At this time, according to her, the masses "did not complicate matters by creating a separate semi-literate public to interfere with the book market." The advantage of such a time was that "the rate of absorption of the lowest class into the middle class was slow enough to prevent any lowering of standards."[23] Not surprisingly, her ideal era for literary culture was the eighteenth century. This was a time, she averred, before capitalist industrialism thoroughly penetrated subject formation, and when the bourgeois sector of the public assimilated itself to the dominant aristocratic culture by adopting and mimicking aristocratic anti-materialist ideals. The coded language of the following assertion reveals her class biases:

> The difference between the popular novels of the eighteenth century and of the nineteenth is that the new fiction instead of requiring its readers to co-operate in a sophisticated entertainment discovers "the great heart of the public." Whereas Sterne's successors at any rate represent a cultivation of the emotions founded on a gentle code, Dickens stands primarily for a set of crude emotional exercises.[24]

The "gentle" or gentrified code which in organic cultural style is "cultivated" in the eighteenth century is replaced, in her mythology, by "crude," i.e. lower class, exploitation of the labile emotions through repetitive, as the word suggests, "exercises." Gentle and crude operate in her sentence as signifiers of the class differences characterizing the different reading publics of the eighteenth and nineteenth centuries. With the increased reading public of the nineteenth century, she suggests, arrived the formulaic machinations of mass-cultural literature. Q. D. Leavis implies that while the bawdiness of Sterne may have been all right for the eighteenth-century connoisseur of sensation, it was not all right for the masses.

More than other modernist critics, Q. D. Leavis fulfills Andreas Huyssen's suggestion that "to reduce all cultural criticism to the problem of quality is a symptom of the anxiety of contamination."[25] Q. D. Leavis demonstrates this anxiety when discussing the circulation of cheap fiction. Her response can be compared with those of Victorian cultural critics cited in chapter two who were anxious about the spread of literacy and pornography. Acknowledging that the popular taste in the 1930s was for "thrillers," she said:

> The reading habit is now often a form of drug habit. In suburban side-streets and even village shops it is common to find a stock of worn and greasy novels let out at 2d or 3d a volume; and it is surprising that a clientele drawn from the poorest class can afford to change the books several times a week, or even daily; but so strong is the reading habit that they do.[26]

Just as Victorian critics were apprehensive about the seemingly endless circulation of penny papers among the working classes, Q. D. Leavis reveals her anxiety about the circulation of cheap novels. More specifically, she exposes a curious disdain for the circulation of pleasure (for whatever the outcome of taking drugs, the impetus is always the pursuit of pleasure) among the lower classes which is continuous with a fear of contamination (note the description of the novels as "greasy") by the lower classes. The suburban location is significant in that it indicates a *rising* lower middle class, the class of clerks and typists that troubled so many reviewers of *Ulysses* and *The Yellow Book*.

While it is true that modernist criticism demonstrated a high level of anxiety with regard to the potential evils of mass-cultural contamination both of society at large and of high-cultural products, it is also true that no prior period of English literary criticism was as influenced by such a force. After various forms of mass culture, such as newspapers, penny novels, and pornography, gained popularity in the second half of the nineteenth century, their identification *as* mass culture became the effect of early twentieth-century artists' and writers' attempts to label and segregate those forms that had already begun to penetrate the sphere of dominant high culture. *Ulysses, Lady Chatterley's Lover*, and Beardsley's illustrations of *Salome* offer clear evidence of this fact in their incorporation of popular music, sentimental fiction, and pornography within frameworks which, as modernist critics would have us believe, are larger than the sum of their individual parts.

Eliot's and Q. D. Leavis's differing class assessment of mass-cultural consumptive practices aside, their terminology with regard to aesthetic reception accords. Mass-cultural consumers are "lulled" into "listless apathy" by a "set of crude emotional exercises" which take the form of a "drug habit." Conversely, consumers of "real" culture "co-operate" on a level with the artist. They engage in a "collaboration of the audience with artist," which participates in their "interest," sometimes at the level of shock. Strikingly, receptivity is reinscribed into an active role. Where prior to modernist criticism apprehension of cultural phenomena was described by "stasis" as opposed to motion and interest, in Eliot, Richards, and the Leavises such modes are positively described. As discussed in chapters one and two, motion and interest were behavioral and aesthetic patterns negatively associated by eighteenth-century proponents of taste and Victorian cultural defenders as incongruent with the disembodiment of the middle class and the aesthetic that emerged alongside it. Continuous with post-Kantian aesthetic practices, motion and interest were considered lower-class, or mass-cultural, strategies of aesthetic consumption, and were especially identified with pornography. Stephen Dedalus makes this point clear in *A Portrait of the Artist as a Young Man* when he mimics the aesthetic in the tradition of Shaftesbury and

Kant and classifies pornography as an improper art because, "Beauty expressed by the artist cannot awaken in us an emotion which is kinetic or a sensation which is purely physical. It awakens, or ought to awaken, or induces, or ought to induce, an esthetic stasis."[27]

In a gesture that shifted the emphases of post-Kantian aesthetics, modernist criticism appropriated mass-cultural consumptive strategies. The effect of such an appropriation dramatically shaped notions not simply of proper modes of aesthetic consumption, but in concert with this, of what constitutes an aesthetic experience. To phrase the transition in Kantian terminology, if the nineteenth century was the century of the beautiful, a time that favored an aesthetic mode of receptivity that set the mind into "restful contemplation," the twentieth century was the century, as Jean-François Lyotard has told us, of the sublime, favoring an aesthetic mode of receptivity that "sets the mind into motion."[28] Training for this specific mode of receptivity was the project of modernist criticism, as the following section will demonstrate.

The art of response/the response to art

The training of sensibility, or responsiveness to art, was I. A. Richards's primary project and his work in this aspect deeply informs the Leavises' critical aims. Richards took a moral stand with regard to aesthetic reception by declaring, "Bad taste and crude responses are not mere flaws in an otherwise admirable person. They are actually a root evil from which other defects follow. No life can be excellent in which the elementary responses are disorganised and confused."[29] Richards's statement provides the attendant argument to modernist criticism's vituperation of mass culture. If the crude and vulgar are defined by their dulled consumptive practices with regard to mass culture, so the refined, indeed the morally superior, are given shape through a keen receptivity and organized response to the conflicting impulses of genuine art. Art is that which possesses the capability of raising and organizing one's level of response.

If, through the onslaught of mass culture, art should disappear, Richards claimed "a *biological* calamity of the first order will have occurred . . . the raising of the standard of response is as immediate a problem as any, and the arts are the chief instrument by which it may be raised *or lowered*" (my italics).[30] To Richards, mass culture impaired one's ability to function at both the moral and biological level. Seven years later, the *Scrutiny* manifesto echoed Richards's sentiments and, in characteristically shrill address, declared that "there is a necessary relationship between the quality of the individual's response to art and his general fitness for a humane existence,"[31] "humane" in this instance working tautologically in cooperation with the quality of response as a way of redefining the socially elite, "polite" or "humane" studies. In the same issue of *Scrutiny* F. R. Leavis made his homage to Richards's teaching overt by stating that with regard to the literary mind, "the defect of intelligence is a default on the part of sensibility; a failure to keep closely enough in touch with responses to particular arrangements of words."[32] In order to avoid this defect "Everything must start from and be related to the training of sensibility, the kind of training of which Mr. Richards has been a pioneer."[33] To both Leavis and Richards, aesthetic consumption is a physical, emotional, and cognitive act, requiring the entirety of one's being, one's sensibility, to react.

For Eliot, sensibility is mostly psychological. Poetry, he remarked in *The Use of Poetry and the Use of Criticism*, " may make us from time to time a little more aware of the deeper unnamed feelings which form the substratum of our being, to which we rarely penetrate; for our lives are mostly a constant evasion of ourselves, and an evasion of the visible and sensible world."[34] Interestingly, Eliot suggests that poetry works on both a metaphysical and an empirical level, confronting readers with the realities of the sensible and psychological, or perhaps ontological, worlds they inhabit. The "self-realizing" capacity Eliot describes as enabled through accessing a high-cultural product like poetry was central to modernist criticism's ability to persuade a generation of readers of the value of a specific mode of "close" reading. Readers engaged texts in order to "know" themselves.

By applying specific reading practices to literature, readers engaged a process of cultural distinction. It was the process, modernist critics averred, that informed or gave shape to the subject, not the text itself. Reading oneself into distinction in the modernist critical method is a circular and self-confirming process. While the readerly stance masquerades as a form of complete receptivity, a psychological void awaiting cultural fulfillment, its very proactive stance with regard to that form of receptivity belies the nature of reading as an already-formed performance of selfhood, a set of attitudes brought to the text under the name of "receptivity." When Leavis declares that "The education of sensibility implied in my phrase, '"English" as a discipline of thought', aims at fostering the completest receptivity that can be attained," his concept of receptive openness is not in fact a specular emptiness, as consumers of mass culture are conceived, but rather a "disciplined" vessel of sensibility, the twentieth-century reconfiguration of Kantian "taste."[35] Where Kantian taste referred solely to the cognitive faculties, sensibility as described by modernist critics refers to the entire person.

"Sensibility," Leavis said, "is more complex in its ambiguity than 'taste'."[36] Conceived as a reader's full mental and sensual dialogic relation with a text, sensibility is supposedly "more complex" because it allows not only a fuller reciprocity between subject and object, but a more complete subject, whose aesthetic judgment is not confined to the cognitive faculties, but rather to a more complete "sensibility." This theory, however, enforces an absolute moral distinction between works of high and low literature, and privileges originality as that which can "shock," rather than "lull," a reader into fresh reception.

Modernist critics perceived a dialogic relation between text and reader, and in turn they began to incorporate shock and invigoration, the senses, into the consumptive practices of high-brow literature. Q. D. Leavis, for example, distinguished high from low by suggesting that readers of best-sellers "mistake the relief of meeting the expected, and being given the desired picture of life, for the exhilarating shock that a novel coming from the first-class fully aware mind gives." Further, she noted, "The peculiar property of a good novel . . . is the series of shocks it gives the reader's preconceptions . . . a configuration of special instances which serve as a test for our mental habits and show us the necessity of revising them."[37] Shock is configured as a positive experience, as that which sets the reader into dialogic engagement with the text. It is thus curious to note that shock in the sensation literature debate of the 1860s, or shock in the mass-culture debate of the 1920s and 1930s, was seen as the simple tool of emotional exploitation, as that which provokes a non-intellectual response.[38] Yet in high culture this invigoration of mental and emotional lassitude is a common rallying point in modernist critiques of the cultural dilemma, and only "real" cultural phenomena can arouse the mental acuity that accompanies shock.

In *A Survey of Modernist Poetry* (1927) Robert Graves and Laura Riding similarly advocated shock, or mental excitement, to their so-called "plain reader," or middle- and low-brow consumer, as a way of approaching modernist poetry. Acknowledging that the difficulty of modernist poetry seemed "to be only part of the game of high-brow baiting low-brow," Graves and Riding concluded that value in the difficult and abstruse poetry of the modern day could be found only if the plain reader would "admit that what is called our common intelligence is the mind in its least active state: that poetry obviously demands more vigorous imaginative effort than the plain reader has been willing to apply to it."[39] As is the message throughout modernist criticism, superior and "true" cultural media demands an interactive mental and physical response from its audience. "Real" culture postulates a full sensibility in all of its disciplined ambiguity. Importantly, the approach to cultural texts advocated by modernist critics differs little from

Modernist criticism

the approach to pornographic texts taken by readers of pornography, who engage their "bodily consciousness" or sensibility in a "disciplined" dialogue with the text in order to receive a specific, sexual form of invigoration from it. In emphasizing sensibility, the modernists were resolutely making a place for the body in cultural consumption, and as such were specifically going against the Shaftesburian and Kantian aesthetic ideal and the trend of more than one-hundred years of literary criticism. For it was Kant who tried to remove the body from the pure aesthetic interaction, separating the agreeable, that which could provoke a pleasurable sensation, from the beautiful, that which was a product of mind as opposed to body. In his third *Critique* Kant noted that "The universal communicability of a pleasure involves in its very concept that the pleasure is not one of enjoyment arising out of mere sensation, but must be one of reflection. Hence aesthetic art, as art which is beautiful, is one having for its standard the reflective judgement and not organic sensation."[40] Richards's aesthetic ideas overturn this notion, specifically in his insistence that "the Mind-Body problem is strictly speaking no problem," that mind and body react to stimuli in concert, and that a purely mental reaction is an impossibility. Directly speaking to this issue, Richards says:

> The identification of the mind with a part of the working of the nervous system, need involve, theology apart, no disturbance of anyone's attitude to the world, his fellow-men, or to himself . . .The nervous system is the means by which stimuli from the environment or from the body, result in appropriate behaviour. All mental events occur in the course of processes of adaptation, somewhere between a stimulus and a response.[41]

Richards's psychological training introduces into literary criticism the idea that the mind and body form one sensibility, and that the experience of literature is the experience of the sensibility in dialogue with the text. Much in line with D. H. Lawrence's thinking as exemplified in *Lady Chatterley's Lover*, Richards suggested that consciousness is formed in part by a physical consciousness. Richards claimed:

> The effects in the body of almost all stimuli of whatever nature are extraordinarily numerous and varied. A lump in the throat, a yearning in the bowels, horripilation, breathlessness, these are their coarser and more obvious forms. Usually they are less salient and fuse with the whole mass of internal sensations to form the *coenesthesia*, the whole bodily consciousness.[42]

Eliot echoed Richards's thinking (and simultaneously alluded to Joyce's elaborate bodily scheme for the chapters of *Ulysses*) in his notion that a writer of the modern age is without Sir Philip Sidney's prerogative to simply look into his heart and write, but rather "One must look into the cerebral cortex, the nervous system, and the digestive tracts."[43] Allowing the body to enter the reading (or writing) process was a technique already practiced by pornographic texts. Indeed, pornography and the sexual practice of reading or looking at pornography played a key role in the formation of the idea of a bodily consciousness in that pornography encouraged a reciprocity and cooperation between body and mind within the reading framework. The body's incorporation into high-cultural reading practices through the legitimating agency of medical psychology made way for the introduction of the pornographic into high art, the domain of the aesthetic. Through the principles of modernist critics, the boundaries between the pornographic and the aesthetic were loosened.

Richards explicitly positioned his ideal reading practice in opposition to Kantian principles. Attacking the notion of disinterest, he noted that a Kantian judgment of taste and "the special form as it is usually described – in terms of disinterestedness, detachment, distance, impersonality, subjective universality, and so forth – this form, I shall try to show later, is sometimes no more than a consequence of the incidence of experience, a condition or an effect of communication."[44] What Richards rejected is the notion that a peculiar aesthetic attitude leads to a peculiar aesthetic value, or a pure art value. Instead, he emphasized that value is found in the experience of aesthetic apprehension itself. Richards, as John Needham has suggested, wanted to defeat those who read poetry in search of an ideological message.[45] Instead his work implies that the "meaning" of a poem is what one goes through in reading it. The "realisation," as Richards termed it, produced by a complex use of language plays a moral part in the production of the reading experience, for what one is "realising" in the end is, just as Eliot's criticism implies, oneself.

It is through the self-realizing, or subject-forming, capacities of culture that modernist criticism further veered away from the aesthetic in the tradition of Shaftesbury and Kant. Instead of focusing on the "subjective universality" (to use Richards's characterization of the Kantian stance) of the aesthetic experience, Eliot, Richards, and F. R. Leavis each stressed the individual particularity of every aesthetic interaction. Where seeking a universal consensus was an important part of Kant's aesthetic, indeed one of the foundational reasons for his critique, universality comes in the modernist era to be associated with mass culture, and, as such, is viewed critically. In fact, for Eliot, good poetry was that which evoked feelings or a response which could *not* be universally communicated. This is an absolute reversal of Kantian aesthetic philosophy, whose very grounds for judgment relied on the communicability of such experiences in order that these encounters with aesthetic phenomena might promote rational community. The response of modernist critics to the seemingly universal appeal of mass culture was to privilege the particular and the individual. Paradoxically, these critics used the individualist capitalist ethic to fight what they saw as capitalist incursions into the soul. Leavis was a fierce defender of particularity and found in D. H. Lawrence a model for both writers and critics: "Without a sustained, tense and living relation with the concrete, with the particulars of experience," Leavis said, "the respectability and the erudition are barren. D. H. Lawrence had a genius for it, and his importance as a 'thinker' is that he could command the concrete by creative art."[46] As opposed to that which leads toward the universal, as in eighteenth-century aesthetic theories, Leavis indicates that the critical assessment, like the creative production, should lead to empirical particularity. Leavis's critical structure suggests that if the act of assessing art or literature is to be instrumental to self-realization, it must proliferate into sensuous and material particularity in order to fall into accord with the individualist ethic of consumer capitalism. Reading becomes as constitutive of individual identity as buying a car, and not so differentiated an act of appropriation. "Judgement" is reconfigured in Leavis from the Kantian norm as "a matter of abstraction," to that which "involves particular immediate acts of choice," and this choice is dependent on the "free and delicate receptivity to fresh experience," that forms one's sensibility.[47]

Sensibility was apotheosized by modernist criticism into a replacement for the famous Kantian concept that a genuine aesthetic interaction should lead to the "free play of reason."[48] Leavis declared instead that aesthetic apprehension should lead to "the free play of sensibility."[49] The valorization of sensibility in the early years of the twentieth century was important to the relationship between the aesthetic and the pornographic in that the "free play of sensibility" at the very least integrates mind and body, allowing the body to participate in valid aesthetic response. More rigorously applided it accommodates, perhaps even mimics, the kind of bodily incitation as interrogation provoked by the pornographic. The modernist mode of aesthetic apprehension is a consumptive practice, epitomized in Leavis's quite famous notion that the critic's task

is to enter into possession of the given poem (let us say) in its concrete fullness, and his constant concern is never to lose his completeness of possession, but rather to increase it. In making value-judgements (and judgements as to significance), implicitly or explicitly, he does so out of that completeness of possession and with that fullness of response.[50]

Leavis's critical approach, a model of appropriation and consumption, is, like Richards's, a "reductive hermeneutic wherein human consciousness moves towards its own completion through the mere possession of a cultural object."[51] Modernist criticism demonstrates not only its complicity in accommodating the acquisitive practices of modernist literature in its appropriation of pornographic tropes and images, but also a mirror image of that impulse. The appropriative impulse is one of the defining characteristics of both modernist literature, in its incorporation of mass-cultural works including pornography into an aesthetico-moral framework, and of modernist criticism, in its notion that the reader literally incorporates his reading into his morally evaluative person. The pornographic or physical impulses of the mass-cultural consumer are acknowl-edged by modernist criticism only to be subsumed into its larger, ethical scheme. In ways that will become clearer in the final section of this chapter, modernist critics acknowledged the body and the sexual in literature in order to preclude the pornographic.

Distanced readings

Modernist criticism quite significantly evokes, and/or mimics, the forms it eval-uated. This becomes particularly clear in Eliot's and Richards's similar concepts of irony and complexity. Richards's theory of irony and disinterest is one of the centerpieces of his literary theory, and is evocative of the very techniques used by James Joyce and Aubrey Beardsley in incorporating explicit sexual represen-tations into their works. Richards's theory begins with the concept that every reader is the subject of certain impulses triggered in response to the stimuli gen-erated by whatever he or she is reading.[52] Irony orders those impulses in such a way that they provide their own system of checks and balances. "Irony," Richards said, "consists in the bringing in of the opposite, the complementary impulses."[53] In poetry of the highest order, Richards claimed, "the most obvious feature is the heterogeneity of the distinguishable impulses" which are "more than hetero-geneous, they are opposed."[54] This opposition is necessary to a moral and phys-ical sense of balance, which was described by Richards as *disinterest*, a response brought about most effectively through the oppositional impulses of irony:

> The equilibrium of opposed impulses, which we suspect to be the ground-plan of the most valuable aesthetic responses, brings into play far more of our personality than is possible in experiences of a more defined emotion. We cease to be oriented in one direction; more facets of the mind are exposed and, what is the same thing, more aspects of things are able to affect us. To respond, not through one narrow channel of

interest, but simultaneously and coherently through many, is to be *disinterested* in the only sense of the word which concerns us here. A state of mind which is not disinterested is one which sees things only from one standpoint or under one aspect. At the same time since more of our personality is engaged the independence and individuality of other things becomes greater. We seem to see "all round them", to see them as they really are; we see them apart from any one particular interest which they may have for us. Of course without some interest we should not see them at all, but the less any one particular interest is indispensable, the more *detached* our attitude becomes. And to say that we are *impersonal* is merely a curious way of saying that our personality is more *completely* involved.[55]

In this passage Richards helps to more fully articulate the self-actuating principles behind Arnold's dictum to "see the object as in itself it really is."

Interestingly, Richards's theory advocates that any impulse toward action experienced by a reader be stifled by competing impulses so that the reader remain in a state of engaged but immobile detachment. As he, C. K. Ogden, and James Wood stated in *The Foundations of Aesthetics* (1925), superabundance of expression "produces an equilibrium of impulses, which prevents the fundamental tendency from breaking forth into overt action."[56] In that most of his work appeared between the two World Wars, Richards's concern for preventing the canalization of interest and any subsequent selfish action can be seen to enact a political analogy. Richards himself made that analogy clear in references throughout his works to the political events of his time. The need for an ironic equilibration of impulses was given stronger impetus by the reminder that "The extent to which reference is interfered with by needs and desires is underestimated even by those who, not having yet forgotten the events of 1914–1918, are most skeptical as to the independence of opinions and desires. Even the most ordinary and familiar objects are perceived as it pleases us to perceive them rather than as they are."[57] And so in *Science and Poetry* (1925) he suggested:

> Our impulses must have some order, some organization, or we do not live ten minutes without disaster. In the past, Tradition, a kind of Treaty of Versailles assigning frontiers and spheres of influence to the different interests, and based chiefly upon conquests, ordered our lives in a moderately satisfactory manner. But Tradition is weakening. Moral authorities are not as well backed by the beliefs as they were; their sanctions are declining in force. We are in need of something to take the place of the old order. Not in need of a new balance of power, a new arrangement of conquests, but of a League of Nations for the moral ordering of impulses; a new order based on conciliation, not on attempted suppression.[58]

Like many of the eighteenth-century philosophies of taste or the aesthetic, this model is alert to the dangers of one's individual self-controlling or self-starting impulses. Art offers a neutralization of these impulses by putting them into a complex network of competitive relationships so that any selfish, impulsive action that might endanger the whole is preempted. This passage clearly reveals the social and political ideals at stake in Richards's notion of irony and complexity. His emphasis on the ironic equilibrium of contending forces provides a model, as Steven Connor has noted, "not only of the well-adjusted person, but also of the well-balanced [and certainly capitalist] liberal state."[59] The balancing of pluralistic impulses creates an irony that Linda Hutcheon describes as used to set up "an egalitarian, indeed, democratizing tension between emotions and even meanings."[60] I would further argue that it is under this notion of conflicting impulses that Beardsley and Joyce became practitioners of an aesthetic of the obscene.

As I showed in chapter three, both Joyce and Beardsley ironically juxtaposed pornographic tropes and images with high-cultural tropes and images, and by doing so defused the potential "interest" or "impulse" that a pornographic representation is designed to arouse. The kind of disinterest fostered is precisely the kind defined above by Richards, the saturation of competing interests, or discourses, so that no one discourse, or impulse, is privileged. Richards's description of the "economy" of great art describes Joyce's style: "Superabundance is a common characteristic of great art, much less dangerous than the preciousness that too contrived an economy tends to produce."[61] *Ulysses* is nothing if not a superabundance of multiple discourses, and it is the very variety of material presented (much of it typically associated with low-cultural forms) that ensures that it transgresses many of the typical boundaries of high literature. Richards's quote again draws attention to the political and social arena, and suggests what Adorno would later say in *Aesthetic Theory*, that "the dialectic of art resembles the social dialectic without consciously imitating it."[62]

If Richards's ideal art rendered the social dialectic as an abundant economy tempered through a rendering of ironic impulses, then what kind of social dialectic can *Ulysses* be said to represent? On the one hand, *Ulysses* contains greater representation than most high-cultural works before it. On the other hand, the text represents greater manipulation of those representations, a virtuoso performance of aesthetic control. Linda Hutcheon suggests that all irony has an evaluative edge that challenges the material ironized. Irony creates a triangulated structure between the author, the reader, and the target of irony. Hutcheon says, "There is an affective 'charge' to irony that cannot be ignored and that cannot be separated from its politics of use if it is to account for the range of emotional response (from anger to delight) and the various degrees of proximity (from distanced detachment to passionate engagement)."[63] To apply

Hutcheon's understanding of irony to *Ulysses* is to suggest that the novel embodies a political struggle for control that makes the deployment of pornographic tropes a demonstration of dominant, or high-cultural, control over such tropes. Molly's soliloquy, in which the pornographic is juxtaposed with other competing discourses in a very formlessness that is an aggressive assertion of form, could be said to exemplify such an irony. In this reading the body (politic) is given order and shape by a higher, more dominant force.

Alternatively, however, post-structuralist readings of the novel have focused on the inability to fix meaning at any single point in the text. For instance, Stephen Heath has suggested that "What is in question in Joyce's writing is not the proclamation of irony or ridicule against the model imitated, but a copying that fixes no point of irony between model and imitation, that rests, in this respect, in a hesitation of meaning."[64] The model suggested by this reading is a leveling of representational modes so that no one mode is prioritized over another. The possibility of reading *Ulysses* in this way was exactly what generated F. R. Leavis's panicky distaste for Joyce's "chaotic" work. Heath's reading supports Frederic Jameson's idea that in postmodern representations all parody loses its critical edge and melts into pastiche.[65] In this approach, *Ulysses* is but one text in the continuum of proliferating mass culture. All cultural forms become generated by repetition, and meaning is supposedly stifled altogether by its inability to lodge in any one space.

I have hesitated between these two readings – the incorporation of the pornographic as a mode of aesthetic control and the incorporation of the pornographic as a leveling of all representational modes – throughout this work under the supposition that both models are contingent on the institutional practices used to decipher the novels or illustrations. Neither explanation is, on its own, entirely sufficient. Meaning is always formulated in relation to a set of institutional practices, and the practices that these works helped to trigger were not the ones in place at the time of their first reading. From our turn-of-the-twenty-first century viewpoint it is easy to overlook the foreignness with which sexual representations would have emerged onto the pages of high art.

The ability of meaning to occupy any space successfully, however (even if only temporarily), can be demonstrated in T. S. Eliot's legendary influence over the way generations of readers approached *Ulysses* in the twentieth century. Though he never focused specifically on irony, Eliot shared Richards's views that art holds complexity in tense balance. In an editorial in *Criterion* that echoes Richards's statements on disinterest above, Eliot remarked that artistic and/or critical consciousness composes the flux of disparate experience into an ordered unity which forms what he called "the classical moment of stasis."[66] In his essay on Marvell he came closest to Richards's theories with the idea that wit "involves, probably, a recognition, implicit in the expression of every experience, of other kinds of experience which are possible." Further, wit demonstrates "internal equilibrium," an "equipoise, and proportion of tones," and in the style of Coleridge's imagination, "reveals itself in the balance or reconcilement of opposite or discordant qualities."[67] Finding order in apparent discord, as in Richards's work, is the defining impetus behind Eliot's work, critical and creative. While Eliot highly valued work that is heterogeneous (e.g., "The Metaphysical Poets"), allusive, and reflective of the complexity of modern experience, he equally valued that such heterogeneity should be "compelled into unity by the operation of the poet's mind."[68] Thus while in an early reference to *Ulysses* he approved that Joyce "uses allusions suddenly and with great speed, part of the effect being the extent of the vista opened to the imagination by the lightest touch," he showed several years later that he more greatly valued the order given to those suddenly contrasted associations.[69]

Eliot's famous essay, "*Ulysses*, Order and Myth" (1923) in which he proclaimed "I hold this book to be the most important expression which the present age has found," has had a profound impact on both the book's acceptance into the literary canon and the way it has been read.[70] Dismissing the potential influence on readers by the obscene representations in *Ulysses* as "an irrelevance," Eliot chose to abandon even his own theories of literary self-realization in order to focus on and champion the aesthetic techniques of the novel, as if the two notions were completely unrelated. Indeed they are related, and as I have tried to argue throughout this work, aesthetic style is as socially denominative as content. Eliot's assessment of *Ulysses* reveals his bias that the kind of social model the text deploys is not one of democratized ambiguity, but of high-cultural ordering. The novel's manipulation of a parallel between contemporaneity and antiquity is, according to Eliot, "simply a way of controlling, of ordering, of giving a shape and a significance to the immense panorama of futility and anarchy which is contemporary history."[71] To Eliot, the aesthetic technique of *Ulysses* is a mode of social and physical ordering, and that order is intentionally imposed. To contrast this model with Richards's is to see the specific difference between equipoise and order. Each offers a potential way to interpret *Ulysses*'s appropriative impulses. Richards's model appears to allow for pluralistic representation, but the impulses (or impulsive people, as it were) must be kept stultifyingly stimulated so as not to allow any one impulse to break away. Eliot's model potentially obscures or distorts entire constituencies in order to give shape to a specific idea.

Modernist criticism

The sexual representations in *The Waste Land* are an example of Eliot's use of order. More than Joyce, Eliot's incorporation of sexual representations into his poetry (while not containing the pornographic explicitness of Joyce's or Lawrence's work, the poem is still representational of sexual actions) is an example of manipulating such representations in order to control them. It is significant in his case that the sexual representations in *The Waste Land* only take place among the degraded working class, the typist and clerk or the soldier's wife. Representations of the lower and working classes, and of the body, then, achieve representation in Eliot's high-cultural work, but only in a presentation that is clearly controlling, evaluative, and ironic. *The Waste Land*'s sexualized working-class characters are the subjects of loathing. There is a political evaluation attached to such representations. In Adorno's words, "the unresolved antagonisms of reality reappear in art in the guise of immanent problems of artistic form."[72] Eliot's ironic ordering, as other critics have pointed out, is the result of an impulse against mass or popular culture, and his instinct is to incorporate it into his works in order to control and survey it under the auspices of high-cultural order.[73] Reading his own motives into Joyce's work, he applauded the potential of form to structure the amorphous masses. Students of *Ulysses* have attributed this ordering impulse to Joyce's work since the publication of Eliot's influential essay, but it is important to realize that this reading may have been generated out of Eliot's own interests. To read *Ulysses* through Eliot's essay is to see the incorporation of pornographic tropes as a mode of social control whereby the body (politic) is made visible in order to be subjected to increased high-cultural control. Eliot's reading perpetuates the aesthetic in the tradition of Shaftesbury and Kant in that the discursive exposure of the body as controlled form in high art is but a continuation of its distancing and objectification.

In contrast with Eliot and Richards, F. R. Leavis did not favor irony. He distrusted it on the basis that it "suggests a lack of seriousness or intensity towards oneself or one's subject matter."[74] Instead of seeking an equilibrium based on complex and competing impulses as arranged by the author, Leavis looked for a unity based on the consciousness of the author. In his critique of *The Waste Land*, he approved of the "rich disorganization" of the poem on the basis that "The unity the poem aims at is that of an inclusive consciousness."[75] That consciousness, Leavis admitted, is an elite one. "The poem in any case exists," Leavis said, "and can exist, only for an extremely limited public equipped with special knowledge." The limited audience of *The Waste Land* is a symptom, Leavis argued, "of the state of culture that produced the poem. Works expressing the finest consciousness of the age in which the word 'high-brow' has become current are almost inevitably such as to appeal only to a tiny minority."[76]

A small minority of educated thinkers was central to Leavis's solution to what he saw as the social problems of his day. The elite, he said, had a duty to work toward "controlling the machine" of modern, capitalist society.[77] He conceived that the minority could be cultivated in the universities and take responsibility for "the implicit standards that order the finer living of an age."[78] Demonstrating the will to order that he shared with Eliot, Leavis defined the university as the center of a "unified sensibility" that could fight against "the machine." This "unified sensibility" would in turn provide an ordering center to society as a whole:

> There can be no control [of the machine] without (to revert to the metaphors of "organism" and "mind") a higher coordination. An urgent necessary work, consequently, is to explore the means of bringing the various kinds of specialist knowledge and training into effective relation with informed general intelligence, humane culture, social conscience and political will. Indicated here we have the function that is pre-eminently the university's.[79]

Through his notion of controlling centers, whether it be the human psyche controlling and integrating sensible consciousness, or the university acting as the controlling center of the sensibility of a civilization (two allegorical models of the mind–body paradigm), Leavis championed writers whose works demonstrate the complexity of the modern situation in a resolute order. This is perhaps one of the primary reasons why Leavis so fervently endorsed D. H. Lawrence's work throughout his career. Lawrence's work, according to Leavis, "is an immense body of living creation in which a supreme vital intelligence is the creative spirit – a spirit informed by an almost infallible sense for health and sanity."[80] The language of this statement recreates the same political paradigm used in his philosophy of the university's role in society. The vital intelligence, or the minority, university-educated culture, is responsible for ordering and giving shape to the "immense body of living creation" that is the masses. In Leavis's model the entire organism, or social body, is represented, but only under the ordering force of the "supreme vital intelligence," minority culture. Leavis's principles were fully informed by Lawrence's, and each distrusted the abstractions of intelligence. Thus by "vital" Leavis means to imply intelligence's debt to the entire organism, their interconnectedness.

Leavis's sensuously empirical approach to literature (what Terry Eagleton has called "*Scrutiny*'s naive sensuous empiricism"), his idea that criticism is a matter of "sensibility, of responding sensitively and with precise discrimination to the words on the page,"[81] accords with Lawrence's work in that this sensuous empiricism is given ontological status. Through his work with Lawrence's texts,

Leavis came to privilege being over knowing, and from this fulminated his zeal-ously anti-theoretical attitude. Stressing the empirically concrete, Leavis praised in Lawrence that "His gift lay, not in thinking, but in experiencing, and in fixing and evoking in words the feelings and perceptions that seemed to him the most significant. Lawrence's commentary on experience, his doctrine, must be approached by way of the concrete, the successful art."[82] Leavis, too, shied away from the abstract or ideological in favor of the concrete. Yet as Terry Eagleton has noted, "To combat 'ideology,' *Scrutiny* pointed to 'experience' – as though that, precisely, were not ideology's homeland."[83] Leavis attempted to avoid the ideological by focusing on the particular and the concrete. He nevertheless advocated aesthetic excursions into the concrete through the con-cepts of health and vitality that were eventually to become as self-confirming as any ideology. Leavis's approach, like Richards's, was a synthesized amalgam of idealism and empiricism in which, as Pamela McCallum points out, "The inherent contradictions converge in the difficulty of comprehending a living interrelatedness through a hybrid form which is polarized, on the one side, towards the observation of crude facticity or the content of empirical reality and, on the other side, towards the atemporal conceptualisation of human capacities."[84] This contradiction is borne throughout Leavis's work, and is in many ways indicative of the powerful hold over his thinking which Lawrence's work exercised.

The "vital" and "organic" originality of Lawrence's work was contrasted by Leavis to "the contrivances of Joyce," whose "insistent will and ingenuity"[85] created a literature in which "the spurious, mechanical manipulation is perva-sive," and the "cosmopolitan" (i.e., non-agriculturally based and therefore corrupt) project is "so far from promising a revival of cultural health, [it] is (it does not need Lawrence's nostril to detect) a characteristic symptom of dissolu-tion."[86] Leavis consistently privileged Lawrence's work over Joyce's as an example of the moral and social health he thought it was the critic's duty to safeguard.

All three critics believed that literature and its proper criticism contributed to "cultural health," and it is the definition of what "health" is that enabled each to develop his literary theory. To Richards, "The critic is as closely occupied with the health of the mind as the doctor with the health of the body . . . the healthi-est mind is that capable of securing the greatest amount of value."[87] His concern was rooted in his psychological training, and his method was to keep the mind so actively engaged through disparate impulses that it stimulated and subse-quently stultified all bodily consciousness. Richards's ideas made way for an appreciative reading of *Ulysses* under the rubric of high-cultural, bourgeois academic approval. As I have shown above, *Ulysses* enacts, perhaps even informs, the very model Richards offers of an aesthetic object that provokes equilibrium and disinterest. While literary critics of the period were not looking at Beardsley's work, I would similarly argue that his work falls under the province of provoking disinterest through a multiply channeled series of competing discourses and high-cultural, stylistic control. Like Joyce's work, it provokes the bodily consciousness even while it works to displace it. The physical arousal of a viewer is deferred or displaced both by the competing impulses as manifest in the content of the text as well as by the aesthetic stylization which continually prevents the representations of sexual bodies from assimilating the pornographic.

Richards's role in making such an aesthetic of the obscene culturally dominant was not in openly advocating the authors of such writing, as both Leavis and Eliot did in championing Lawrence and Joyce respectively, but rather in making a way for readers of such an aesthetic to reconcile a bodily reading with competing intellectual and moral impulses. Richards's immense influence over literary studies in the first half of the twentieth century contributed to the development of a reading technique that allowed for the complex body–mind dialectic of the aesthetic of the obscene, in part because it made a claim for the naturalness of such a reading practice through a biological universality. According to Richards, readers had always read that way. The success of explicit sexual representations in literature with aspirations to high-art status has depended in large part on texts' effectiveness in reconciling differing sexual, intellectual, and social impulses. The works of Beardsley, Joyce, and Lawrence each participate in this process. It was Richards's theoretical work, though he did not write at length on Beardsley, Joyce, or Lawrence, that convinced readers, and especially university-trained readers, of this criterion, which was in turn used to validate such representations.

Eliot's notion of cultural health, as displayed most prominently in his concept of the "dissociation of sensibility," was focused in part on divided class sensibilities. In "Notes Toward a Definition of Culture" he said that "class itself possesses a function, that of maintaining that part of the total culture of the society which pertains to that class. We have only to keep in mind, that in a healthy society this maintenance of a particular level of culture is to the benefit not merely of the class which maintains it, but of the society as a whole."[88] Under what might be called the "separate but equal" policy, Eliot suggested that each class has its own individual culture which contributes to the "healthy society." This separateness is the result of a split Eliot placed in the beginning of the middle class's rise to dominance after the English Civil War. He observed,

What I see, in the history of English poetry, is not so much daemonic possession as the splitting up of personality. If we say that one of these partial personalities may develop in the national mind is that which manifested itself in the period between Dryden and Johnson, then what we have to do is to re-integrate it: otherwise we are likely to get only successive alternation of personality.[89]

The reintegration, Eliot's criticism intimated, had to be brought about through the amalgamation of disparate experience – physical, intellectual, and social – through which a "unified sensibility" could be reconciled. Part of this reintegration, then, lay in reconciling disparate class aesthetics.

The modernist aesthetic which subsumes the pornographic, with its integration of low-cultural, pornographic representations into higher-cultural discourses of varying intellectual, social, and moral import, enacts the process Eliot described. It allows the mythologized "whole" social personality/body to be represented. One aspect of Eliot's approval and life-long critical endorsement of Joyce is the high profile given to order in *Ulysses*. As I stated above, one interpretation of this reading is to see Joyce's appropriation of pornographic tropes not as a pluralistically motivated mode of increasing aesthetic representation, but rather as a method of increasing control over socially subversive forms by introducing them into the dominant cultural order where they could more easily be surveyed and controlled. That Eliot was a strong proponent of sensibility in reading – that is, of the part played by the body and emotions in the reading process – is a signal both of the effect that pornographic and mass-cultural reading practices had on high-cultural practices, as well as a determining factor in the continuing validation of the reading experience as in keeping with those practices.

As with other modernist critics, Eliot was both created by and participated in creating a platform for the subsumption of the pornographic into the aesthetic. The circular process of literary criticism gained particular momentum in the first half of the twentieth century, however, as university study of English became not just a standard but a strong part of the university, and, hence, the middle-class establishment. Just as literature itself received a central place in the university, even as it was being marginalized by culture at large, so criticism began to enjoy a powerful, if imaginary, relationship to the literature it critiqued in that it was a discipline in which all university students could be trained. By the 1950s and 1960s, the education of aesthetic reception was so widespread that the medical and legal regulation of obscenity that dominated the century from the 1850s to the 1950s began to be dismantled in favor of trusting a reader's own personal ability to judge and handle an explicit sexual representation. The Obscene

Publications Act of 1959 revised English obscenity law to say that "publication of the article in question is justified as being for the public good on the ground that it is in the interests of science, literature, art or learning, or of other objects of general concern."[90] The admissibility of literary merit as part of the criteria for obscenity marked a revolutionary shift in the boundaries between pornography and art in the United Kingdom, a shift quickly mirrored in the United States. This was in large part due to the successes of literary critics and literature programs in the universities to make a bodily reading part of an ethical exploration as opposed to a simple sexual, physical exploration.

Leavis played a key role in identifying a reader's sensibility, or bodily consciousness, with ethical exploration. "Literary criticism," Leavis said, "enters overtly into questions of emotional hygiene and moral value – more generally (there seems no adequate phrase) of spiritual health."[91] He focused his concern for cultural health on the ability of individuals to respond keenly and fully to the representations of literature. In distinct opposition to the model of aesthetic interaction of Shaftesbury and Kant in which the body is marginalized, Leavis believed a reader's aesthetic reception ought to include a "full-bodied response." The reader must embody, or take into the body, the text. As Leavis said, "Words in poetry invite us, not to 'think about' and judge but to 'feel into' or 'become' – to realize a complex experience that is given in words. They demand, not merely a fuller-bodied response, but a completer responsiveness."[92] This reading practice, which incorporates the body into the reader's imaginative reflections, is little different from the bodily interrogation as incitation that is the practice of the reader of pornography. The body, and a bodily response, is a necessary constituent of the modern reading practice.

To avoid a purely pornographic reading, then, the body had to be attached to a greater ethical project. That project was both the equation of sex with health (a project that Leavis claimed to reject, but in which he nevertheless participated)[93] and the reconciliation of the body with the intellectual, moral, and social aspects of existence. The body was incorporated into cultural phenomena in such a way that increased its visibility, but also rendered its pure physicality less powerful by mediating it through other faculties. The creation of a "unified sensibility" by modernist critics worked toward the integration of faculties that included, but mediated, the body, while extending this project to as many members of society as possible.

The modernist critical project worked toward class leveling through the idea that the development of the sensible faculties through classic, difficult literature was a project worthy of all sectors of society. In fact, as the century has progressed Leavis's role in the establishment of institutionalized literary studies has erroneously led to a view of him as a conservative elitist. To those in the early and middle decades of the last century, his critical approach was quite liberating. As Peter Miles and Malcolm Smith have commented, "To, for example, the university-educated grammar school product of mid-century Britain Leavis meant the possibility of participation in authority through a route which seemed dependent on mind and sensibility rather than class, inheritance or institutional background."[94] Leavis was involved in the development of a mode of cultural distinction independent of the traditional routes of the nineteenth century, and again, part of that cultural distinction was based on the ability of individuals to organize a new relation to themselves, one which required them to identify, differentiate, intensify, and harmonize the sensuous and the moral-reflective faculties.[95]

Novels such as *Lady Chatterley's Lover* and *Ulysses*, and works of art such as Beardsley's, underscore a process of aesthetic reception and representation that gained tremendous ground in the twentieth century. The body entered art, and quite specifically literary art. The fact that the works studied in this book contain explicit sexual representations simply makes the incorporation of the body into artistic representational and reception practices more obvious. While Leavis eventually withdrew his support for *Lady Chatterley's Lover*, calling it a bad novel after it was vindicated in the renowned Penguin trial of the 1960s, his earlier criticism went a long way toward creating an aesthetic and moral justification for it.[96] Just as Leavis made a forceful case for Lawrence's work, and for a type of aesthetic apprehension that accommodated the aesthetic of the obscene, so Eliot forged a path for Joyce's work, and for a mode of aesthetic structuring which should house explicit sexual representations within a larger framework. The role that the institutionalization and professionalization of literary criticism within the university played in establishing both a forum for such works to be read as well as a legitimating tool for the methods by which they should be read should not be underestimated. The pedagogical use of sexually explicit literature disseminated, in the words of Hunter, Saunders, and Williamson, "an aesthetic capacity to make sexuality central to the supervised construction of personal identity."[97]

In looking at the trajectory of the two novels that most boldly introduced an aesthetic of the obscene into high-cultural – or as it primarily has become in this century, bourgeois academic – discourse, *Ulysses* and *Lady Chatterley's Lover*, it is interesting to note that while *Ulysses* has had greater currency within the universities, where *Lady Chatterley's Lover* is rarely taught, Lawrence's novel is more widely read outside of the university, distinctly because of its reputation *as* pornography. Both novels could be said to be equally pornographic in the sense that they position the reader as a voyeur to their representations of explicitly sexualized bodies engaged in sexual acts, and engage relatively equal amounts of historically accurate pornographic tropes and images. Joyce's more conservative method of appropriative parody introduced the pornographic to readers in a way that allowed them to feel mentally and socially superior to the representations, and therefore less threatened by them. In contrast, Lawrence's work evaluated not the subjects of his novel so much as its readers. His alignment of sexuality with health, and with a new social order based on bodies as disinterested bearers of an unconstrained freedom, challenged his readers to agree. While these ideas experienced their efflorescence in the 1960s, helping to popularize Lawrence's work, much of what Lawrence fought against in the novel – the complete industrialization and penetration of capital into individual lives – has materialized. A good part of his battle has been lost. The test of his work in the future will be whether or not it can survive the passing vogue of its own ideas.

Though differing in approach, both works established landmarks in the literary consciousness of this century. Perhaps the greatest measure of such a mark can be found in simply browsing the fiction on the shelves of any bookstore. It is rare to find a book nowadays that does not incorporate some form of sexual representation into its pages. It is equally rare to find a reader who does not expect, or perhaps even want, to find it there. This incorporation is part of a literary tradition forged from the works that followed Joyce's and Lawrence's, perhaps including, but not exclusively derived from, the pornography to which modern artists were almost wholly indebted. Explicit sexual representations in literature have become naturalized into readers' expectations about aesthetic experience. Twentieth-century writers have continued to explore their discursive limits, not only testing the relationship between the sensuous and the moral-reflective faculties, but incorporating ideas and images from such a variety of sources that, as is characteristic of the art we have labeled "postmodern," "the line between high art and commercial forms seems increasingly difficult to draw."[98]

Today's readers have, perhaps unknowingly, adopted reading strategies that were in the nineteenth, and even the beginning of the twentieth, century attributed to mass-cultural and pornographic reading practices: they have learned to read with their bodies. This is due in part to the work of the omnipresent but subterranean pornographic discourse since its emergence in the eighteenth century. Readers of pornography were the first to expose their bodies to a personal interrogation as incitation, a dialogue with their own bodily consciousness, even as Kant was writing against the admissibility of the body into any "true" or "pure" aesthetic interaction. That pornographic reading and representational practices made their way into high-cultural modernist literature and criticism in the late nineteenth and early twentieth centuries is a tribute both to pornography's ability to exert pressure on high-cultural aesthetic practices, and to modernist writers' and critics' ability to appropriate such practices in a way that subsumed them within, or at least reconciled them to, high culture.

Just as the lines between pornography and aesthetics were softened and redistributed in the twentieth century, collapsing many of the distinctions set up between them in the eighteenth century, so the lines between mass and high culture became blurred. Due in part to the efforts of modernist criticism and the project of English literature studies in the twentieth century, the site of social accountability was transferred from the realm of production to the realm of consumption, from texts to their readers and viewers. The project of literary studies is now rooted in the ironic belief that if we know how to read, then what we read cannot affect us. Pornography, in a paradox that asserts a complicated victory for Kantian aesthetics in its effort to translate sensations into cognitions, is regarded as merely a state of mind, a reading practice.

Notes

1 Civil society: aesthetics and pornography in the eighteenth century

1 T. W. Adorno, *Aesthetic Theory*, trans. C. Lenhardt (London: Routledge & Kegan Paul, 1984) 16.

2 An argument for the derealization of the body in the modern period is forcefully made in Francis Barker, *The Tremulous Private Body: Essays on Subjection* (New York: Methuen, 1984).

3 To speak of the senses in terms of sublimation is to accept Freud's premise that there is in fact an "instinctual energy" that is refined and/or displaced into socially acceptable patterns. Pornographic practices, in this sense, seem to me to be not so much a de-sublimation as an alternate sublimation, an alternate way of channeling one's energy. Viewed by some segments of society as a socially unacceptable act, reading pornography is nevertheless a socially channeled act. The pornographic and the aesthetic together suggest that the senses can only exist in relative states of sublimation, as they can only manifest themselves in social outlets, never in the Darwinian myth of "instinctual" form.

4 Geoffrey Robertson, *Obscenity: An Account of Censorship Laws and their Enforcement in England and Wales* (London: Weidenfeld & Nicolson, 1979) 15–19.

5 Quoted in Donald Thomas, *A Long Time Burning* (New York: Frederick A. Praeger, 1969) 15–16.

6 I use the word technology to indicate that pornography was considered a practical, as opposed to a liberal, art with deliberate aims. Though the shift toward empirical thinking began in the work of René Descartes (1596–1650), I am primarily referring to the writings of John Locke (1632–1704), whose *Essay Concerning Human Understanding* (1690) marked a watershed in empirical philosophy. The invention of pornography is overdetermined, and many have conjectured about the forces behind

it. In *Sexual Underworlds of the Enlightenment* (Chapel Hill: University of North Carolina Press, 1988), the editors, G. S. Rousseau and Roy Porter, suggest that Linnaeus's highly influential taxonomy created a narrative of the fundamental sexuality of all living beings that was furthered by Erasmus Darwin's evolutionary theories which "enshrined sexuality as the fundamental agent of progress, order and happiness in the universe" (1). Margaret C. Jacob in "The Materialist World of Pornography," *The Invention of Pornography: Obscenity and the Origins of Modernity, 1500–1800*, ed. Lynn Hunt (New York: Zone Books, 1993) argues that pornography was enabled by the new materialist sciences of the seventeenth and eighteenth centuries that mechanized and atomized nature. "Materialism," Jacob claims, "is the logical outcome when nature is abstractly mechanized and bodies in motion are made wholly sufficient, encapsulated by the experimental gaze of the natural philosophers. When that logic could not be readily perceived, or was vehemently resisted, a large and generally clandestine literature emerged, much of it pornographic, that drew the inevitable pornographic conclusion" (161).

7 Hunt, "Introduction," *The Invention of Pornography*, 10.

8 Pepys's diary entries about the purchase and use of *L'Ecole des filles* reveal the deep sense of shame attached to reading such works. His quick disposal of the work suggests a pattern of behavior that makes it difficult to reconstruct accurately the field of pornography throughout the centuries. On February 8, 1668 he wrote, "Thence away to the Strand, to my booksellers, and there stayed an hour and bought that idle, roguish book which I have bought in plain binding (avoiding the buying of it better bound) because I resolve, as soon as I have read it, to burn it, that it may not stand in the list of books, nor among them, to disgrace them if it should be found." *The Diary of Samuel Pepys*, ed. Robert Latham and William Matthews, vol. ix (Berkeley: University of California Press, 1976) 57–58. On February 9, 1668 he read the work: "We sang till almost night, and drank my good store of wine, and then they parted and I to my chamber, where I did read through *L'escholle des Filles*; a lewd book, but what doth me no wrong to read for information sake (but it did hazer my prick para stand all the while, and una vez descharger); and after I had done it, I burned it, that it might not be among my books to my shame; and so at night to supper and to bed" (59).

9 David Foxon, *Libertine Literature in England, 1660–1745* (London: The Book Collector, 1964) 48.

10 Thomas, *A Long Time Burning*, 22–23.

11 See Hunt, "Introduction," *The Invention of Pornography*, 30.

12 Foxon, *Libertine Literature in England*, 48.

13 Joan DeJean, in her argument "The Politics of Pornography: *L'Ecole des Filles*," *The Invention of Pornography*, 109–123, develops this claim in relation to French pornography in the seventeenth century.

14 The bawdy works of the Earl of Rochester, while not constituting pornography, *per*

se, do demonstrate the ways that works of an explicit sexual nature can collapse boundaries between private and public. For instance, lines from *Sodom* (1684) (quoted in Thomas, *A Long Time Burning*, 24), spoken by Bolloxinian, the king, demonstrate the shriveling of that abstract concept, the king's body, into sensuous particularity:

> Thus in the zenith of my lust I reign;
> I eat to swive, and swive to eat again;
> Let other monarchs, who their sceptres bear
> Keep their subjects less in love than fear
> Be slaves to crowns, my nation shall be free;
> My pintle only shall my sceptre be,
> My laws shall act more pleasure than command,
> And with my prick I'll govern the land.

15 For a history of the naming of pornography in the nineteenth century, see Walter Kendrick, *The Secret Museum: Pornography in Modern Culture* (New York: Viking, 1987) ch. 1. For more on eighteenth-century sexual literature see Foxon, *Libertine Literature in England*; *The Invention of Pornography*; G. S. Rousseau and Roy Porter, *Sexual Worlds of the Enlightenment* (Chapel Hill: University of North Carolina Press, 1988); and Roy Porter and Lesley Hall, *The Facts of Life: The Creation of Sexual Knowledge in Britain, 1650–1950* (New Haven: Yale University Press, 1995).

16 *The Adventures of Lady Harpur: Her Life of Free Enjoyment and Ecstatic Love Adventures*, vol. 1 (Glasgow [sic]: William Murray, 1894) 1.

17 See Steven Marcus, *The Other Victorians* (New York: Basic Books, 1964) 208, 240, 279–280.

18 Michel Foucault, *The History of Sexuality*, vol. 1 (New York: Vintage Books, 1978) 20. Foucault, of course, positions this move toward self-examination as originating out of Catholic confession and the injunction to inspect one's sensations and desires minutely so that all traces of guilty sensuality may be related to the priest-confessor. The Anglican church does not participate in this ritual and so the move towards sexual self-interrogation must be seen as participating in a broader cultural shift. In terms of English cultural history, Foucault becomes more convincing in suggesting that the success of sexual medicine in making health understood in sexual terms was central to the interest in the very sensations, thoughts, acts, and desires it sought to regulate in the nineteenth and twentieth centuries.

19 Quoted in Thomas, *A Long Time Burning*, 335.

20 John Cleland, *Fanny Hill, or Memoirs of a Woman of Pleasure* (London: Penguin Books, 1995) 40–42.

21 Quoted in Thomas, *A Long Time Burning*, 336.

22 The *OED* was behind society in observing the use of terms about masturbation. Roy Porter and Lesley Hall in *The Facts of Life: The Creation of Sexual Knowledge in Britain, 1650–1950* claim that such works as the anonymously written *Onania* (1710) and

Tissot's *Onanism* (1760) articulated the concept to a public concerned about the spread of self-abuse (96). Porter and Hall also note that "the special feature of masturbation is that it was a sex act portrayed in the advice and warning literature as entirely pernicious – a vice doubly dangerous as it could be so easily savoured in secret with the aid of nothing but a lurid imagination and perhaps some stimulus material" (96).

23 Marcus makes the claim in *The Other Victorians* that pornography came into "full meaningful existence" in the latter part of the eighteenth century (282). In her introduction to *The Invention of Pornography*, Lynn Hunt suggests that "If we take pornography to be the explicit depiction of sexual organs and sexual practices with the aim of arousing sexual feelings, then pornography was almost always an adjunct to something else until the middle or end of the eighteenth century" (9–10). As a term, pornography came into widespread use in the nineteenth century. Its development as a genre is thus critically placed at the turn of the nineteenth century, the period we call Romantic.

24 Quoted in Thomas, *A Long Time Burning*, 345.

25 See David Loth, *The Erotic in Literature* (London: Secker & Warburg, 1961) 94–100. Though Loth maintains that Griffiths earned £10,000 for publishing *Fanny Hill*, David Foxon suggests that such information may be exaggerated myth. See David Foxon, *Libertine Literature in England, 1660–1745*, 48–49.

26 I am not suggesting that pornography shared the same distribution as popular novels or periodicals. It had its own discrete mode of distribution. That all forms were produced in increasing numbers and sold to private citizens, however, is evidence of an autonomous market's emergence in the eighteenth century and its concomitant proliferation of niche markets.

27 Donatien-Alphonse de Sade, *The 120 Days of Sodom*, trans. Austryn Wainhouse and Richard Seaver (New York: Grove Press, 1966) 271.

28 See Howard Caygill, *Art of Judgement* (Oxford: Basil Blackwell, 1989) 100–101.

29 See Linda Dowling, *The Vulgarization of Art: The Victorians and Aesthetic Democracy* (Charlottesville: University Press of Virginia, 1996).

30 John Barrell, *The Birth of Pandora and the Division of Knowledge* (Philadelphia: University of Pennsylvania Press, 1992) 52, 63.

31 See Preben Mortensen, *Art in the Social Order: The Making of the Modern Conception of Art* (Albany: State University Press of New York, 1997) 71.

32 Anthony Ashley Cooper, the third Earl of Shaftesbury, *Characteristics of Men, Manners, Opinions, Times*, vol. II (Hampshire, England: Gregg International Publishers, 1968) 425. Shaftesbury's analogy between the aesthetic and social order inaugurates, as John Guillory claims in *Cultural Capital: The Problem of Literary Canon Formation* (University of Chicago Press, 1993), "a major topos of moral philosophy, variously developed by Hutcheson, Kames, Burke, and others" (305). Howard

Caygill, in *Art of Judgement* also asserts that "The theory of civil society was haunted by the problem of taste" (37). Caygill develops the broad connections between theories of civil society and European aesthetic philosophy up to Kant throughout his work.

33 Dowling, *The Vulgarization of Art*, 2.

34 Immanuel Kant, *The Critique of Judgment*, trans. James Creed Meredith (Oxford: Clarendon Press, 1991) 68. Henceforth all citations from this text will be referred to as *CJ*.

35 *Weekly Register* (February 6, 1731). Reprinted in Bernard Denvir, *The Eighteenth Century: Art, Design, Society, 1689–1789* (Essex: Longman Group Limited, 1983) 63.

36 Also in the *Weekly Register* article by Shaftesbury is a comment on the work necessary to acquire taste: "Taste is a peculiar relish for an agreeable object, by judiciously distinguishing its beauties; is founded on truth, or verisimilitude at least, and is acquired by toil and study, which is the reason so few are possessed of it." *Weekly Register* (February 6, 1731). Reprinted in Denvir, *The Eighteenth Century*, 63.

37 Quoted in Denvir, *The Eighteenth Century*, 70.

38 Ronald Paulson, *The Beautiful, the Novel, and the Strange: Aesthetics and Heterodoxy* (Baltimore: Johns Hopkins University Press, 1996) 6.

39 See Ernst Cassirer, *The Philosophy of Enlightenment*, trans. Fritz C. A. Koelln and James Pettgrove (Princeton University Press, 1951) 315.

40 Three particularly good accounts of this relationship can be found in Lawrence E. Klein's *Shaftesbury and the Culture of Politeness* (Cambridge University Press, 1994), John Barrell's *The Birth of Pandora and the Division of Knowledge* (Philadelphia: University of Pennsylvania Press, 1992) and Preben Mortensen's *Art in the Social Order: The Making of the Modern Conception of Art* (Albany: State University of New York Press, 1997).

41 Barrell, *The Birth of Pandora and the Division of Knowledge*, 41–42.

42 Quoted in ibid., 47.

43 Shaftesbury, *Characteristics*, vol. I, 129.

44 Shaftesbury discusses this most thoroughly in "An Essay on the Freedom of Wit and Humour," ibid., vol. 4, 64–143.

45 Klein, *Shaftesbury and the Culture of Politeness*, 63.

46 Shaftesbury, *Characteristics*, vol. II, 128.

47 Caygill, *Art of Judgement*, 43.

48 Shaftesbury, *Characteristics*, vol. I, 332.

49 Quoted in Thomas, *A Long Time Burning*, 345.

50 William Hogarth, *Analysis of Beauty*, ed. Ronald Paulson (New Haven: Yale University Press, 1996) 18.

51 Francis Hutcheson, *An Inquiry into the Original of our Ideas of Beauty and Virtue* (Hampshire, England: Gregg International Publishers, 1969) 94.

52 Ronald Paulson, "Introduction," *Analysis of Beauty*, xxiii.

53 Ibid., xi.

54 Monroe Beardsley, *Aesthetics: From Classical Greece to the Present* (University of Alabama, 1966) 192.

55 Guillory, *Cultural Capital*, 307.

56 Quoted in Caygill, *Art of Judgement*, 65.

57 Joseph Addison, "Taste and the Pleasures of the Imagination," *Critical Essays from the Spectator*, ed. Donald F. Bond (New York: Oxford University Press, 1970) 177. Despite a similar motive for developing a theory of aesthetics, Addison's aesthetics more closely resembles Hogarth's than Shaftesbury's. As Paulson has described in *The Beautiful, the Novel, and the Strange*, Addison's spectatorship could not be called "beautiful" in the Shaftesburian sense. Addison identifies the "Pleasures of the Imagination" with the sense of sight, one of the perceived lower faculties. Hogarth also privileges the sense of sight.

58 Katharine Everett Gilbert and Helmut Kuhn, *A History of Esthetics* (New York: Macmillan & Co., 1939) 248.

59 Caygill, *Art of Judgement*, 98; in a footnote, Caygill also claims that Kant knew all of the eighteenth-century British philosophers of taste in translation, 406, n.14. Also see Ernst Cassirer, *The Philosophy of the Enlightenment*, trans. Fritz C. A. Koelln and James Pettgrove (Princeton University Press, 1951), Frances Ferguson, *Solitude and the Sublime: Romanticism and Individuation* (New York: Routledge, 1992) and R. L. Brett, *The Third Earl of Shaftesbury: A Study in Eighteenth Century Literary Theory* (New York: Hutchinson's University Library, 1951).

60 Ferguson, *Solitude and the Sublime*, 6.

61 Three different accounts of these differences can be found in Caygill's *Art of Judgement*, Mortensen's *Art in the Social Order*, and Martha Woodmansee, *The Author, Art, and the Market* (New York: Columbia University Press, 1994).

62 Two particularly good accounts of this movement can be found in Guillory's *Cultural Capital* and Woodmansee's *The Author, Art, and the Market*.

63 Caygill, *Art of Judgement*, 42.

64 Paul de Man, "Phenomenality and Materiality in Kant," *Aesthetic Ideology*, ed. Andrzej Warminski (Minneapolis: University of Minnesota Press, 1996) 83.

65 Kant sees gratification as rooted in the body and comments that "perhaps Epicurus was not wide of the mark when he said that at bottom all gratification is bodily sensation" (*CJ* 197). The pleasure formed in the estimate of beauty, however, depends on reason and expresses "the conformity of the object to the cognitive faculties brought into play in the reflective judgement" (*CJ* 30).

66 Cassirer, *The Philosophy of the Enlightenment*, 326.

67 Shaftesbury is often cited as the originator of the concept of disinterest, and his views on it are expounded in "The Moralists," *Characteristics*, vol. II. Hutcheson,

Shaftesbury's disciple, agreed with him that the perception of beauty must be divorced from any personal utility or desire, claiming in the *Inquiry* that "Our Sense of Beauty from Objects, by which they are constituted good to us, is very distinct from our Desire of them when they are thus constituted" (12).

68 Shaftesbury, *Characteristics*, vol. II, 404.

69 Paulson, *The Beautiful, the Novel, and the Strange*, 4–5.

70 Guillory, *Cultural Capital*, 313.

71 Pierre Bourdieu, *Distinction: A Social Critique of the Judgement of Taste*, trans. Richard Nice (Cambridge: Harvard University Press, 1984) 5.

72 Jürgen Habermas, *The Structural Transformation of the Public Sphere*, trans. Thomas Burger (Cambridge: MIT Press, 1992) 168.

73 Joseph Addison, *The Spectator*, no. 1 (March 1, 1711).

74 This idea is developed more fully in Peter Stallybrass and Allon White, *The Politics and Poetics of Transgression* (Ithaca: Cornell University Press, 1986). See especially pp. 27–80.

75 Joseph Addison, *Critical Essays from the Spectator*, ed. Donald F. Bond (New York: Oxford University Press, 1970) 177.

76 Bourdieu, *Distinction*, 490.

77 See Ferguson on Adorno and Kant, *Solitude and the Sublime*, 63–64.

78 Jean-Luc Nancy, "The Sublime Offering," *Of the Sublime: Presence in Question*, trans. Jeffrey S. Librett (Albany: State University of New York, 1993) 31.

79 Bourdieu, *Distinction*, 491.

80 In the nineteenth century pornography does enact its own mode of cultural distinction, as is discussed in chapter two.

81 While this would seem to strike a note of difference from British empirical philosophers of taste, their conclusions are strikingly similar. Hutcheson (*An Inquiry Concerning Beauty, Order, Harmony and Design*, 1725) and Burke (*A Philosophical Inquiry into the Origin of our Ideas of the Sublime and Beautiful*, 1757) are the most "Lockean" in their prioritization of sensation (Addison's "Pleasures of the Imagination" also works in the Lockean tradition). Burke even presaged twentieth-century aesthetics in his suggestion that the explanation of aesthetic enjoyment is to be sought on the physiological level (see Monroe C. Beardsley, *Aesthetics: From Classical Greece to Present* [University of Alabama Press, 1966] 196). Despite starting from the senses, however, the British empiricists almost invariably invoked providence as being responsible for their workings. Even the skeptic Hume concluded that the standard of taste is fixed by God (see David Hume, "Of the Standard of Taste," *David Hume Essays: Moral, Political, and Literary*, ed. Eugene F. Miller [Indianapolis: Liberty Classics, 1985]). Where Kant diverged from these thinkers is most obviously in the displacement of divine law onto reason.

82 An earlier example can be found in Shaftesbury, who writes "there is nothing so

divine as beauty, which belonging not to body, nor having any principle or existence except in mind or reason, is alone discovered and acquired by this diviner part, when it inspects itself, the only object worth of itself" (*Characteristics*, vol. II, 260).

83 Georg Wilhelm Friedrich Hegel, *The Philosophy of Fine Art*, trans. F. P. B. Osmaston, in *Philosophies of Art and Beauty*, ed. Albert Hofstadter and Richard Kuhns (University of Chicago Press, 1964) 383. Henceforth all citations in text will be referred to as *PFA*.

84 Terry Eagleton, *The Ideology of the Aesthetic* (Oxford: Blackwell UK, 1990) 158.

85 Arthur Schopenhauer, *The World as Will and Idea*, trans. R. B. Haldane and J. Kemp, in Hofstadter and Kuhns, *Philosophies of Art and Beauty*, 457.

86 Ibid., 462.

87 Ibid., 476.

88 René Wellek, *Immanuel Kant in England, 1793–1838* (Princeton University Press, 1931) 260–261.

89 W. David Shaw, *The Lucid Veil: Poetic Truth in the Victorian Age* (Madison: University of Wisconsin Press, 1987) 26, 129–135, 130, 138, 161–168, 209, 235–236.

90 Karl Marx, *Marx and Engels on Art and Literature*, ed. Lee Baxandall and Stefan Morawski (St. Louis: Telos Press, 1973) 52.

91 Ibid., 51.

92 Karl Marx, *Economic and Philosophical Manuscripts*, in *Karl Marx: Early Writings* (London: Harmondsworth, 1975) 355.

93 Eagleton, *The Ideology of the Aesthetic*, 201.

94 Friedrich Nietzsche, *Beyond Good and Evil*, trans. Walter Kaufmann (New York: Vintage, 1989) 17.

95 Ibid., 11.

96 Quoted in Luc Ferry, *The Invention of Taste in the Democratic Age*, trans. Robert de Loaiza (University of Chicago Press, 1993) 175.

97 Leo Bersani, *The Freudian Body* (New York: Columbia University Press, 1986) 4.

98 Sigmund Freud, *The Ego and the Id*, trans. Joan Riviere, ed. James Strachey (New York: W. W. Norton & Company, 1969) 4–5.

99 Ibid., n. 20.

100 Sigmund Freud, *Civilization and its Discontents*, trans. and ed. James Strachey (New York: W. W. Norton & Co., 1961) 33. Also of interest, Freud goes on to say that "the genitals themselves, the sight of which is always exciting, are, nevertheless hardly ever judged to be beautiful, the quality of beauty seems, instead, to attach to certain secondary sexual characters" (34).

101 Just as their revolution was more dramatic than the English, so French literature, beginning with the Marquis de Sade and continuing through the works of Jean Genet and Georges Bataille, developed a more radical aesthetic of the obscene throughout the nineteenth and early twentieth century. Two works that take into account the French tradition and compare it with the relatively tame one in English

are Peter Michelson, *Speaking the Unspeakable* (Buffalo: State University Press, 1993), and Susan Sontag, "The Pornographic Imagination," in *Styles of Radical Will* (New York: Doubleday, 1969).

102 See Lynda Nead, "'Above the Pulp-line': The Cultural Significance of Erotic Art," *Dirty Looks: Women Pornography Power*, ed. Pamela Church Gibson and Roma Gibson (London: BFI Publishing, 1993) 146.

103 Ibid., 146.

2. *Victorian obscenities: the new reading public, pornography, and Swinburne's sexual aesthetic*

1 See Edmund Gosse, *The Life of Algernon Charles Swinburne* (New York: The Macmillan Co., 1917) 134–140.

2 Ibid., 147.

3 *Swinburne: The Critical Heritage*, ed. Clyde K. Hyder (New York: Barnes & Noble, 1970) 24.

4 Gosse, *The Life of Algernon Charles Swinburne*, 150.

5 Donald Thomas, *Swinburne: The Poet in his World* (New York: Oxford University Press, 1979) 114.

6 Ibid., 114.

7 Hotten's books number frequently among the pornographic bibliographies of Henry Spencer, Lord Ashbee. There is clear evidence that he was actively publishing pornography when he took on Swinburne's poems. Cecil Y. Lang, in his introduction to *The Swinburne Letters* (New Haven: Yale University Press, 1959), also suggests that before his death in 1873, Hotten blackmailed Swinburne for some pornographic work they did together: "It is obvious . . . that Swinburne cooperated (*collaborated* might be a more precise word) with Hotten in the issue of certain books from which both publisher and poet seemed to have derived both satisfaction and income – *Flagellation* and *Romance of the Rod* are two named by Swinburne" (xlvii). Swinburne is known to have enjoyed the literature of flagellation. He wrote several long poems about school-boy floggings, both for the *Whippingham Papers* and *The Pearl*. He characteristically signed the poems "By an Etoniensis."

8 While it is common to attribute these changes to the Elementary Education Act of 1870, which broadened school attendance within the working classes, it is clear that changes throughout the century led up to what in the last two decades of the century amounted to near universal literacy in England and Wales. Throughout the century, via religious bodies, charity schools, Sunday schools, and some National schools, the rudiments of elementary education were being administered in small doses to men and women of the working classes. Horace Mann's educational census of 1851 estimated that about one child in every three under the age of fifteen attended day school. Though few working-class children attended for more than one or two years, it is likely that a much larger portion received some instruction at one time or

another. Eventually the state shouldered the primary burden of education, increasing its financial aid between 1851 and 1870 to such an extent that it bore a larger share of the costs than the voluntary bodies and the parents together. See Harold Perkin, *The Structured Crowd* (New Jersey: Barnes & Noble, 1981) 49–50. R. K. Webb in *The British Working Class Reader, 1790–1840* suggests that in the 1840s between two-thirds and three-quarters of the working class, and possibly more of the men, could read.

9 The Endowed Schools Act of 1869 took money that had originally been left to schools for other purposes and used it to create many new grammar schools with places for girls.

10 Joseph Ackland, "Elementary Education and the Decay of Literature," *The Nineteenth Century*, 35:203 (March 1894) 413.

11 Edward Royle, *Modern Britain: A Social History, 1750–1985* (London: Edward Arnold, 1987) 360.

12 Ibid., 61–70.

13 E. G. Bulwer Lytton, *England and the English*, reprinted in *The English Ruling Class*, ed. W. L. Guttsman (London: Weidenfeld and Nicolson, 1969) 27.

14 Peter Miles and Malcolm Smith, *Cinema, Literature, and Society: Elite and Mass Culture in Interwar Britain* (New York: Croom Helm, 1987) 60.

15 In creating his own taxonomy of the English social classes in *Culture and Anarchy* (New York: Cambridge University Press, 1988), Matthew Arnold admitted that such divisions were general, and that "in every one of us, whether we be properly Barbarians [aristocracy], Philistines [middle class], or Populace [working class], there exists, sometimes more or less developed, the same tendencies or passions which have made our fellow-citizens of other classes what they are . . . Thus, an English Barbarian who examines himself will, in general, find himself to be not so entirely a Barbarian but that he has in him, also, something of the Philistine, and even something of the Populace as well. And the same with Englishmen of the two other classes as well" (105–106).

16 Elite English education has still not lost its distaste for the materialist, practical interests of a business-dominated society. In 1996, Oxford University turned down a gift of $34 million to build a business school on its premises. "The Daily Telegraph, a conservative newspaper, called the 259-to-214 vote against the offer, among university dons who came to a meeting about the issue on November 5, elitist bias against business. It is, it said, 'an old British disease that lies behind much of our industrial decline into not-so-genteel poverty.'" Quoted in "We Can't Do Business, the Dons Tell a Big Donor," *The New York Times* (November 26, 1996) A4.

17 Linda Dowling, *The Vulgarization of Art: The Victorians and Aesthetic Democracy* (Charlottesville: University Press of Virginia, 1996) xii.

18 Ibid., xii.

19 Ibid., 24.

20 Judith Stoddart, "The Morality of *Poems and Ballads*," *The Whole Music of Passion*, ed. Rikky Rooksby and Nicholas Shrimpton (Hants, England: Scolar Press, 1993) 102.

21 Matthew Arnold, "The Function of Criticism at the Present Time," *Essays Literary and Critical by Matthew Arnold* (London: J. M. Dent & Sons, 1928) 15.

22 The first quotation in the OED that uses culture in the sense of intellectual development is ironically from Wordsworth's 1805 *Prelude*, book XIII, line 197, "Where grace of culture hath been utterly unknown." What's important to note about this use is that the *Prelude* was not published until 1850. Thus Arnold's use of the term in 1876 in *Literature and Dogma*, as quoted in the OED, can be said to participate in defining a specifically modern use of the word.

23 Matthew Arnold, *Culture and Anarchy* (New York: Cambridge University Press, 1988) 45, 47.

24 Reprinted in Patrick Brantlinger, *Bread and Circuses: Theories of Mass Culture as Social Decay* (Ithaca: Cornell University Press, 1983) 122.

25 An article on "Penny Fiction" published in *The Quarterly Review*, 171:341 (1890) 150–171, noted that "It is hardly necessary to say that the gentlemen who accept engagements of this kind are not as a rule very distinguished members of the Republic of Letters, though in some few instances their antecedents are better than might be expected." The author tells of a university educated clergyman who, having argued with his bishop, abandoned his career to write penny fiction. Of the working-class authors, the author relays "a still more amusing illustration of the social status of some of our popular instructors . . . related by a lady, the wife of a well-known physician. Her cook having repeatedly neglected to send up the dinner with the punctuality which is desirable in a well-ordered household, she remonstrated with some sharpness, and to her astonishment was informed that the young person in question was so much occupied with the novel she was writing that she had been unable to pay due attention to her duties in the kitchen."

26 Ackland, "Elementary Education and the Decay of Literature," 412–423.

27 Ibid., 421.

28 "Penny Fiction," 156.

29 E. L. Godkin, "Newspapers Here and Abroad," *Review of Reviews*, 1 (January–June 1890) 203.

30 In his *Notes sur l'Angleterre* (1872), H. Taine described Victorian-era English gentlemen as those with "cultivated minds, a liberal education, travel, information, good manners and ease in society." Further he added that, "The real 'gentleman' is . . . a *disinterested man of integrity*"(my emphasis) (rpt. in *The English Ruling Class*, 36–38). Similarly, Edward Royle described the English gentleman as one whose "largeness of mind and generosity of spirit were based on a classical education. He was a man of leisure, an amateur capable of *detachment* and philosophical reflection" (my emphasis) (Royle, *Modern Britain*, 391). These descriptions confirm that, though more men in the nineteenth century were able to call themselves gentlemen, the

206.

qualifications for the designation were in keeping with those of the eighteenth century. One's ability to detach from one's own interests and show disinterest was foremost in classifying one's behavior as a gentleman. One of the ironies of disinterestedness is that it purportedly enlarges an individual beyond selfish personal interest and, in doing so, further contributes to a social-subjective, or ideological, viewpoint that reinforces the subjectivity of that individual. Arguably, one is as invested in one's disinterest as in any other personal attribute.

31 Arnold, *Culture and Anarchy*, 17.

32 Jürgen Habermas, in *The Structural Transformation of the Public Sphere* (Cambridge: MIT Press, 1992), cites art-historian A. Hauser with regard to this development. According to Hauser, after the bourgeoisie rose to dominance in the mid-nineteenth century, intellectuals found themselves alienated from a self-satisfied public: "the cultural elite, and especially its literary productive section, thereby lost the feeling of having a mission to fulfill in society. It saw itself cut off from the social class of which it had hitherto been a mouthpiece and it felt completely isolated between the uneducated classes and the bourgeoisie. It was this feeling that first gave rise to the replacement of the earlier cultural stratum with its roots in the middle class by the social group we call the 'intelligentsia'" (174).

33 William Morris, lecture delivered to the Birmingham Society of Arts and School of Design, February 19, 1880, reprinted in *Strangeness and Beauty: An Anthology of Aesthetic Criticism, 1840–1910*, ed. Eric Werner and Graham Hough (Cambridge University Press, 1983) 91.

34 Matthew Arnold, *Culture and Anarchy*, 105.

35 Quoted in Steven Marcus, *The Other Victorians* (New York: Basic Books, 1964) 146–147n.

36 Edwin Chadwick, *Report . . . from the Poor Law Commissioners on an Inquiry into the Sanitary Conditions of the Labouring Population of Great Britain* (London: 1842) 369–372.

37 This article from an 1886 volume of the *Contemporary Review* was quoted in "Evening Continuation Schools," *New Review*, 51 (August 1893) 135.

38 "Penny Fiction," 154.

39 Regenia Gagnier outlines this shift in "On the Insatiability of Human Wants: Economic Man and Aesthetic Man," *Victorian Studies*, 36:2 (winter 1993) 125–153. Lawrence Birken, in *Consuming Desire: Sexual Science and the Emergence of a Culture of Abundance 1871–1914* (Ithaca: University of Cornell Press, 1988) makes the point that it was the sexologists who overturned the typical belief in individuals as producers and began to see them instead as consumers.

40 Gagnier, "On the Insatiability of Human Wants," 143–144.

41 Walter Kendrick, *The Secret Museum: Pornography in Modern Culture* (New York: Viking Books, 1987) 167.

42 Max Nordau, *Degeneration* (Lincoln: University of Nebraska Press, 1993) 557.

43 Ian Hunter, David Saunders, and Dugald Williamson, *On Pornography: Literature, Sexuality, and Obscenity Law* (New York: St. Martin's Press, 1993) 64–65.

44 Peter Fryer, ed., *Forbidden Books of the Victorians* (London: The Odyssey Press, 1970) 19.

45 Iwan Bloch, *The Sexual Life of Our Time*, trans. M. Eden Paul (London: William Heinemann, 1920) 734.

46 See Steven Marcus, *The Other Victorians* (New York: Basic Books, 1964), Peter Gay, *The Education of the Senses* (New York: Oxford University Press, 1984), Walter Kendrick, *The Secret Museum: Pornography in Modern Culture* (New York: Viking Books, 1987); and Roy Porter and Lesley Hall, *The Facts of Life: The Creation of Sexual Knowledge in Britain, 1650–1950* (New Haven: Yale University Press, 1995).

47 H. Montgomery Hyde, *A History of Pornography* (New York: Farrar, Straus and Giroux, 1964) 180.

48 Edward J. Bristow, *Vice and Vigilance: Purity Movements in Britain since 1700* (Dublin: Gill and Macmillan, 1977) 49.

49 According to several sources, after the passage of the Obscene Publications Act in 1857, Lord Chief Justice John Campbell informed his diary that half of the Holywell Street shops had closed down and the other half were stocking only respectable wares. See David Loth, *The Erotic in Literature* (London: Secker & Warburg, 1961) 120, and Ian Hunter et al., *On Pornography* (New York: St. Martin's Press, 1993) 57–91.

50 Gay, *The Education of the Senses*, 358.

51 Cited by Ashbee in his introduction to the *Index Librorum Prohibitorum*, reprinted in Fryer, n.17.

52 Royle, *Modern Britain*, 21, 87.

53 Guinevere L. Griest, *Mudie's Circulating Library and the Victorian Novel* (Bloomington: Indiana University Press, 1970) 79.

54 Fryer, *Forbidden Books of the Victorians*, 26.

55 Gay, *Education of the Senses*, 372.

56 Lynn Hunt, "Pornography and the French Revolution," *The Invention of Pornography: Obscenity and the Origins of Modernity, 1500–1800*, ed. Lynn Hunt (New York: Zone Books, 1993) 301–339. Hunt also notes that the variety of engravings that can be seen in pornography of the 1790s, from high brow to low brow, "signals the beginning of the democratization of pornography as a genre during the Revolution. The libertine literature of the *ancien régime*, destined exclusively for upper-class men, now becomes partly, perhaps even predominantly, a popular genre" (317–318).

57 Quoted in Roy Porter and Lesley Hall, *The Facts of Life*, 24–25.

58 For instance, *Aphrodisiacs and Anti-Aphrodisiacs*, a volume issued in 1869 by J. C. Hotten, the publisher who took on Swinburne's *Poems and Ballads* after Moxon withdrew it, is catalogued by Ashbee as "beautifully printed on toned paper" with a fleuron on the title page and a Roxburghe binding (Fryer, *Forbidden Books of the*

Victorians, 59). A Roxburghe binding, according to John Carter, *ABC for Book Collectors* (New York: Granada, 1985) 181, was a style "originally designed for publications of the Roxburghe Club, founded by a group of patrician bibliophiles after the Duke of Roxburghe's sale in 1812, this special style of binding has a gilt-lettered smooth leather spine, usually brown or green, and dark-red paper-board sides, with no leather corners." Only one-hundred copies (according to Hotten's advertisement) were sold for private distribution.

59 Fryer, *Forbidden Books of the Victorians*, 124, 223.

60 Ibid., 76–124.

61 The prices quoted are taken from two catalogues, dated 1901 and 1903, found in the British Library's "Album 7."

62 Kendrick, *The Secret Museum*, 48.

63 Bristow suggests in *Vice and Vigilance* that by 1908, 800 million obscene picture postcards had been handled by the Post Office (208).

64 Pisanus Fraxi, *Catena Librorum Tacendorum* (London: privately printed, 1885) 181.

65 Tracy C. Davis, "The Actress in Victorian Pornography," *Victorian Scandals: Representations of Gender and Class*, ed. Kristine Ottesen Garrigan (Athens: University of Ohio Press, 1992) 99–134.

66 My thanks to Britt Salvesen of the University of Chicago for supplying me with this information from his incomplete dissertation on stereoscopes.

67 Iaian McCalman, *Radical Underworld: Prophets, Revolutionaries and Pornographers in London, 1795–1840* (Cambridge University Press, 1988) 204.

68 Ibid., 205.

69 The British Library houses many examples of the bawdy street literature produced in the 1830s and 1840s. Tiny 2 inch × 3 inch duodecimo chap-books such as *The Cockchafer: "A Choice selection of Flash, Frisky, and Funny Songs Never before printed and adapted for Gentlemen only"* (c.1840), house numerous bawdy music-hall songs apparently in common circulation among the literate working classes. Ashbee lists about fifty such chap-books in *Index Librorum Prohibitorum* (London: privately printed, 1878) and notes that "These are songs which, some 30 years ago, were sung publicly by J. H. Munyard, H. Hall, Ross, Sharp, and others, in the various music halls of the metropolis . . . the death blow to these jovial smutty ditties was struck when the doors of the Canterbury and Weston's Music Halls were opened to women; the entertainment had then to be modified, and suited to female ears; vice was not checked, but its aspects changed; and instead of being places of resort where men could indulge in coarse and bawdy songs, the music halls became meeting-places for prostitutes" (135–136).

70 McCalman, *Radical Underworld*, 219.

71 Ibid., 209.

72 Lynn Hunt, "Introduction," *The Invention of Pornography*, 43–44.

73 McCalman, *Radical Underworld*, 225; Jeffrey Weeks, *Sex, Politics, and Society* (New

York: Longman, 1981) 21; Thomas F. Boyle, "Morbid Depression Alternating with Excitement: Sex in Victorian Newspapers," *Sexuality and Victorian Fiction*, ed. Don Richard Cox (Knoxville: University of Tennessee Press, 1984) 213.

74 Boyle, "Morbid Depression Alternating with Excitement," 212–213.

75 Judith Walkowitz, *City of Dreadful Delight: Narrative of Sexual Danger in Late-Victorian London* (University of Chicago Press, 1992) 97. In the British Library's "Album 7" there is an undated penny pamphlet titled "Astounding Revelations Concerning Supposed Massage Houses, or Pandemoniums of Vice Frequented by Both Sexes." The pamphlet compares its own discoveries to those of Stead's "Maiden Tribute" and notes that "it is not for us to moralise upon the present social scandal, but to publish facts – unsavory though they be – and thus cause official notice to be taken of Modern Babylon's latest development of immorality." The pamphlet is clearly intended to sexually stimulate its readers.

76 Walkowitz, *City of Dreadful Delight*, 124.

77 McCalman, *Radical Underworld*, 223.

78 Over its three-year publication (1842–1844), *The Exquisite* moved from a magazine concerned with health and radical, populist causes to a more graphically oriented sex magazine. In the middle of its second year it began to introduce illustrations, and eventually printed English translations of French pornographic tales. By its eighty-fifth issue it raised its price to six pence. Without any research into its publishing decisions, one must speculate as to the reasons for its changes. Was it answering the demands of the market?

79 *The Exquisite*, vol. 1 (London: H. Smith, 37 Holywell Street, 1842) 6.

80 This entire account has been taken from Boyle, "Morbid Depression Alternating with Excitement," 224–225.

81 Though the *chroniques scandaleuses* are almost invariably about the seduction of a woman, upper-class women do seduce their servants, male and female, in various pornographic texts. One such example is *The Modern Eveline* (Paris: Charles Carrington, 1904) in which the eponymous heroine seduces her footman, John. John, as it turns out, is a willing victim. Of equal interest, Eveline enjoys a fascination for "the other half." She engages with many servants, enjoys forced copulation with strangers below her class, and goes slumming by affecting a cockney accent and offering herself as a street girl to be photographed naked in Pimlico.

82 *My Secret Life* is thought to have been published in the late 1880s in Belgium. The small number of copies (accounts vary from six to thirty) were paid for by its anon-ymous author at a cost of over £1,000. As such, it ranks among the elite forms of pornography that would have been available only to gentleman-collectors.

83 Marcus, *The Other Victorians*, 128.

84 *My Secret Life* (New York: Blue Moon Books, 1988) 158. All references cited in the text will hereafter be referred to as *MSL*.

85 Such verbal repetition is central to the work of pornography and can be found in

most texts. An example from the same period can be found in *The Adventures of Lady Harpur* (Glascow [sic]: William Murray, 1894), where Lady Harpur's mulatto mother, Miss Queenie, is exhorted by a lover "Now, Queenie, now – hold me in your arms put both hands on my bottom – squeeze the cheeks of my Arse! Oh my love, say with me; Prick; Cunt; Arse; Pissing; Fucking; Prick; Cunt; Arse; Fuck; Fuck!" (vol. II, 8).

86 Michel Foucault, *The History of Sexuality*, vol. I (New York: Vintage Books, 1978) 20–23.

87 Coral Lansbury, *The Old Brown Dog: Women, Workers, and Vivisection in Victorian England* (Madison: University of Wisconsin Press, 1985), 115.

88 Ibid., 120. A more clearly pornographic example of the female-style narrative to which Lansbury refers can be found in Ashbee's bibliography: "*The Confessions of a Lady's Maid*, Or Boudoir Intrigue: disclosing many startling scenes and voluptuous incidents as witnessed by her in the various Families of Distinction with whom she lived: forming a wonderful picture of fashionable Frailty, Passion, and Seduction. Beautifully illustrated with Coloured Plates, by an eminent French artist. W. Johns, 35 Holywell Street, Strand, London" (Fryer, *Forbidden Books of the Victorians*, 213).

89 Andreas Huyssen, in *After the Great Divide: Modernism, Mass Culture, Postmodernism* (Bloomington: Indiana University Press, 1986) makes the convincing claim that mass culture is frequently figured as female at the turn of the twentieth century; see especially pp. 44–65.

90 "From the Maid's Point of View," *New Review*, 5:27 (1891) 170. Hereafter all citations in the text will be referred to as "MP".

91 Weeks, *Sex, Politics and Society*, 73–74.

92 Raymond Williams, *Marxism and Literature* (New York: Oxford University Press, 1977) 121–128. Of residual culture Williams says "The residual, by definition, has been effectively formed in the past, but as an effective element of the present. Thus certain experiences, meanings, and values which cannot be expressed or substantially verified in terms of the dominant culture, are nevertheless lived and practised on the basis of residue – cultural as well as social – of some previous social and cultural institution or formation. It is crucial to distinguish this aspect of the residual, which may have an alternative or even oppositional relation to the dominant culture, from that active manifestation of the residual (this being its distinction from the archaic) which has been wholly or largely incorporated into the dominant culture" (122). The necessity of incorporating Swinburne's residual culture into the dominant culture is not fully realized until early in the twentieth century.

93 Quoted in Marcus, *The Other Victorians*, 214.

94 *Swinburne: The Critical Heritage*, ed. Clyde K. Hyder (New York: Barnes & Noble, 1970) 22.

95 Ibid., 24.

96 Ibid.

97 Ibid., 31.

98 Ibid., 27.

99 Ibid., 29.

100 Ibid., 30.

101 Kathy Alexis Psomiades, *Beauty's Body: Femininity and Representation in British Aestheticism* (Stanford University Press, 1997) 76.

102 Hyder, *Swinburne*, 27.

103 A fascinating side effect of this demarcation is the association of women and the lower classes as those more easily prone to affect, and hence very much outside the separate economy of the masculinized, pure aesthetic.

104 Such a definition suggests that pornography could equally create a sense of harmony in a reader, who, employing a specific practice of reading, is reified by pornography in sexual stimulation – the purpose sought there.

105 It is interesting to note that while his publicly published poems dwell on female charms, his poems of flagellation deal specifically with the bodies of adolescent boys. "Charlie Collingwood's Flogging," a poem published under the pen-name "Etoniensis" in the September 1879 edition of *The Pearl* (New York: Grove Press, 1968) 86–92, lingers over the fleshy details of Charlie Collingwood's bottom, as seen in the following excerpt:

> And again we can see his great naked red bottom, round, fleshy and plump,
> And the bystanders look from the Master's red rod, to the schoolboy's red rump:
> There are weals over weals, there are stripes upon stripes, there are cuts after cuts,
> All across Charlie Collingwood's bottom, and isn't the sight of it nuts?
> There, that cut on the fleshiest part of the buttocks, high up on the right,
> He got that before supper last evening, oh! isn't his bottom a sight?
> And that scar that's just healed, don't you see where the birch cut the flesh?
> That's a token of Charlie's last flogging, the rod will soon stamp it afresh. (lines 19–26)

106 Psomiades, *Beauty's Body*, 87.

107 W. M. Rossetti, *Swinburne's Poems and Ballads* (London: John Camden Hotten, 1866) 71.

108 Ibid., 20.

109 Charles Algernon Swinburne, "Notes on Poems and Reviews," *Swinburne Replies*, ed. Clyde Kenneth Hyder (Syracuse University Press, 1966) 19, 31.

110 Ibid., 30.

111 Ibid., 27.

112 Here I make a distinction between the socially transgressive work of Swinburne and that of other artists like Thomas Hardy and George Moore, whose works were also accused of obscenity. While Hardy's and Moore's works addressed sexuality in terms of content, their representations of sexuality remained implied and metaphorical. Swinburne, by contrast, used the very language and techniques of pornography, albeit in a disjunctive and prolix manner, and this was the source of his literary scandal.

113 Hyder, *Swinburne Replies*, 32.

3. The mastery of form: Beardsley and Joyce

1 Osbert Burdett, *The Beardsley Period* (London: John Lane, the Bodley Head Ltd., 1925) 265.

2 In Joyce's case, some of the sexually explicit language he uses can be traced to medical tracts and advertising. The "Circe" episode, for instance, is often linked to the medical writings of Richard von Krafft-Ebing's *Psychopathia Sexualis* (1886). An explicit, genitally focused sexual discourse developed out of a medical-scientific discourse, enabling the pornographic genre. Such a discourse remained solely within the province of pornography and medicine until the early decades of the twentieth century.

3 For a discussion of Kant's influence in England, see chapter one. See also Martha Woodmansee, *The Author, Art, and the Market: Rereading the History of Aesthetics* (New York: Columbia University Press, 1994), especially chapter 6, "The Uses of Kant in England," pp. 111–148. Woodmansee points out, as others have also done, that the primary disseminator of Kantian aesthetic philosophy in England was Coleridge. Also see René Wellek, *Immanuel Kant in England, 1793–1838* (Princeton University Press, 1931), and W. David Shaw, *The Lucid Veil: Poetic Truth in the Victorian Age* (Madison: University of Wisconsin Press, 1987).

4 Immanuel Kant, *The Critique of Judgment*, trans. J. C. Meredith (Oxford: Clarendon Press, 1991). See especially sections 10–14.

5 Anthony Ashley Cooper, third Earl of Shaftesbury, *Characteristics of Men, Manners, Opinions, Times*, vol. II (Hampshire, England: Gregg International Publishers, 1968) 425.

6 Samuel Weber, *Mass Mediauras: Form, Technics, Media* (Stanford University Press, 1996) 20.

7 Arthur Symons, *Aubrey Beardsley* (London: J. M. Dent & Co., 1905) 37.

8 Burdett, *The Beardsley Period*, 8.

9 Peter Michelson, "Beardsley, Burroughs, decadence and the poetics of obscenity," *TriQuarterly*, no. 12 (spring 1968) 140.

10 James Joyce, *Stephen Hero* (London: Jonathan Cape, 1956) 82. Hereafter citations in text will be referred to as *SH*.

11 T. S. Eliot, "*Ulysses*, Order, and Myth," *Selected Prose of T. S. Eliot*, ed. Frank Kermode (London: Faber & Faber, 1975) 177.

12 Burdett, *The Beardsley Period*, 55.

13 Ibid., 15.

14 John K. M. Rothenstein, *A Pot of Paint: The Artists of the 1890s* (1929; New York: Books for Libraries Press, 1970) 23, 164.

15 Bridget J. Elliott, in "Sights of Pleasure: Beardsley's Images of Actresses and the New Journalism of the Nineties," *Reconsidering Aubrey Beardsley*, ed. Robert Langenfeld

(Ann Arbor: UMI Research Press, 1989) provides a useful discussion of these ideas on pp. 94–96.

16 James Joyce, *A Portrait of the Artist as a Young Man* (New York: Penguin, 1976) 205.

17 Francis Barker, *The Private Tremulous Body: Essays on Subjection* (New York: Methuen, 1984) 64.

18 Barker's view may seem to be at odds with Foucault's well-known theory expressed in *The History of Sexuality*, vol. I (New York: Vintage Books, 1978) that the middle-classes were in fact talking quite constantly about their sexuality in the nineteenth century through a proliferation of discourses, medical and otherwise. However, these discourses can be seen to be consistent with Barker's point in that they address one's sexuality indirectly, substituting themselves for more direct attempts to realize the body. They are, like the Kantian aesthetic, distancing, rational accounts of the irrational body.

19 Barker, *The Private Tremulous Body*, 59.

20 T.W. Adorno, *Aesthetic Theory*, trans. C. Lenhardt (London: Routledge & Kegan Paul, 1984) 16.

21 Gustave Le Bon, *The Crowd* (London: T. Fisher Unwin, 1913) 40.

22 Le Bon's work is based on a late nineteenth-century psychiatric distinction between an unconscious level of emotion, reflex and automatism, and consciousness as associated with reason and conscious memory. Consciousness was, in Le Bon's view, a relatively recent development. The state of being in the crowd was therefore identical to being unconscious, a state in which individuality is absorbed into the crowd or the mass.

23 While 1904 marks the date of "popular" as first defined in the sense of "ephemeral publications intended for a general readership" its use dated back to 1817, Coleridge's *Biographia Literaria*. See also Michael Hayes, "Popular Fiction and Middle-Brow Taste," *Literature and Culture in Modern Britain, 1900–1929*, ed. Clive Bloom (Essex: Langma Group UK, 1993) 76–100.

24 Walter Benjamin, "The Work of Art in the Age of Mechanical Reproduction," *Illuminations*, trans. Harry Zohn (New York: Schocken Books, 1968) 239.

25 Ibid., 223.

26 Adorno, *Aesthetic Theory*, 339.

27 Benjamin, "The Work of Art in the Age of Mechanical Reproduction," 223.

28 Ibid., 222.

29 *The National Observer* (April 21, 1894), 588.

30 Ibid., 599.

31 Quoted in Elliott, "Sights of Pleasure: Beardsley's Images of Actresses and the New Journalism of the Nineties," 94.

32 "The Scandal of Ulysses," *The Sporting Times* (April 1, 1922) 4.

33 *Daily Herald*, no. 921 (March 17, 1922) 4.

34 Shane Leslie, *Quarterly Review*, 238 (October 1922) 219–234.

35 George Rehm, *Chicago Tribune* (February 13, 1922) 2.

36 Shane Leslie, *Dublin Review*, 9 (September 1922) 119.

37 Linda Hutcheon, *A Theory of Parody* (New York: Methuen, 1985) 53.

38 See Pierre Bourdieu "The Field of Cultural Production," *The Field of Cultural Production* (New York: Columbia University Press, 1993) 31.

39 Frederic Jameson, "Postmodernism and Consumer Society, *The Anti-Aesthetic: Essays on Postmodern Culture*, ed. Hal Foster (Seattle: Bay Press, 1983) 114.

40 Mikhail Bakhtin, *Rabelais and his World*, trans. Helene Iswolsky (Bloomington: Indiana University Press, 1984) 1–59.

41 Hutcheon, *A Theory of Parody*, 75.

42 Roland Barthes, *Critical Essays*, trans. Richard Miller (New York: Hill & Wang, 1972) 119.

43 Susan Sontag, "The Pornographic Imagination," *Styles of Radical Will* (New York: Doubleday, 1969) 51.

44 See Holbrook Jackson, *The Eighteen Nineties* (1913; London: Jonathan Cape, 1931) 101; Ian Fletcher, *Aubrey Beardsley* (Boston: G. K. Hall & Co., 1987) 29; Linda Gerstner Zatlin, *Aubrey Beardsley and Victorian Sexual Politics* (Oxford: Clarendon Press, 1990) 143–151; Richard Brown, *James Joyce and Sexuality* (Cambridge University Press, 1985) 64, 79, 86, 132–133; Richard Ellman, *The Consciousness of Joyce* (London: Faber & Faber, 1977) 117. It is often suggested that Beardsley would have had access to pornography through his friend and publisher Leonard Smithers, who collected and published pornography for a period of time before going bankrupt around the turn of the century. Smithers's library is lost, though a catalogue of an auction held by Sotheby, Wilkinson, & Hodge on November 14, 1895 (found in "Album 7," The British Library), shows that Smithers (as well as Havelock Ellis) was present and purchased a number of erotic and/or pornographic French and English titles of the eighteenth and nineteenth centuries. Smithers's purchases may have been available to Beardsley, as their correspondence shows that Beardsley often borrowed Smithers's pornographic works.

45 Laura Kipnis, *Ecstasy Unlimited: On Sex, Capital, Gender, and Aesthetics* (University of Minneapolis Press, 1993) 30.

46 Jennifer Wicke, "Through a Gaze Darkly: Pornography's Academic Market," *Dirty Looks: Women Pornography Power*, ed. Roma Gibson and Pamela Church Gibson (London: BFI, 1993) 67–68.

47 Michael Koetzle, *1000 Nudes* (Cologne: Benedikt Taschen, 1994) 310.

48 Garry Leonard, in "Power, Pornography, and the Problem of Pleasure: The Semerotics of Desire and Commodity Culture in Joyce," *James Joyce Quarterly*, vols. 30–31, nos. 4–1 (summer–fall 1993) 615–665, writes of erotic postcards and their effect on erotic fantasy in "The Dead."

49 Joyce, *Portrait*, 115.

215.

50 Ibid., 98.
51 James Joyce, *Ulysses* (New York: Vintage, 1961) 566. Henceforth all citations in text will be referred to as *Ulysses*.
52 *My Secret Life* (*c*.1880) (New York: Blue Moon, 1988). In John Cleland's *Fanny Hill or Memoirs of a Woman of Pleasure* (1748–1749) (London: Penguin Books, 1995) a sexually uninitiated Fanny first discovers sexual intercourse by hiding in a closet where "seeing everything minutely, I could not myself be seen" (40). In *Romance of Lust* (1873; New York: Blue Moon Books, 1992) the protagonist and his wife visit a bawdy house in Paris where "through cleverly arranged peep-holes, any operation in the next room could be distinctly seen" (461).
53 Sander Gilman, *The Jew's Body* (New York: Routledge, 1991) 124.
54 The pornography here may very well be playing on the Renaissance tradition of painting Eros and Aphrodite, and as such it underscores the mutually parodic, mutually constitutive, nature of both the aesthetic and the pornographic.
55 Such erotic photocards were extremely common in the early decades of the twentieth century. A catalogue advertising "Erotic Photos – Scenes of Copulation" (*c*.1902) lists as its item no. 20 "Carmen and Pepito: A Spanish torero with an Andalusian maid. 20 cabinets £0.15.0, each cabinet £0.1.0." Spanish scenes feature frequently in turn-of-the-century erotic postcards.
56 M. M. Bakhtin, *The Dialogic Imagination*, trans. Caryl Emerson and Michael Holquist (Austin: University of Texas Press, 1992) 323.
57 Ibid., 355.
58 John Middleton Murray, *Nation and Athenaeum*, 31 (April 22, 1922) 124–125.
59 John Carey, *The Intellectuals and the Masses* (Boston: Faber & Faber, 1992) 20.
60 Jackson, *The Eighteen Nineties*, 100.
61 Bridget Elliott, "New and Not So 'New Women' on the London Stage: Aubrey Beardsley's *Yellow Book* Images of Mrs. Patrick Campbell and Rejane," *Victorian Studies*, vol. 31, no. 1 (autumn 1987) 33–34.
62 Linda Gerstner Zatlin, in "Aubrey Beardsley Counts the Ways," *Victorian Newsletter*, 67 (spring 1985) 1–6, outlines Beardsley's reliance upon eighteenth-century sexual iconography.
63 Jackson, *The Eighteen Nineties*, 103.
64 Robert Ross, *Aubrey Beardsley* (London: John Lane, the Bodley Head, 1921) 48.
65 Christopher Snodgrass convincingly makes this argument in *Aubrey Beardsley: Dandy of the Grotesque* (New York: Oxford University Press, 1995), chapter 3, "The Craving for Authority."
66 Quoted in Ian Fletcher, *Aubrey Beardsley* (Boston: G. K. Hall & Co., 1987) 7.
67 Snodgrass, *Aubrey Beardsley*, 171.
68 A classic example of this can be found in *Fanny Hill* when the heroine describes the penis of a young messenger in the following manner: "I saw, with wonder and surprise, what? not the plaything of a boy, not the weapon of a man, but a maypole of

so enormous a standard that, had proportions been observed it must have belonged to a young giant" (94). As is typical of pornography, the penis evokes the sublime. In Fanny's words, "it stood, an object of terror and delight" (95).

69 Snodgrass, *Aubrey Beardsley*, 210.

70 Throughout *My Secret Life* Walter thinks of masturbation as a shameful, harmful act. In one particular scene he secretly watches a couple make love and in response notes, "my prick stood stiff, but I resisted my desire to masturbate" (338).

71 Snodgrass, *Aubrey Beardsley*, 65. Snodgrass's interesting and detailed reading of *The Toilete of Salome*, first version, provides a portion of the observations I enumerate here.

72 Ibid., 65.

73 Linda Gerstner Zatlin, in "Félicien Rops and Aubrey Beardsley: The Naked and the Nude," *Reconsidering Aubrey Beardsley*, ed. Robert Langenfeld (Ann Arbor: UMI Research Press, 1989) 167–207, makes the case that Beardsley was familiar with Rops's work.

74 Linda Gerstner Zatlin, "Aubrey Beardsley's 'Japanese' Grotesques," *Victorian Literature and Culture*, 25:1 (spring 1997) 87–108.

75 *Priapeia* (London: Smithers, 1888) 51.

76 Margot Norris, *Joyce's Web: The Social Unraveling of Modernism* (Austin: University of Texas Press, 1992) 177.

77 Steven Marcus, *The Other Victorians* (New York: Basic Books, 1964) 253. Evidence counter to this, however, is found in Henry Spencer Ashbee's *Index Librorum Prohibitorum* (London: privately printed, 1877) where Ashbee comments in an entry on *Exhibition of Female Flagellants* that "the mania has possessed all classes for chastising and being chastised" (240). Indeed, Ashbee's bibliography includes a pamphlet entitled *Mysteries of Flagellation* (1863) priced at two pence, suggesting that the literature of flagellation was in fact a matter of mass consumption. Of *Mysteries* Ashbee notes "The pamphlet, considering its class, is not badly written" (311). Within *Exhibition of Female Flagellants* (London: William Dugdale, c.1860), flagellation is figured deliberately as upper class. Its central character Flirtilla coaches her protégée with this in mind: "Know then thou silly girl there is a manner in handling this sceptre of felicity [whip], that few ladies are happy in: it is not the impassioned and awkward brandish of a vulgar female that can charm, but the deliberate and elegant manner of a woman of rank and fashion, who displays all that dignity in every action, even to the flirting of her fan, that leaves an indelible wound. What a difference between high and low-life in this particular!" (4).

78 This is likely relating to its public school affiliation as well as to its most famous proponent, Leopold von Sacher-Masoch, who wrote of male subjection to domineering females in the late nineteenth century.

79 Snodgrass, *Aubrey Beardsley*, 13.

80 Ellman, *The Consciousness of Joyce*, 126

81 Brown, *James Joyce and Sexuality*, 86.

82 The following account and drawn similarities are taken from Brown, *James Joyce and*

Sexuality, 86. In my own research in the British Library's "Private Case," the English translation, *Gynococracy* (London, 1893), is attributed to the authorship of, among others, Havelock Ellis or Leonard Smithers. That the names in the French version found in Joyce's library are British suggests that his version was a translation from an originally English text. *Gynococracy* is a fascinating text on many accounts, and seems to inform several of the strands of the "Circe" episode. For instance, Julian's experience under "petticoat rule" leads him to a fear of emasculation. In an attempt to assert his masculinity he asks the governess to marry and have sex with him. When she rejects him he says "I felt as though I had potentially lost a child and my spirit was grieved" (136). A footnote to this sentence says "Emasculation was prohibited among the Jews. According to Josephus, it killed beforehand children who might otherwise have been begotten. The reason is intelligible, but illogical" (n.136). The emasculation and masochism in relation to women Bloom endures in "Circe" may be linked to his guilt over his son Rudi's death, a guilt that *Gynococracy* locates within the Jewish tradition. The theme of male subjection to female punishment and emasculation flourishes in pornography of the early twentieth century, and versions of the *Gynococracy* story can be found in *A Man and 3 Maids: A Snappy Spanking Story* (*c*.1930) as well as in *Miss High-Heels* (Paris: Groves & Michaux, 1931).

83 Linda Gerstner Zatlin, *Aubrey Beardsley and Victorian Sexual Politics* (Oxford: Clarendon Press, 1990) 131. In a small pocketbook containing music-hall songs called *The Rambler's Flash Songster* (London: W. West, 57 Wych Street, *c*.1840–1850), a ditty entitled "Master Humphrey's Clock" confirms the slang usage of the word clock for a woman's genitalia. The lyrics read: "Women unto clocks great resemblance bear, / Some clocks split and crack, I say / But use well your key, and you'll soon make way" (6).

84 Zatlin, *Aubrey Beardsley and Victorian Sexual Politics*, 131.

85 Snodgrass, *Aubrey Beardsley*, 254.

86 *The Letters of Aubrey Beardsley*, ed. Henry Maas, J. C. Duncan, and W. G. Good (Rutherford: Farleigh Dickinson University Press, 1970) 158.

87 Edward Said, *Orientalism* (New York: Pantheon Books, 1978) 1–2, 188, 190.

88 In *Gynococracy* Julian eroticizes the yashmak, wondering "Was it wicked to kiss the mouth of an Eastern woman because when walking around it was covered by a yashmak?" (61).

89 *The Orientalists: European Painters in North Africa and the Near East*, ed. MaryAnne Stevens (London: Royal Academy of Arts, 1984) 139.

4. Being disinterested: D. H. Lawrence

1 Throughout this chapter I will refer to *John Thomas and Lady Jane*, *The First Lady Chatterley*, and *Lady Chatterley's Lover* as the *Lady Chatterley* novels. Lawrence wrote each of these novels as successive drafts, discarding the first two upon their completion. I see referring to each of them as important in that they contribute to

the development and articulation of the ideas Lawrence was refining for the final 1928 version, *Lady Chatterley's Lover*.

2 Immanuel Kant, *Critique of Judgment*, trans. James Creed Meredith (Oxford: Clarendon Press, 1991) 91.

3 Jean-Luc Nancy, "The Sublime Offering," *Of the Sublime: Presence in Question*, trans. Jeffrey F. Librett (Albany: State University Press of New York, 1993) 38.

4 Kant, *Critique of Judgment*, 106.

5 Michel Foucault, *The History of Sexuality*, vol. 1 (New York: Vintage Books, 1978) 51–75. In the section titled "Scientia Sexualis," Foucault argues that sexologists constructed a discourse around and apropos of sex and that "sex was not only a matter of sensation and pleasure, of law and taboo, but also of truth and falsehood, and that the truth of sex became something fundamental, useful, or dangerous, precious or formidable; in short, that sex was constituted as a problem of truth" (56).

6 Lawrence Birken, in *Consuming Desire: Sexual Science and the Emergence of a Culture of Abundance, 1871–1914* (Ithaca: Cornell University Press, 1988), firmly establishes Darwin as "the first real sexologist" (60) and dates the emergence of sexology with the publication of Darwin's *The Descent of Man, and Selection in Relation to Sex* in 1871. His claim is based on the idea that Darwin was the first to articulate an epistemology of individuals (see his "Introduction", 1–21).

7 The verb "to know" has its etymological derivation from a number of sources, the Latin *(g)noscere* and French *connaître* suggesting "to know by the senses" and the German *wit*, French *savoir*, and Latin *scire* suggesting to "know by the mind." Knowing has historically in the West always been divided into material and ideal forms.

8 Richard von Krafft-Ebing, *Psychopathia Sexualis*, trans. Franklin S. Klaf (New York: Bell Publishing Co., 1965) 1.

9 Geoffrey Galt Harpham in "Aesthetics and the Fundamentals of Modernity," *Aesthetics and Ideology*, ed. George Levine (New Brunswick: Rutgers University Press, 1994) 124–149, makes the interesting case that Freud reinvents Kantian judgment in the unconscious. If Kantian judgment is based on a series of negations, it is not phenomenal perception, not theoretical reason, not speculative understanding, not desire, not utility, not politics, so the unconscious is based entirely on its negative relation to consciousness. Says Harpham, "Disinterested in time, space, or reality in general, the Freudian unconscious replays the most salient features of Kantian judgment" (136).

10 Grant Allen, *Physiological Aesthetics* (New York: D. Appleton and Co., 1877) 1.

11 Ibid., 34, 42.

12 See Allen, *Physiological Aesthetics*, 261, and Herbert Spencer *The Principles of Psychology*, vol. II (New York: D. Appleton and Co., 1901) 647.

13 Havelock Ellis, "Sexual Selection in Man," *Studies in the Psychology of Sex*, vol. II (New York: Random House, 1936) 136.

14 Sigmund Freud, *Three Essays on the Theory of Sexuality*, trans. and ed. James Strachey (New York: Basic Books, 1962) n. 22.

15 Sublimation itself may not be as disinterested as it at first seems. As Leo Bersani has pointed out in *The Freudian Body* (New York: Columbia University Press, 1986), "sublimation is not a mechanism by which desire is denied, but a self-reflexive activity by which desire multiplies and diversifies its representations. There is, to be sure, a certain purification of the desiring impulse, but purification should be understood here as an abstracting process which is not necessarily desexualizing" (43).

16 Ellis, "Sexual Selection in Man," 138.

17 Ibid., 138.

18 Kant, *Critique of Judgment*, 68.

19 Ellis, "Sexual Selection in Man," 154.

20 Freud diverged from this theory in his notion of "naturally competing" drives, itself an overdetermined model also found in late nineteenth-century economic and biological theories.

21 Nigel Kelsey, *D. H. Lawrence: Sexual Crisis* (New York: St. Martin's Press, 1991) 82.

22 Terry Eagleton, *The Ideology of the Aesthetic* (Oxford: Basil Blackwell, 1990) 23.

23 My account here is based on several theorists, including Paul de Man, "Aesthetic Formalization: Kleist's *Über das Marionettentheater*," *The Rhetoric of Romanticism* (New York: Columbia University Press, 1984) 263–291; Terry Eagleton, *The Ideology of the Aesthetic*, and Regenia Gagnier, "A Critique of Practical Aesthetics," *Aesthetics and Ideology*, ed. George Levine (New Brunswick: Rutgers University Press, 1994) 264–282.

24 Peter Brooks, "Aesthetics and Ideology – What Happened to Poetics?" *Aesthetics and Ideology*, ed. George Levine (New Brunswick: Rutgers University Press, 1994) 160.

25 Emile Delavenay argues in *D. H. Lawrence and Edward Carpenter: A Study in Edwardian Transition* (New York: Taplinger Publishing Co., 1971) that Lawrence's thinking was essentially pre-Freudian, and very much derived from or similar to Carpenter's stand for the emancipation of the individual from the political, economic, and moral constraints of the Victorian middle class.

26 Edward Carpenter, *Love's Coming of Age* (Manchester: Labour Press, 1896) 15.

27 See Roland Barthes, *The Pleasure of the Text*, trans. Richard Miller (New York: The Noonday Press, 1975).

28 D. H. Lawrence, *Lady Chatterley's Lover* (New York: Bantam Books, 1983). Hereafter citations of the text will be marked parenthetically as *LCL*.

29 Karl Marx, *Karl Marx: Selected Writings in Sociology and Social Philosophy*, ed. and trans. T. B. Bottomore (New York: McGraw-Hill Book Co., 1956) 70–71.

30 Graham Hough, *The Dark Sun* (New York: The Macmillan Company, 1957) 159.

31 D. H. Lawrence, *John Thomas and Lady Jane* (New York: The Viking Press, 1972) 46–47. Hereafter citations of the text will be marked parenthetically as *JTLJ*.

32 D. H. Lawrence, *The First Lady Chatterley* (New York: Dial Press, 1944) 65–66. Hereafter citations of the text will be marked parenthetically as *FLC*.

33 Jay A. Gertzman, *A Descriptive Bibliography of* Lady Chatterley's Lover (New York: Greenwood Press, 1989) 244.

34 Forster's *Howards End* (1910) also notably strives to level class differences through the baby of Leonard Bast and Helen Schlegel.

35 E. M. Forster, *Maurice* (New York: W. W. Norton & Co., 1987) 118. Hereafter citations of the text will be marked parenthetically as *M*.

36 Gertzman, *A Descriptive Bibliography of* Lady Chatterley's Lover, 237–243.

37 Anonymous, *Lady Chatterley's Husbands* (New York: William Faro, Inc. 1931) 9.

38 Ibid., 10.

39 Ibid., 9.

40 The circulation of *Lady Chatterley's Lover* through private subscription was, as Ian Hunter, David Saunders, and Dugald Williamson have suggested in *On Pornography: Literature, Sexuality and Obscenity Law* (London: Macmillan, 1993), in "the same manner as pornography and was a minor catalyst to the pornography trade since, without copyright protection, it was open to piracy" (95).

41 Excerpted from a letter to Compton Mackenzie and reprinted in Adam Parkes, *Modernism and the Theater of Censorship* (New York: Oxford University Press, 1996) 107.

42 George Levine, in *The Realistic Imagination* (University of Chicago Press, 1981), has characterized this as the general rhetorical strategy of all realistic modes. "Realism," he writes, "as a literary method, can in these terms be defined as a self-conscious effort, usually in the name of some moral enterprise of truth telling and extending the limits of human sympathy, to make literature appear to be describing directly not some other language but reality itself (whatever that may be taken to be); in this effort, the writer must self-contradictorily dismiss pervious conventions of representation while, in effect, establishing new ones" (8).

43 *Autobiography of a Flea* (London, c.1887; though the imprint reads "Cytheria: 1789") 43.

44 John Cleland, *Fanny Hill* (New York: Penguin Books, 1995) 128–131.

45 *The Way of a Man With a Maid* (Hertfordshire: Wordsworth Classics, 1996) 68.

46 See chapter three, n. 68, for an elaboration of the sublime penis in pornography.

47 Anne Fernilough, *D. H. Lawrence: Aesthetics and Ideology* (Oxford: Clarendon Press, 1993) 3. That Lawrence's ideas about sexual union form part of a larger social movement can be seen in Marie Stopes's description of sexual intercourse in her best-selling sex and marriage manual, *Married Love* (1918), where Stopes, whose sexual metaphors sound much like Lawrence's, writes:

> When two who are mated in every respect burn with the fire of innumerable forces within them, which set their bodies longing toward each other with desire to interpenetrate and encompass one another, the fusion of joy and rapture is not purely physical. The half-swoon-

ing sense of flux which overtakes the spirit in that eternal moment at the apex of rapture sweeps into its flaming tides the whole essence of man and woman, and as it were, the heat of contact vapourises their consciousness so that it fills the whole of cosmic space. For the moment they are identified with divine thoughts, the waves of eternal force, which to the mystic often appear in terms of golden light.

The similarities are quite obvious despite Lawrence's avowed hatred for Stopes's work.

48 James Joyce, *Ulysses* (New York: Vintage Books, 1961) 366.

49 Fernilough, *D. H. Lawrence*, 99.

50 See *The Private Case: An Annotated Bibliography of the Private Case Erotica Collection in the British (Museum) Library*, compiled by Patrick J. Kearney (London: Jay Landesman Ltd., 1981).

51 Such a scene can be found in *The Romance of Lust* (1873; New York: Blue Moon Books, 1992) where the hero, Charlie, and his sisters Lizzie and Mary, each receive an initiation into anal sex by a Mr. James MacCallum (141–149).

52 Cleland, *Fanny Hill*, 94–95. More modern examples that further support this fact are plentiful. For instance, *A Night in a Moorish Harem* (1906; Hertfordshire: Wordsworth Classics, 1995) contains the following revelation of the penis: "He undressed himself without stopping till his Herculean form stood entirely naked before me in all its gigantic but complete proportions. His immense shaft was proudly erect and huge even for such a giant" (69). A 1925 book, *The Adventures of Grace and Anna* (Hertfordshire: Wordsworth Classics, 1996) shows that such scenes are archetypal: "He certainly was a man fully gifted in these parts, his prong being fully a foot long and some inches in diameter, and being naked as he was, his huge balls dangling below his horse-like prick, it was enough to startle any girl, and Anna gave a little scream at the sight and buried her head in the cushions" (86).

53 Eliseo Vivas, *D. H. Lawrence: The Failure and Triumph of Art* (Evanston: Northwestern University Press, 1960) 6.

54 Ibid., 8–9.

55 Ibid., 142.

56 Hunter, Saunders, Williamson, *On Pornography*, 110.

57 Frederick Carter, *D. H. Lawrence and the Body Mystical* (London: Dennis Archer, 1932) 58, 24.

58 Horace Gregory, *Pilgrim of the Apocalypse* (New York: The Viking Press, 1933) 81.

59 F. R. Leavis, *D. H. Lawrence: Novelist* (New York: Alfred A. Knopf, 1956) xiii.

60 Ibid., 17.

61 Ibid., 17, 74.

62 Ibid., 177.

63 Ibid., 373.

64 Hough, *The Dark Sun*, 159.

65 Each of the above writers has written in homage to Lawrence. One such work, Henry Miller's *The World of Lawrence:A Passionate Appreciation*, ed. Evelyn J. Hinz and John J. Teunissen (Santa Barbara: Capra Press, 1980), reflects the common ideology of the age in which Lawrence participated: "Lawrence was right, when in his Introduction to *Fantasia*, he said that Freud did accomplish one good thing: he made us aware of our animal nature, of the body which we have repressed. For it is here that we have a chance to connect again with the universe, through the dark gods within. And the analyst is to be praised who has this for his aim: to reveal to the patient the true nature of the self, of personality" (199).

5. *Modernist criticism: the battle for culture and the accommodation of the obscene*

1 The most notorious of such critics is John Carey, whose book *The Intellectuals and the Masses* (Boston: Faber & Faber, 1992) claims that the project of modernism was one of distinguishing between the masses and the elite. Andreas Huyssen's more scholarly *After the Great Divide: Modernism, Mass Culture, Postmodernism* (Bloomington: Indiana University Press, 1986) does not see the divide between mass and elite culture as simply as Carey, but does focus on the tensions created between different cultural practices associated with high and low culture.

2 David Chinitz has written persuasively of T. S. Eliot's collaborations and uses of mass-cultural practices in "T. S. Eliot and the Cultural Divide," *PMLA*, 110:2 (March 1995) 236–247.

3 Oxford University established its English program in the 1890s and modeled it after its intellectually respectable Classical Moderations. English at Cambridge was lumped with the recently established Modern Language Tripos in the first years of the twentieth century and the first chair in English was not established until 1912, when Sir Arthur Quiller-Couch was established the King Edward VII Chair of English Literature. Eventually an English Tripos was proposed and accepted in 1917 when, according to Bernard Bergonzi in *Exploding English: Criticism, Theory, Culture* (Oxford: Clarendon Press, 1990), "many of the dons who might have opposed it were away at war" (43). Interesting in light of the current expansion of literary studies into cultural studies, the original Cambridge degree was called "Literature, Life, and Thought," whereas the Oxford degree was more strictly confined to "English Language and Literature" (43).

4 Barry Cullen, "'I thought I had provided something better' – F. R. Leavis, Literary Criticism and Anti-Philosophy," *The British Critical Tradition*, ed. Gary Day (New York: St. Martin's Press, 1993) 188.

5 Bernard Bergonzi, *Exploding English: Criticism, Theory, Culture*, 43–44.

6 Pamela McCallum, *Literature and Method:Towards a Critique of I.A. Richards,T. S. Eliot, and F. R. Leavis* (Dublin: Gill and MacMillan Humanities Press, 1983) 155. One measure of Leavis's impact on reading in this century can be found in *Roget's*

Thesaurus of English Words and Phrases, ed. Susan M. Lloyd (New York: Penguin Books, 1982) in which the word "Leavisite" is listed as a synonym for "interpreter" (266).

7 By the word 'culture' I am referring both to society at large as well as the body of cultural artifacts viewed as peculiarly of value to that social body by a specific group of individuals concerned in its maintenance.

8 Q. D. Leavis, *Fiction and the Reading Public* (1932; New York: Russell & Russell, 1965) 74.

9 T. S. Eliot, "Dante," *Selected Essays* (New York: Harcourt Brace Jovanovich, 1978) 200.

10 Modernist critics are responsible for augmenting the meaning of sensibility in the twentieth century. Where before the 1920s and 1930s "sensibility" had primarily meant the power of sensation or emotion as distinguished from cognition and will, Eliot's use of the term in his "dissociation of sensibility" reconfigured it to imply the conjunction of thought and feeling. In Eliot, Richards, and Leavis, the term almost always implies an organic relationship between the body's senses and the mind's faculties.

11 McCallum, *Literature and Method*, 3–4.

12 *Scrutiny*, 1:1 (May 1932) 2.

13 T. S. Eliot, "The Metaphysical Poets," *Selected Essays*, 247.

14 Christopher Norris has made this observation in his preface to Michael Bell's *F. R. Leavis* (New York: Routledge, 1988) ix. Terry Eagleton, in *Literary Theory: An Introduction* (Oxford: Blackwell Books, 1983), also makes a similar claim that by locating the dissociation of sensibility in the seventeenth century, "Eliot was in fact assaulting . . . the whole ideology of middle-class liberalism, the official ruling ideology of industrial capitalist society" (39).

15 T. S. Eliot, "Philip Massinger" *Selected Essays*, 189.

16 F. R. Leavis, "Joyce and the Revolution of the Word," *Scrutiny* 2:2 (September 1933) 199, 198.

17 Ibid., 199.

18 Raymond Williams, *Culture and Society, 1780–1950* (1958; Harmondsworth, England: Penguin Books, 1968) 252. An important parallel should be drawn between the work of the British modernist critics and the work of American New Critics. In the United States, English literature studies were deeply influenced by the work of John Ransom Crowe, Allen Tate, and Robert Penn Warren, whose work, contemporaneous with Leavis's involvement with *Scrutiny*, originated out of the recognition that the American South needed to develop forms of cultural production that could combat the industrial dominance of northern US, capitalist culture. Their work offered an agrarian critique of industrial capitalism, as is described by Mark Janovich in *The Cultural Politics of New Criticism* (New York: Cambridge University Press, 1993).

19 I. A. Richards, *Principles of Literary Criticism* (New York: Harcourt Brace Jovanovich, 1925) 202–203.

20 Q. D. Leavis, *Fiction and the Reading Public*, 67, 74, 224.

21 F. R. Leavis, "Mass Civilisation and Minority Culture," *For Continuity* (Cambridge: The Minority Press, 1933) 18, 20–21.

22 T. S. Eliot, "Marie Lloyd," *Selected Essays*, 407.

23 Q. D. Leavis, *Fiction and the Reading Public*, 146.

24 Ibid., 156.

25 Andreas Huyssen, *After the Great Divide*, ix.

26 Q. D. Leavis, *Fiction and the Reading Public*, 7.

27 James Joyce, *A Portrait of the Artist as a Young Man* (New York: Penguin Books, 1976) 206.

28 Immanuel Kant, *The Critique of Judgment*, trans. James Creed Meredith (Oxford: Clarendon Press, 1991) 94. See Jean-François Lyotard, *The Postmodern Condition: A Report of Knowledge*, trans. Geoff Bennington and Brian Massumi (University of Minneapolis Press, 1993).

29 I. A. Richards, *Principles of Literary Criticism*, 62.

30 Ibid., 234.

31 *Scrutiny*, 1:1 (May 1932) 5.

32 F. R. Leavis, "The Literary Mind," *Scrutiny*, 1:1, 25.

33 Ibid., 31.

34 T. S. Eliot, *The Use of Poetry and the Use of Criticism* (Cambridge: Harvard University Press, 1933) 149.

35 F. R. Leavis, "Valuation in Criticism," *Valuation in Criticism*, ed. G. Singh (Cambridge University Press, 1986) 286.

36 Ibid., 285.

37 Q. D. Leavis, *Fiction and the Reading Public*, 74, 256.

38 Sensation literature of the 1860s presaged the mass-culture explosion of the 1920s and 1930s, and public debate about it mirrors modernist criticism's concerns about mass culture. Susan David Bernstein, in "Dirty Reading: Sensation Fiction, Women, and Primitivism," *Criticism*, 36:2 (spring 1994), says "The critical campaign against sensation fiction can be understood as an effort to guard 'culture' from the encroachment of underclass modes of entertainment" (222). Margaret Oliphant, in a review of novels for *Blackwood's Edinburgh Magazine* in 1867, called sensation fiction, "feverish productions" and noted how terrible it was that "We have grown accustomed to . . . the narrative of many thrills of feeling" (quoted in Bernstein, "Dirty Reading," 213). Shock, in this context, is oddly numbing. Similarly, in a review of "Our Female Sensation Novelists" in *Littel's Living Age*, 103 (August 1863), the author suggested that sensationalism arouses the "lower" order of feeling "by drugging thought and reason, and stimulating the attention through the lower and more animal instincts" (352–353). Shock, as configured in the sensation novel debate, excites the body at the same time that it numbs or drugs the mind.

39 Laura Riding and Robert Graves, *A Survey of Modernist Poetry* (London: William Heinemann, Ltd., 1927) 10.

40 Kant, *The Critique of Judgment*, 166.

41 I. A. Richards, *Principles of Literary Criticism*, 85.

42 Ibid., 85.

43 T. S. Eliot, "Metaphysical Poets," *Selected Essays*, 250.

44 I. A. Richards, *Principles of Literary Criticism*, 15.

45 John Needham, *The Completest Mode: I. A. Richards and the Continuity of English Literary Criticism* (Edinburgh University Press, 1982) 29.

46 F. R. Leavis, "The Literary Mind," *Scrutiny*, 1:1 (May 1932) 28.

47 F. R. Leavis, "Restatement for Critics," *Scrutiny*, 1:4 (March 1933) 316.

48 See Kant, *The Critique of Judgment*, 39, 58, 88, 107.

49 Ibid., 316.

50 F. R. Leavis, "Literary Criticism and Philosophy," *Scrutiny*, 6:1 (June 1937) 61.

51 McCallum, *Literature and Method*, 182.

52 Richards explained impulses in *Principles of Literary Criticism* as follows: "The process in the course of which a mental event may occur, a process apparently beginning in a stimulus and ending in an act, is what we have called an impulse. In actual experience single impulses of course never occur. Even the simplest human reflexes are very intricate bundles of mutually dependent impulses, and in any actual human behaviour the number of simultaneous and connected impulses occurring is beyond estimation" (86). Richards regarded a stimulus as that which "must not be conceived as an alien intruder which thrusts itself upon us and, after worming a devious way through our organism as through a piece of cheese, emerges at the other end as an act. Stimuli are only received if they serve some need of the organism and the form which the response to them takes depends only in part upon the nature of the stimulus, and much more upon what the organism 'wants', i.e. the state of equilibrium of its multifarious activities"(87).

53 Ibid., 250.

54 Ibid., 250.

55 Ibid., 252–253.

56 I. A. Richards, C. K. Ogden, and James Wood, *The Foundations of Aesthetics* (New York: Lear Publishers, 1925) 90.

57 I. A. Richards, *Principles of Literary Criticism*, 263–264.

58 I. A. Richards, *Sciences and Poetries: A Reissue of Science and Poetry* (New York: W. W. Norton & Co., 1970) 40.

59 Steven Connor, *Theory and Cultural Value* (Oxford: Basil Blackwell Books, 1992) 37.

60 Linda Hutcheon, *Irony's Edge: The Theory and Politics of Irony* (New York: Routledge, 1994) 38.

61 I. A. Richards, *Principles of Literary Criticism*, 270.

62 T. W. Adorno, *Aesthetic Theory*, trans. C. Lenhardt (London: Routledge & Kegan Paul, 1984) 7.

226.

63 Linda Hutcheon, *Irony's Edge*, 15.

64 Stephen Heath, "Ambiviolences," *Poststructuralist Joyce: Essays from the French*, ed. Derek Attridge and Daniel Ferrer (New York: Cambridge University Press, 1984) 141–142.

65 Frederic Jameson, "Postmodernism and Consumer Society," *The Anti-Aesthetic: Essays on Postmodern Culture*, ed. Hal Foster (Seattle: Bay Press, 1983) 111–125.

66 T. S. Eliot, *Criterion*, 2:7 (April 1924) 232.

67 T. S. Eliot, "Marvell," *Selected Essays*, 303, 304, 302, 256–257.

68 T. S. Eliot, "The Metaphysical Poets," *Selected Essays*, 243.

69 T. S. Eliot, "A Note on Ezra Pound," *To-day*, 4 (September 1918) 6.

70 T. S. Eliot, "*Ulysses*, Order and Myth," *Selected Prose of T. S. Eliot*, ed. Frank Kermode (New York: Harcourt Brace Jovanovich, 1975) 175.

71 Ibid., 177.

72 T. W. Adorno, *Aesthetic Theory*, 8.

73 This does not mitigate the question of whether or not Eliot's work escapes his critical intentions. Should we choose not to read through Eliot's lens, the sexual, lower-class bodies haunt and subvert the poem's very high-cultural aims. They are bodies, as it were, that will not stay buried.

74 Daniel R. Schwarz, *The Humanistic Heritage* (Philadelphia: University of Pennsylvania Press, 1986) 70.

75 F. R. Leavis, *New Bearings in English Poetry* (Ann Arbor: University of Michigan Press, 1960) 103.

76 Ibid., 103–104.

77 F. R. Leavis, "Why Universities?" *Scrutiny*, 3:2 (September 1934) 120.

78 F. R. Leavis, "Mass Civilisation and Minority Culture," *For Continuity*, 15.

79 F. R. Leavis, "Why Universities?" 120.

80 F. R. Leavis, *D. H. Lawrence: Novelist* (New York: Alfred A. Knopf, 1956) 73.

81 F. R. Leavis, "Towards Standards of Criticism," *Towards Standards of Criticism: A Selection from 'The Calendar of Modern Letters'* (London: Wishart & Co., 1933) 17.

82 F. R. Leavis, "The Literary Mind," *Scrutiny*, 1:1 (May 1932) 26.

83 Terry Eagleton, *Criticism and Ideology*, 15.

84 Pamela McCallum, *Literature and Method*, 7.

85 F. R. Leavis, *D. H. Lawrence: Novelist*, 17.

86 F. R. Leavis, "Joyce and the Revolution of the Word," 198.

87 I. A. Richards, *Principles of Literary Criticism*, 35.

88 T. S. Eliot, "Notes Toward the Definition of Culture," *Christianity and Culture* (New York: Harcourt Brace Jovanovich, 1949) 107.

89 T. S. Eliot, *The Use of Poetry and the Use of Criticism*, 77.

90 Quoted in Edward de Grazia, *Girls Lean Back Everywhere: The Law of Obscenity and the Assault on Genius* (New York: Vintage Books, 1992) n.430.

91 F. R. Leavis, "Thought and Emotional Quality," *Scrutiny*, 13:1 (spring 1945) 55.

92 F. R. Leavis, "Literary Criticism and Philosophy: A Reply," 60–61.

93 In "Restatement for Critics," *Scrutiny*, 1:4 (March 1933), Leavis differentiated himself from T. S. Eliot on this point when, accused of rejecting Eliot when he turned to orthodox Christianity, he said "if it means the kind of rejection of life implicit in Mr. Eliot's attitude towards sex, then we do certainly dissociate ourselves at that point" (318). For explorations of the equation of sex with health, see Roy Porter and Lesley Hall, *The Facts of Life: The Creation of Sexual Knowledge in Britain, 1650–1950* (New Haven: Yale University Press, 1995); Ian Hunter, David Saunders and Dugald Williamson, *On Pornography: Literature, Sexuality and Obscenity Law* (London: Macmillan, 1993), and Jeffrey Weeks, *Sex, Politics and Society* (New York: Longman, 1981).

94 Peter Miles and Malcolm Smith, *Cinema, Literature, and Society: Elite and Mass Culture in Interwar Britain* (New York: Croom Helm, 1987) 90.

95 The idea of harmonizing the sensuous and moral reflective faculties is developed quite effectively in Ian Hunter, David Saunders, and Dugald Williamson, *On Pornography*. See especially chapter three.

96 See F. R. Leavis, "The Orthodoxy of Enlightenment," *Anna Karenina and Other Essays* (London: Chatto & Windus, 1967) 235–241.

97 Hunter, Saunders, and Williamson, *On Pornography*, 129.

98 Frederic Jameson, "Postmodernism and Consumer Society," *The Anti-Aesthetic*, 112.

Bibliography

Ackland, Joseph. "Elementary Education and the Decay of Literature." *The Nineteenth Century*. 35.203 (March 1894): 412–423.

Addison, Joseph. "Taste and the Pleasures of the Imagination." *Critical Essays from the Spectator*. Ed. Donald F. Bond. New York: Oxford University Press, 1970. *The Spectator*, no. 1.1 (March 1711).

Adorno, T. W. *Aesthetic Theory*. Trans. C. Lenhardt. London: Routledge & Kegan Paul, 1984.

The Adventures of Grace and Anna. Hertfordshire: Wordsworth Classics, 1996.

The Adventures of Lady Harpur: Her Life of Free Enjoyment and Ecstatic Love Adventures, vol. 1. Glascow [sic]: William Murray, 1894.

Allen, Grant. *Physiological Aesthetics*. New York: D. Appleton and Co., 1877.

Aphrodisiacs and Anti-Aphrodisiacs. London: J. C. Hotten, 1869.

Arnold, Matthew. *Culture and Anarchy*. New York: Cambridge University Press, 1988.

"The Function of Criticism at the Present Time." *Essays Literary and Critical by Matthew Arnold*. London: J. M. Dent & Sons, 1928.

Autobiography of a Flea. London: c.1889.

Bakhtin, Mikhail. *The Dialogic Imagination*. Trans. Caryl Emerson and Michael Holquist. Austin: University of Texas Press, 1992.

Rabelais and his World. Trans. Helene Iswolsky. Bloomington: Indiana University Press, 1984.

Barker, Francis. *The Private Tremulous Body: Essays on Subjection*. New York: Methuen, 1984.

Barrell, John. *The Birth of Pandora and the Division of Knowledge*. Philadelphia: University of Pennsylvania Press, 1992.

Barthes, Roland. *Critical Essays*. Trans. Richard Miller. New York: Hill & Wang, 1972. *The Pleasure of the Text*. Trans. Richard Miller. New York: The Noonday Press, 1975.

Beardsley, Monroe C. *Aesthetics: From Classical Greece to Present.* University of Alabama Press, 1966.

Benjamin, Walter. "The Work of Art in the Age of Mechanical Reproduction." *Illuminations.* Trans. Harry Zohn. New York: Schocken Books, 1968.

Bergonzi, Bernard. *Exploding English: Criticism, Theory, Culture.* Oxford: Clarendon Press, 1990.

Bersani, Leo. *The Freudian Body.* New York: Columbia University Press, 1986.

Birken, Lawrence. *Consuming Desire: Sexual Science and the Emergence of a Culture of Abundance, 1871–1914.* Ithaca: Cornell University Press, 1988.

Bloch, Iwan. *The Sexual Life of Our Time.* Trans. M. Eden Paul. London: William Heinemann, 1920.

Bourdieu, Pierre. *Distinction: A Social Critique of the Judgement of Taste.* Trans. Richard Nice. Cambridge: Harvard University Press, 1984.

The Field of Cultural Production. New York: Columbia University Press, 1993.

Boyle, Thomas F. "Morbid Depression Alternating with Excitement: Sex in Victorian Newspapers." *Sexuality and Victorian Fiction* Ed. Don Richard Cox. Knoxville: University of Tennessee Press, 1984.

Brantlinger, Patrick. *Bread and Circuses: Theories of Mass Culture as Social Decay.* Ithaca: Cornell University Press, 1983.

Brett, R. L. *The Third Earl of Shaftesbury: A Study in Eighteenth-Century Literary Theory.* New York: Hutchinson's University Library, 1951.

Bristow, Edward J. *Vice and Vigilance: Purity Movements in Britain since 1700.* Dublin: Gill and Macmillan, 1977.

Brooks, Peter. "Aesthetics and Ideology – What Happened to Poetics?" *Aesthetics and Ideology.* Ed. George Levine. New Brunswick: Rutgers University Press, 1994.

Brown, Richard. *James Joyce and Sexuality.* Cambridge University Press, 1985.

Bulwer Lytton, E. G. "England and the English." *The English Ruling Class.* Ed. W. L. Guttsman. London: Weidenfeld and Nicolson, 1969.

Burdett, Osbert. *The Beardsley Period.* London: John Lane, the Bodley Head Ltd., 1925.

Carey, John. *The Intellectuals and the Masses.* Boston: Faber & Faber, 1992.

Carpenter, Edward. *Love's Coming of Age.* Manchester: Labour Press, 1896.

Carter, Frederick. *D. H. Lawrence and the Body Mystical.* London: Dennis Archer, 1932.

Carter, John. *ABC for Book Collectors.* New York: Granada, 1985.

Cassirer, Ernst. *The Philosophy of the Enlightenment.* Trans. Fritz C. A. Koelln and James Pettgrove. Princeton University Press, 1951.

Caygill, Howard. *Art of Judgement.* Oxford: Basil Blackwell, 1989.

Chadwick, Edwin. *Report . . . from the Poor Law Commissioners on an Inquiry into the Sanitary Conditions of the Labouring Population of Great Britain.* London: 1842.

Cleland, John. *Fanny Hill, or Memoirs of a Woman of Pleasure.* London: Penguin Books, 1995.

The Cockchafer: "A Choice selection of Flash, Frisky, and Funny Songs Never before Printed and Adapted for Gentlemen Only." London: W. West, c.1840.

Connor, Steven. Theory and Cultural Value. Oxford: Basil Blackwell Books, 1992.

Cullen, Barry. "'I Thought I Had Provided Something Better' – F.R. Leavis, Literary Criticism and Anti-Philosophy." The British Critical Tradition. Ed. Gary Day. New York: St. Martin's Press, 1993.

Daily Herald. 921 (March 17, 1922): 4.

Davis, Tracy C. "The Actress in Victorian Pornography." Victorian Scandals: Representations of Gender and Class. Ed. Kristine Ottesen Garrigan. Athens: University of Ohio Press, 1992.

De Grazia, Edward. Girls Lean Back Everywhere: The Law of Obscenity and the Assault on Genius. New York: Vintage Books, 1992.

De Man, Paul. "Aesthetic Formalization: Kleist's Über das Marionettentheater." The Rhetoric of Romanticism. New York: Columbia University Press, 1984: 263–291.

"Phenomenality and Materiality in Kant." Aesthetic Ideology. Ed. Andrzej Warminski. Minneapolis: University of Minnesota Press, 1996.

De Sade, Donatien-Alphonse. The 120 Days of Sodom. Trans. Austryn Wainhouse and Richard Seaver. New York: Grove Press, 1966.

DeJean, Joan. "The Politics of Pornography: L'Ecole des Filles." The Invention of Pornography: Obscenity and the Origins of Modernity, 1500–1800. Ed. Lynn Hunt. New York: Zone Books, 1993.

Delavenay, Emile. D. H. Lawrence and Edward Carpenter: A Study in Edwardian Transition. New York: Taplinger Publishing Co., 1971.

Denvir, Bernard. The Eighteenth Century: Art, Design, Society, 1689–1789. Essex: Longman Group Ltd., 1983.

Dowling, Linda. The Vulgarization of Art: The Victorians and Aesthetic Democracy. Charlottesville: University of Virginia Press, 1996.

Eagleton, Terry. Criticism and Ideology. London: Verso Books, 1976.

The Ideology of the Aesthetic. Oxford: Blackwell UK, 1990.

Literary Theory: An Introduction. Oxford: Blackwell Books, 1983.

Eliot, T. S. Criterion. 2:7 (April 1924).

"A Note on Ezra Pound." To-day. 4 (September 1918): 6.

"Notes Toward the Definition of Culture," Christianity and Culture. New York: Harcourt Brace Jovanovich, 1949.

Selected Essays. New York: Harcourt Brace Jovanovich, 1978.

"Ulysses, Order and Myth." Selected Prose of T. S. Eliot. Ed. Frank Kermode. New York: Harcourt Brace Jovanovich, 1975.

The Use of Poetry and the Use of Criticism. Cambridge: Harvard University Press, 1933.

Elliott, Bridget J. "New and Not So 'New Women' on the London Stage: Aubrey Beardsley's Yellow Book Images of Mrs. Patrick Campbell and Rejane." Victorian Studies, 31.1 (autumn 1987):33–56.

"Sights of Pleasure: Beardsley's Images of Actresses and the New Journalism of the

Nineties." *Reconsidering Aubrey Beardsley.* Ed. Robert Langenfeld. Ann Arbor: UMI Research Press, 1989.

Ellis, Havelock. "Sexual Selection in Man." *Studies in the Psychology of Sex,* vol. II. New York: Random House, 1936.

Ellman, Richard. *The Consciousness of Joyce.* London: Faber & Faber, 1977.

"Evening Continuation Schools." *New Review.* 51 (August 1893): 135.

Exhibition of Female Flagellants. London: William Dugdale, c.1860.

The Exquisite, vol. I. London: H. Smith, 37 Holywell Street, 1842.

Ferguson, Frances. *Solitude and the Sublime: Romanticism and Individuation.* New York: Routledge, 1992.

Fernilough, Anne. *D. H. Lawrence: Aesthetics and Ideology.* Oxford: Clarendon Press, 1993.

Ferry, Luc. *The Invention of Taste in the Democratic Age.* Trans. Robert de Loaiza. University of Chicago Press, 1993.

Fletcher, Ian. *Aubrey Beardsley.* Boston: G. K. Hall & Co., 1987.

Forster, E. M. *Maurice.* New York: W. W. Norton & Co., 1987.

Foucault, Michel. *The History of Sexuality,* vol. I. New York: Vintage Books, 1978.

Foxon, David. *Libertine Literature in England, 1660–1745.* London: The Book Collector, 1964.

Frances Barker, *The Private Tremulous Body.* Ann Arbor: University of Michigan Press, 1995.

Fraxi, Pisanus. *Catena Librorum Tacendorum.* London: privately printed, 1885.

Index Librorum Prohibitorum. London: privately printed, 1878.

Freud, Sigmund. *Civilization and its Discontents.* Trans. and Ed. James Strachey. New York: W. W. Norton & Co., 1961.

The Ego and the Id. Trans. Joan Riviere. Ed. James Strachey. New York: W. W. Norton & Company, 1969.

Three Essays on the Theory of Sexuality. Trans. and Ed. James Strachey. New York: Basic Books, 1962.

"From the Maid's Point of View." *New Review.* 5.27 (1891): 170–184.

Fryer, Peter, Ed. *Forbidden Books of the Victorians.* London: The Odyssey Press, 1970.

Gagnier, Regenia. "A Critique of Practical Aesthetics." *Aesthetics and Ideology.* Ed. George Levine. New Brunswick: Rutgers University Press, 1994. 264–282.

"On the Insatiability of Human Wants." *Victorian Studies.* 36:2 (winter 1993): 125–153.

Gertzman, Jay A. *A Descriptive Bibliography of Lady Chatterley's Lover.* New York: Greenwood Press, 1989.

Gilbert, Katharine Everett and Helmut Kuhn. *A History of Esthetics.* New York: Macmillan & Co., 1939.

Godkin, E. L. "Newspapers Here and Abroad." *Review of Reviews.* 1 (January–June 1890): 203.

Gosse, Edmund. *The Life of Algernon Charles Swinburne.* New York: The Macmillan Co., 1917.

Gregory, Horace. *Pilgrim of the Apocalypse.* New York: The Viking Press, 1933.

Griest, Guinevere L. *Mudie's Circulating Library and the Victorian Novel.* Bloomington: Indiana University Press, 1970.

Guillory, John. *Cultural Capital: The Problem of Literary Canon Formation.* University of Chicago Press, 1993.

Gynococracy. London: 1893.

Habermas, Jürgen. *The Structural Transformation of the Public Sphere.* Trans. Thomas Burger. Cambridge: MIT Press, 1992.

Harpham, Geoffrey Galt. "Aesthetics and the Fundamentals of Modernity." *Aesthetics and Ideology.* Ed. George Levine. New Brunswick: Rutgers University Press, 1994.

Hayes, Michael. "Popular Fiction and Middle-Brow Taste." *Literature and Culture in Modern Britain, 1900–1929.* Ed. Clive Bloom. Essex: Langma Group UK, 1993.

Heath, Stephen. "Ambiviolences." *Poststructuralist Joyce: Essays from the French.* Ed. Derek Attridge and Daniel Ferrer. New York: Cambridge University Press, 1984. 141–142.

Hegel, Georg Wilhelm Friedrich. *The Philosophy of Fine Art.* Trans. F. P. B. Osmaston. *Philosophies of Art and Beauty.* Ed. Albert Hofstadter and Richard Kuhns. University of Chicago Press, 1964.

Herr, Cheryl. *Joyce's Anatomy of Culture.* Urbana: University of Illinois Press, 1986.

Hogarth, William. *Analysis of Beauty.* Ed. Ronald Paulson. New Haven: Yale University Press, 1996.

Hough, Graham. *The Dark Sun.* New York: The Macmillan Company, 1957.

—— and Eric Werner, Eds. *Strangeness and Beauty: An Anthology of Aesthetic Criticism, 1840–1910.* Cambridge University Press, 1983.

Hume, David. "Of the Standard of Taste." *David Hume Essays: Moral, Political, and Literary.* Ed. Eugene F. Miller. Indianapolis: Liberty Classics, 1985.

Hunt, Lynn. "Pornography and the French Revolution." *The Invention of Pornography: Obscenity and the Origins of Modernity, 1500–1800.* Ed. Lynn Hunt. New York: Zone Books, 1993.

—— Ed. *Eroticism and the Body Politic.* Baltimore: The Johns Hopkins University Press, 1991.

—— Ed. *The Invention of Pornography: Obscenity and the Origins of Modernity, 1500– 1800 .* New York: Zone Books, 1993.

Hunter, Ian, David Saunders, and Dugald Williamson. *On Pornography: Literature, Sexuality, and Obscenity Law.* New York: St. Martin's Press, 1993.

Hutcheon, Linda. *Irony's Edge: The Theory and Politics of Irony.* New York: Routledge, 1994.

—— *A Theory of Parody.* New York: Methuen, 1985.

Hutcheson, Francis. *An Inquiry into the Original of Our Ideas of Beauty and Virtue.* Hampshire, England: Gregg International Publishers, 1969.

Huyssen, Andreas. *After the Great Divide: Modernism, Mass Culture, Postmodernism.* Bloomington: Indiana University Press, 1986.

Hyde, H. Montgomery. *A History of Pornography.* New York: Farrar, Straus and Giroux, 1964.

Hyder, Clyde K. *Swinburne: The Critical Heritage.* New York: Barnes & Noble, 1970.

Jackson, Holbrook. *The Eighteen Nineties.* London: Jonathan Cape, 1931.

Jacob, Margaret C. "The Materialist World of Pornography." *The Invention of Pornography: Obscenity and the Origins of Modernity, 1500–1800*. Ed. Lynn Hunt. New York: Zone Books, 1993.

Jameson, Frederic. "Postmodernism and Consumer Society." *The Anti-Aesthetic: Essays on Postmodern Culture*. Ed. Hal Foster. Seattle: Bay Press, 1983.

Jancovich, Mark. *The Cultural Politics of the New Criticism*. New York: Cambridge University Press, 1993.

Joyce, James. *Portrait of the Artist as a Young Man*. New York: Penguin, 1976.

   Stephen Hero. London: Jonathan Cape, 1956.

   Ulysses. New York: Vintage, 1961.

Kant, Immanuel. *The Critique of Judgment*. Trans. James Creed Meredith. Oxford: Clarendon Press, 1991.

Kearney, Patrick J., Ed. *The Private Case: An Annotated Bibliography of the Private Case Erotica Collection in the British (Museum) Library*. London: Jay Landesman Ltd., 1981.

Kelsey, Nigel. *D. H. Lawrence: Sexual Crisis*. New York: St. Martin's Press, 1991.

Kendrick, Walter. *The Secret Museum: Pornography in Modern Culture*. New York: Viking, 1987.

Kipnis, Laura. *Ecstasy Unlimited: On Sex, Capital, Gender, and Aesthetics*. Minneapolis: University of Minnesota Press, 1993.

Klein, Lawrence E. *Shaftesbury and the Culture of Politeness*. Cambridge University Press, 1994.

Koetzle, Michael. *1000 Nudes*. Cologne: Benedikt Taschen, 1994.

Lady Chatterley's Husbands. New York: William Faro, Inc. 1931.

Lang, Cecil Y. *The Swinburne Letters*. New Haven: Yale University Press, 1959.

Lansbury, Coral. *The Old Brown Dog: Women, Workers, and Vivisection in Victorian England*. Madison: University of Wisconsin Press, 1985.

Lawrence, D. H. *The First Lady Chatterley*. New York: Dial Press, 1944.

   John Thomas and Lady Jane. New York: The Viking Press, 1972.

   Lady Chatterley's Lover. New York: Bantam Books, 1983.

   "Pornography and Obscenity." *Sex, Literature, and Censorship*. Ed. Harry T. Moore. New York: Twayne Publishers, 1953.

Le Bon, Gustave. *The Crowd*. London: T. Fisher Unwin, 1913.

Leavis, F. R. *D. H. Lawrence: Novelist*. New York: Alfred A. Knopf, 1956.

   "Joyce and the Revolution of the Word." *Scrutiny*. 2:2 (September 1933): 193–201.

   "Literary Criticism and Philosophy." *Scrutiny*. 6:1 (June 1937): 59–70.

   "The Literary Mind." *Scrutiny*. 1:1 (May 1932): 20–32.

   "Mass Civilisation and Minority Culture." *For Continuity*. Cambridge: The Minority Press, 1933.

   New Bearings in English Poetry. Ann Arbor: University of Michigan Press, 1960.

   "The Orthodoxy of Enlightenment." *Anna Karenina and other Essays*. London: Chatto & Windus, 1967.

   "Restatement for Critics." *Scrutiny*. 1:4 (March 1933): 315–323.

234.

"Thought and Emotional Quality." *Scrutiny.* 13:1 (spring 1945): 53–72.

"Towards Standards of Criticism." *Towards Standards of Criticism: A Selection from 'The Calendar of Modern Letters.'* London: Wishart & Co., 1933.

"Valuation in Criticism." *Valuation in Criticism.* Ed. G. Singh. Cambridge University Press, 1986.

"Why Universities?" *Scrutiny.* 3:2 (September 1934): 117–132.

Leavis, Q. D. *Fiction and the Reading Public.* New York: Russell & Russell, 1965.

Leonard, Garry. "Power, Pornography, and the Problem of Pleasure: The Semerotics of Desire and Commodity Culture in Joyce." *James Joyce Quarterly,* 30–31.4–1 (summer–fall 1993): 573–591.

Leslie, Shane. *Dublin Review.* 9 (September 1922) 119.

Quarterly Review. 238 (October 1922). 219–234.

Levine, George. *The Realistic Imagination.* University of Chicago Press, 1981.

Ed. *Aesthetics and Ideology.* New Brunswick: Rutgers University Press, 1994.

Loth, David. *The Erotic in Literature.* London: Secker & Warburg, 1961.

Maas, Henry, J. C. Duncan, and W. G. Good, Eds. *The Letters of Aubrey Beardsley,* Rutherford: Farleigh Dickinson University Press, 1970.

Marcus, Steven. *The Other Victorians.* New York: Basic Books, 1964.

Marx, Karl. *Karl Marx: Early Writings.* London: Harmondsworth, 1975.

Marx, Karl: Selected Writings in Sociology and Social Philosophy. Ed. and Trans. T. B. Bottomore. New York: McGraw-Hill Book, Co., 1956.

Marx and Engels on Art and Literature. Ed. Lee Baxandall and Stefan Morawski. St. Louis: Telos Press, 1973.

McCallum, Pamela. *Literature and Method: Towards a Critique of I. A. Richards, T. S. Eliot, and F. R. Leavis.* Dublin: Gill and MacMillan Humanities Press, 1983.

McCalman, Iaian. *Radical Underworld: Prophets, Revolutionaries and Pornographers in London 1795–1840.* Cambridge University Press, 1988.

Michelson, Peter. "Beardsley, Burroughs, decadence and the poetics of obscenity." *TriQuarterly,* no. 12 (spring 1968): 139–145.

Speaking the Unspeakable. Buffalo: State University Press, 1993.

Miles, Peter and Malcolm Smith, *Cinema, Literature, and Society: Elite and Mass Culture in Interwar Britain.* New York: Croom Helm, 1987.

Miller, Henry. *The World of Lawrence: A Passionate Appreciation.* Ed. Evelyn J. Hinz and John J. Teunissen. Santa Barbara: Capra Press, 1980.

Miss High-Heels. Paris: Groves & Michaux, 1931.

The Modern Eveline. Paris: Charles Carrington, 1904.

Mortensen, Preben. *Art in the Social Order: The Making of the Modern Conception of Art.* Albany: State University Press of New York, 1997.

Murray, John Middleton. *Nation and Athenaeum.* 31 (April 22, 1922): 124–125.

My Secret Life. New York: Blue Moon Books, 1988.

Mysteries of Flagellation. London: 1863.

Nancy, Jean-Luc. "The Sublime Offering." *Of the Sublime: Presence in Question*. Trans. Jeffrey S. Librett. Albany: State University of New York, 1993.

The National Observer (April 21, 1894). 588–589.

Nead, Lynda. "'Above the Pulp-line': The Cultural Significance of Erotic Art." *Dirty Looks: Women Pornography Power*. Ed. Roma Gibson and Pamela Church Gibson. London: BFI Publishing, 1993.

The Female Nude: Art, Obscenity, and Sexuality. New York: Routledge, 1992.

Needham, John. *The Completest Mode: I.A. Richards and the Continuity of English Literary Criticism*. Edinburgh University Press, 1982.

Neret, Gilles, Ed. *Erotica Universalis*. Munich: Schocken Books, 1992.

Nietzsche, Friedrich. *Beyond Good and Evil*. Trans. Walter Kaufmann. New York: Vintage, 1989.

A Night in a Moorish Harem. Hertfordshire: Wordsworth Classics, 1995.

Nordau, Max. *Degeneration*. Lincoln: University of Nebraska Press, 1993.

Norris, Christopher. "Introduction". Michael Bell. *F. R. Leavis*. New York: Routledge, 1988.

Norris, Margot. *Joyce's Web: The Social Unraveling of Modernism*. Austin: University of Texas Press, 1992.

Parkes, Adam. *Modernism and the Theater of Censorship*. New York: Oxford University Press, 1996.

Paulson, Ronald. *The Beautiful, the Novel, and the Strange: Aesthetics and Heterodoxy*. Baltimore: Johns Hopkins University Press, 1996.

Ed. *Analysis of Beauty*. New Haven: Yale University Press, 1996.

The Pearl. New York: Grove Press, 1968.

"Penny Fiction." *The Quarterly Review*. 171.341 (1890):150–171

Pepys, Samuel. *The Diary and Correspondence of Samuel Pepys, FRS* vol. III. Ed. Jay Smith. New York: Bigelow, Brown & Co., n.d.

Perkin, Harold. *The Structured Crowd*. New Jersey: Barnes & Noble, 1981.

Porter, Roy and Lesley Hall. *The Facts of Life: The Creation of Sexual Knowledge in Britain, 1650–1950*. New Haven: Yale University Press, 1995.

Psomiades, Kathy Alexis. *Beauty's Body: Femininity and Representation in British Aestheticism*. Stanford University Press, 1997.

The Rambler's Flash Songster. London: W. West, c.1840–1850.

Rehm, George. *Chicago Tribune* (February 13, 1922): 2.

Richards, I. A. *Principles of Literary Criticism*. New York: Harcourt Brace Jovanovich, 1925.

Sciences and Poetries: A Reissue of Science and Poetry. New York: W. W. Norton & Co., 1970.

and C. K. Ogden, and James Wood. *The Foundations of Aesthetics*. New York: Lear Publishers, 1925.

Riding, Laura and Robert Graves. *A Survey of Modernist Poetry*. London: William Heinemann, Ltd., 1927.

236.

Robertson, Geoffrey. *Obscenity: An Account of Censorship Laws and their Enforcement in England and Wales.* London: Weidenfeld and Nicolson, 1979.

Romance of Lust. New York: Blue Moon Books, 1992.

Ross, Robert. *Aubrey Beardsley.* London: John Lane, the Bodley Head, 1921.

Rossetti, W. M. *Swinburne's Poems and Ballads.* London: John Camden Hotten, 1866.

Rothenstein, John K. M. *A Pot of Paint: the Artists of the 1890s.* New York: Books for Libraries Press, 1970.

Rousseau, G. S and Roy Porter. *Sexual Worlds of the Enlightenment.* Chapel Hill: University of North Carolina Press, 1988.

Royle, Edward. *Modern Britain: A Social History 1750–1985.* London: Edward Arnold, 1987.

Said, Edward. *Orientalism.* New York: Pantheon Books, 1978.

"The Scandal of Ulysses." *Sporting Times* (April 1, 1922): 4.

Schopenhauer, Arthur. *The World as Will and Idea.* Trans. R. B. Haldane and J. Kemp. *Philosophies of Art and Beauty.* Ed. Albert Hofstadter and Richard Kuhns. University of Chicago Press, 1964.

Schwarz, Daniel R. *The Humanistic Heritage.* Philadelphia: University of Pennsylvania Press, 1986.

Scrutiny. 1:1 (May 1932): 2–7.

Shaftesbury (Third Earl of), Anthony Ashley Cooper. *Characteristics of Men, Manners, Opinions, Times.* 3 vols. Hampshire, England: Gregg International Publishers, 1968.

"The Moralists." *Philosophies of Art and Beauty.* Ed. Albert Hofstadter and Richard Kuhns. Chicago: University of Chicago Press, 1964.

Shaw, W. David. *The Lucid Veil: Poetic Truth in the Victorian Age.* Madison: University of Wisconsin Press, 1987.

Smith, Jay, Ed. *The Diary and Correspondence of Samuel Pepys, FRS,* vol. III. New York: Bigelow, Brown & Co., n.d.

Snodgrass, Christopher. *Aubrey Beardsley: Dandy of the Grotesque.* New York: Oxford University Press, 1995.

Sontag, Susan. "The Pornographic Imagination." *Styles of Radical Will.* New York: Doubleday, 1969.

Spencer, Herbert. *Essays: Moral, Political and Aesthetic.* New York: D. Appleton and Co., 1866.

The Principles of Psychology. Vol. II. New York: D. Appleton and Co., 1901.

Stallybrass, Peter and Allon White. *The Politics and Poetics of Transgression.* Ithaca: Cornell University Press, 1986.

Stevens, MaryAnne, Ed. *The Orientalists: European Painters in North Africa and the Near East.* London: Royal Academy of Arts, 1984.

Stoddart, Judith. "The Morality of *Poems and Ballads.*" *The Whole Music of Passion.* Ed. Rikky Rooksby and Nicholas Shrimpton. Hampshire, England: Scolar Press, 1993.

Swinburne, Charles Algernon. "Notes on Poems and Reviews." *Swinburne Replies.* Ed. Clyde Kenneth Hyder. Syracuse University Press, 1966.

Symons, Arthur. *Aubrey Beardsley*. London: J. M. Dent & Co., 1905.

Thomas, Donald. *A Long Time Burning*. New York: Frederick A. Praeger, 1969.

Swinburne: The Poet in His World. New York: Oxford University Press, 1979.

Vivas, Eliseo. *D. H. Lawrence: The Failure and Triumph of Art* . Evanston: Northwestern University Press, 1960.

Walker, R. A., Ed. *The Best of Beardsley*. London: The Bodley Head, 1948.

Walkowitz, Judith. *City of Dreadful Delight: Narrative of Sexual Danger in Late-Victorian London*. University of Chicago Press, 1992.

The Way of a Man With a Maid. Hertfordshire: Wordsworth Classics, 1996.

"We Can't Do Business, the Dons Tell a Big Donor." *The New York Times* (26 November 1996): A4.

Webb, R. K. *The British Working Class Reader, 1790–1840*. London: Allen & Unwin, 1955.

Weeks, Jeffrey. *Sex, Politics, and Society*. New York: Longman, 1981.

Wellek, René. *Immanuel Kant in England, 1793–1838*. Princeton University Press, 1931.

Wicke, Jennifer. "Through a Gaze Darkly: Pornography's Academic Market." *Dirty Looks: Women Pornography Power*. Ed. Roma Gibson and Pamela Church Gibson. London: BFI, 1993.

Williams, Raymond. *Culture and Society, 1780–1950*. Harmondsworth, England: Penguin Books, 1968.

Marxism and Literature. New York: Oxford University Press, 1977.

Woodmansee, Martha. *The Author, Art, and the Market*. New York: Columbia University Press, 1994.

Zatlin, Linda Gerstner. "Aubrey Beardsley Counts the Ways." *Victorian Newsletter*. 67 (spring 1985): 1–6.

Aubrey Beardsley and Victorian Sexual Politics. Oxford: Clarendon Press, 1990.

"Aubrey Beardsley's 'Japanese' Grotesques." *Victorian Literature and Culture*. 25:1 (spring 1997): 87–108.

"Félicien Rops and Aubrey Beardsley: The Naked and the Nude." *Reconsidering Aubrey Beardsley*. Ed. Robert Langenfeld. Ann Arbor: UMI Research Press, 1989.

Index